A NOTE FROM
MARY POPE OSBORNE ABOUT THE

MAGIC TREE HOUSE® Fact Trackers

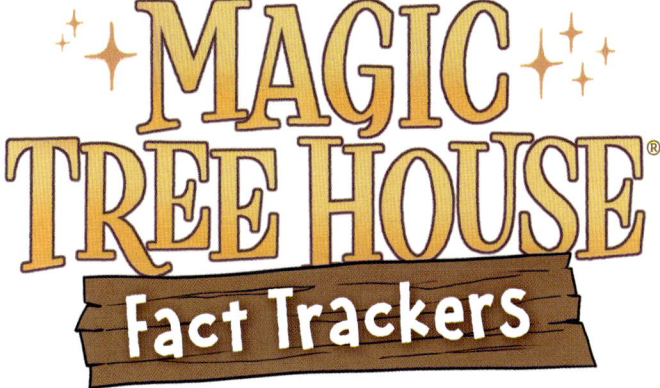

When I write Magic Tree House® adventures, I love including facts about the times and places Jack and Annie visit. But when readers finish these adventures, I want them to learn even more. So that's why we write a series of nonfiction books that are companions to the fiction titles in the Magic Tree House® series. We call these books Fact Trackers because we love to track the facts! Whether we're researching dinosaurs, Pilgrims, sea monsters, or cobras, we're always amazed at how wondrous and surprising the real world is. We want you to experience the same wonder we do—so get out your pencils and notebooks and hit the trail with us. You can be a Magic Tree House® Fact Tracker, too!

Mary Pope Osborne

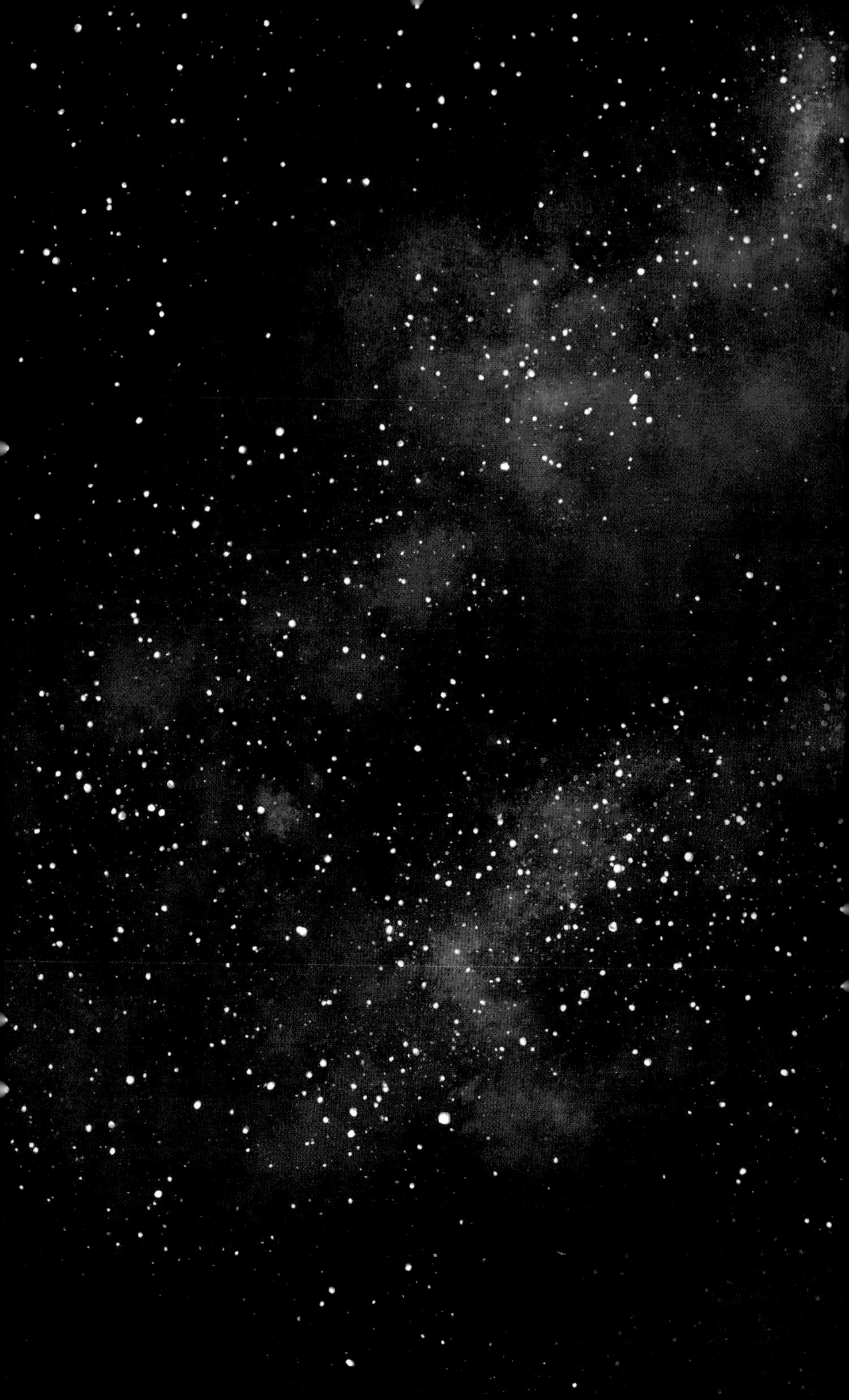

MAGIC TREE HOUSE®
Fact Trackers

SPACE

by WILL OSBORNE
AND MARY POPE OSBORNE
ADAPTED BY MEI NAKAMURA
WITH ART BY JOMIKE TEJIDO
COLOR BY CAI TSE

A STEPPING STONE BOOK™
RANDOM HOUSE 🏠 NEW YORK

Text copyright © 2002 by Will Osborne and Mary Pope Osborne
Cover art and interior illustrations copyright © 2025 by Jomike Tejido
Text adapted by Mei Nakamura

All rights reserved. Published in the United States by Random House Children's Books, a division of Penguin Random House LLC, 1745 Broadway, New York, NY 10019. This work is adapted from *Magic Tree House Fact Tracker: Space*, written by Will Osborne and Mary Pope Osborne and illustrated by Sal Murdocca, text copyright © 2002 by Will Osborne and Mary Pope Osborne and interior illustrations copyright © 2002 by Sal Murdocca. Published in paperback in the United States by Random House Children's Books, a division of Penguin Random House LLC, New York, in 2002.

Random House and the colophon are registered trademarks of Penguin Random House LLC and RH Graphic with the book design and A Stepping Stone Book and the colophon are trademarks of Penguin Random House LLC. Magic Tree House is a registered trademark of Mary Pope Osborne; used under license.

penguinrandomhouse.com
rhcbooks.com
MagicTreeHouse.com

Library of Congress Cataloging-in-Publication Data is available upon request.
ISBN 978-0-593-70589-6 (hardcover) — ISBN 978-0-593-70588-9 (trade)
ISBN 978-0-593-70590-2 (lib. bdg.) — ISBN 978-0-593-70591-9 (ebook)

Editor: Courtney Carbone
Designers: April Ward and Jules Buckley
Copy Editor: Stephanie Bay
Managing Editor: Katy Miller
Production Manager: Luke McCord

MANUFACTURED IN CHINA
10 9 8 7 6 5 4 3 2 1
First Graphic Novel Edition

This book has been officially leveled by using the F&P Text Level Gradient™ Leveling System.

Random House Children's Books supports the First Amendment and celebrates the right to read.

Penguin Random House values and supports copyright. Copyright fuels creativity, encourages diverse voices, promotes free speech, and creates a vibrant culture. Thank you for buying an authorized edition of this book and for complying with copyright laws by not reproducing, scanning, or distributing any part of it in any form without permission. You are supporting writers and allowing Penguin Random House to continue to publish books for every reader. Please note that no part of this book may be used or reproduced in any manner for the purpose of training artificial intelligence technologies or systems.

The authorized representative in the EU for product safety and compliance is Penguin Random House Ireland, Morrison Chambers, 32 Nassau Street, Dublin D02 YH68, Ireland, https://eu-contact.penguin.ie.

With special thanks to our scientific consultant
Amie Gallagher, Planetarium Director
Raritan Valley Community College,
Branchburg, New Jersey

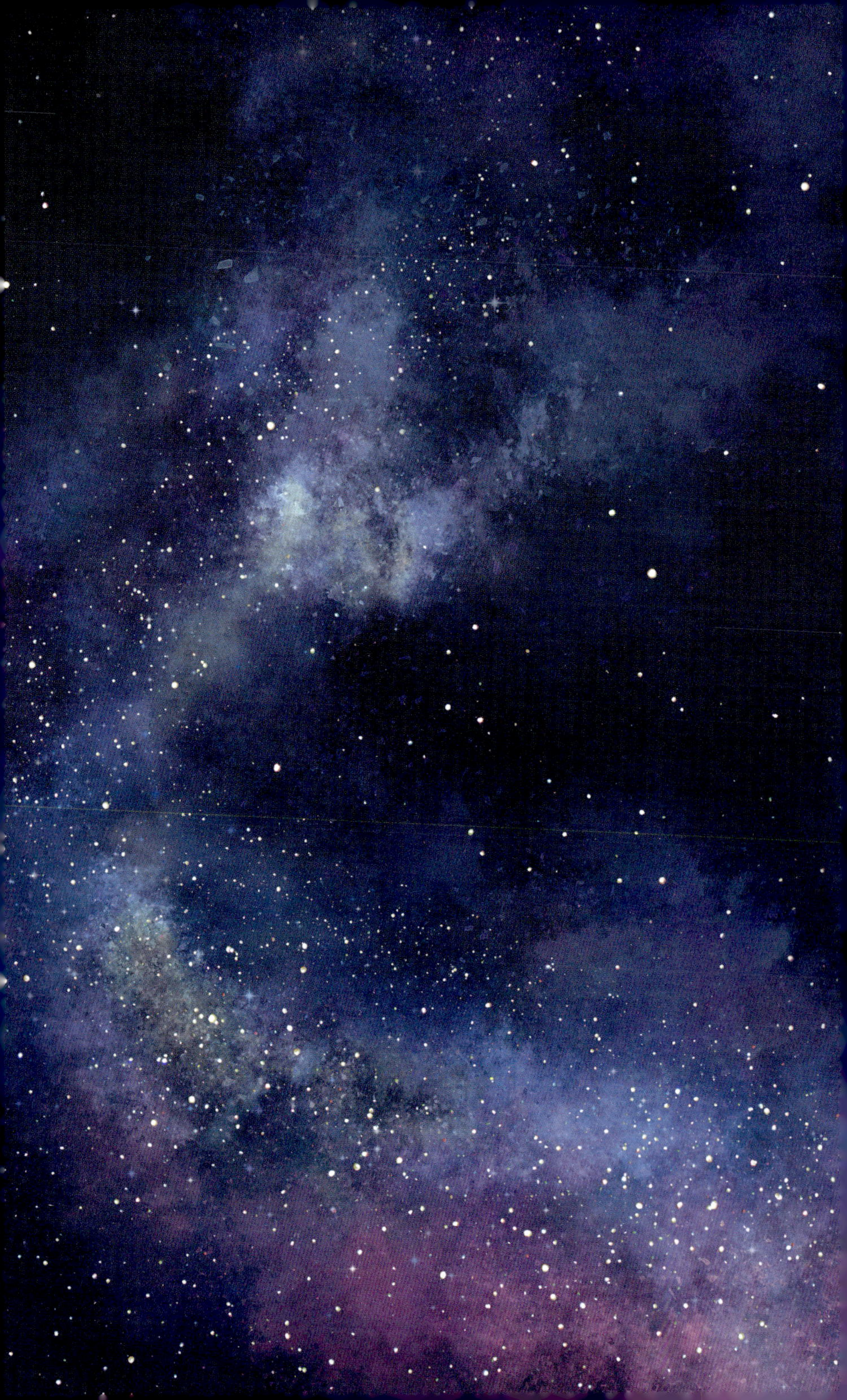

Contents

CHAPTER 1: **Astronomy** 1

CHAPTER 2: **The Universe**.................................. 16

CHAPTER 3: **The Sun** 28

CHAPTER 4: **Our Solar System**........................... 40

CHAPTER 5: **Space Travel** 72

CHAPTER 6: **From Earth to the Moon** 82

CHAPTER 7: **Space Travel Today**.................. 93

CHAPTER 8: **Living and Working in Space**..........108

CHAPTER 9: **The Future**................................. 118

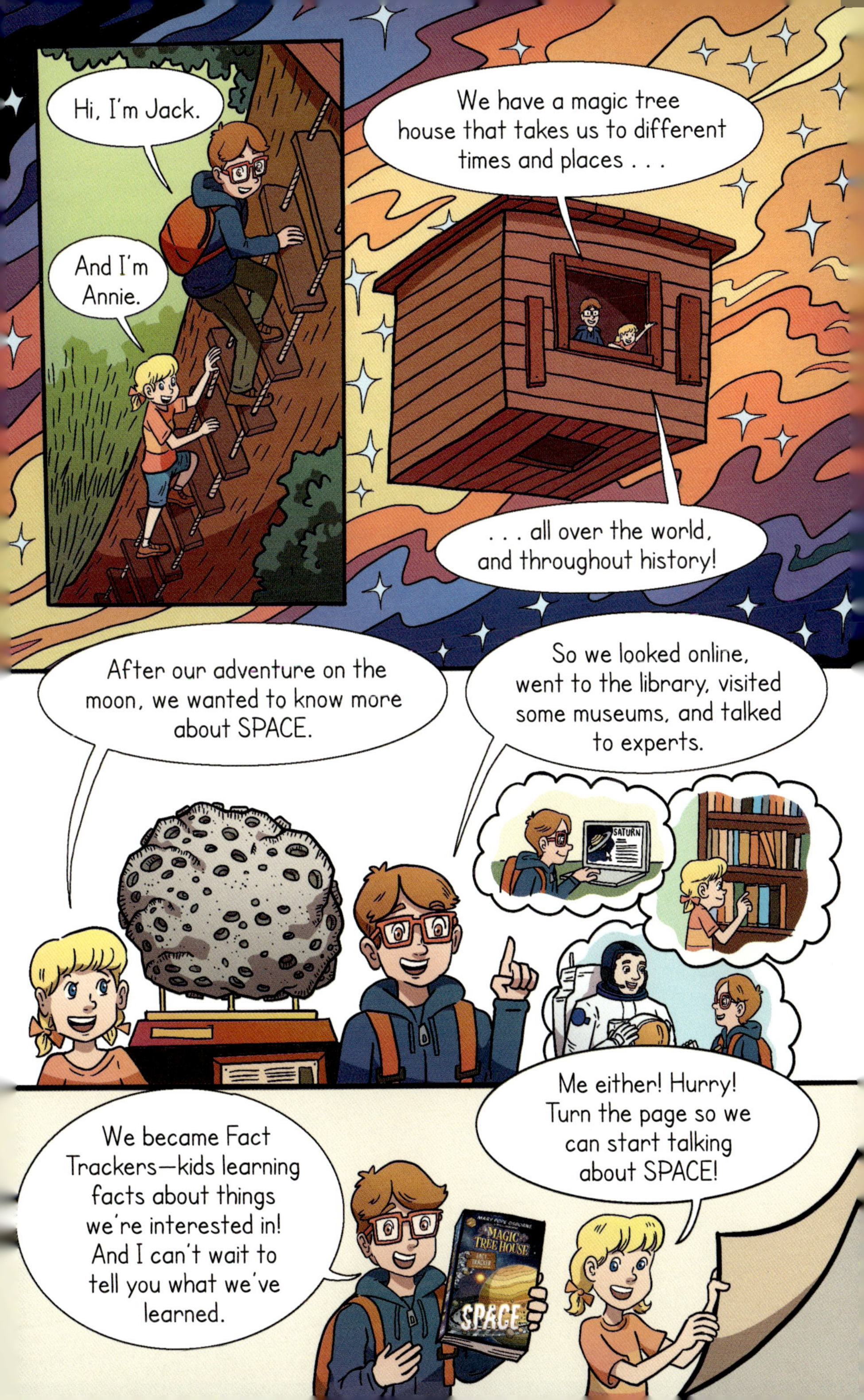

Hi, I'm Jack.
And I'm Annie.
We have a magic tree house that takes us to different times and places . . .
. . . all over the world, and throughout history!
After our adventure on the moon, we wanted to know more about SPACE.
So we looked online, went to the library, visited some museums, and talked to experts.
SATURN
We became Fact Trackers—kids learning facts about things we're interested in! And I can't wait to tell you what we've learned.
MAGIC TREE HOUSE
SPACE
Me either! Hurry! Turn the page so we can start talking about SPACE!

CHAPTER ONE
Astronomy

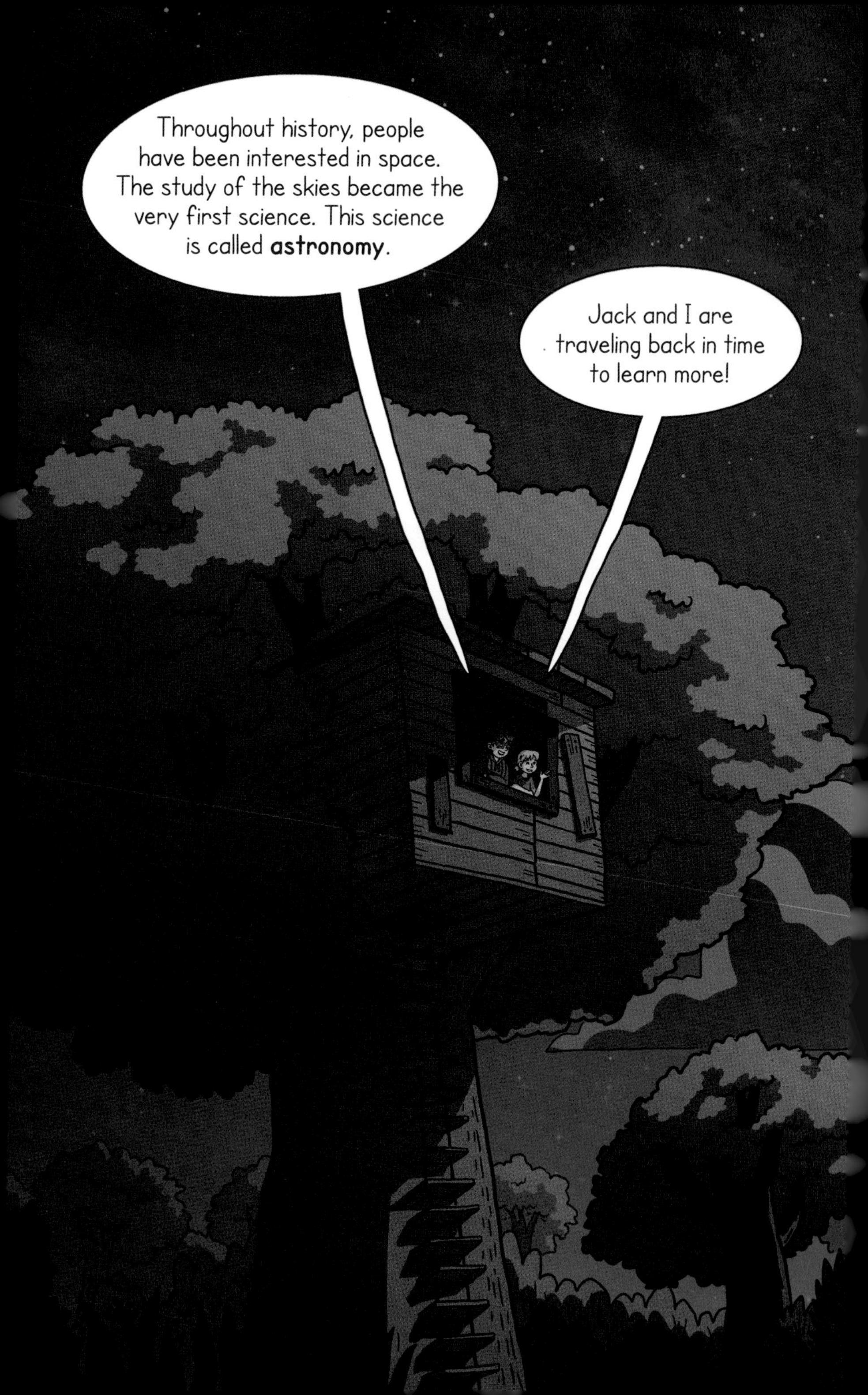
Throughout history, people have been interested in space. The study of the skies became the very first science. This science is called **astronomy**.
Jack and I are traveling back in time to learn more!

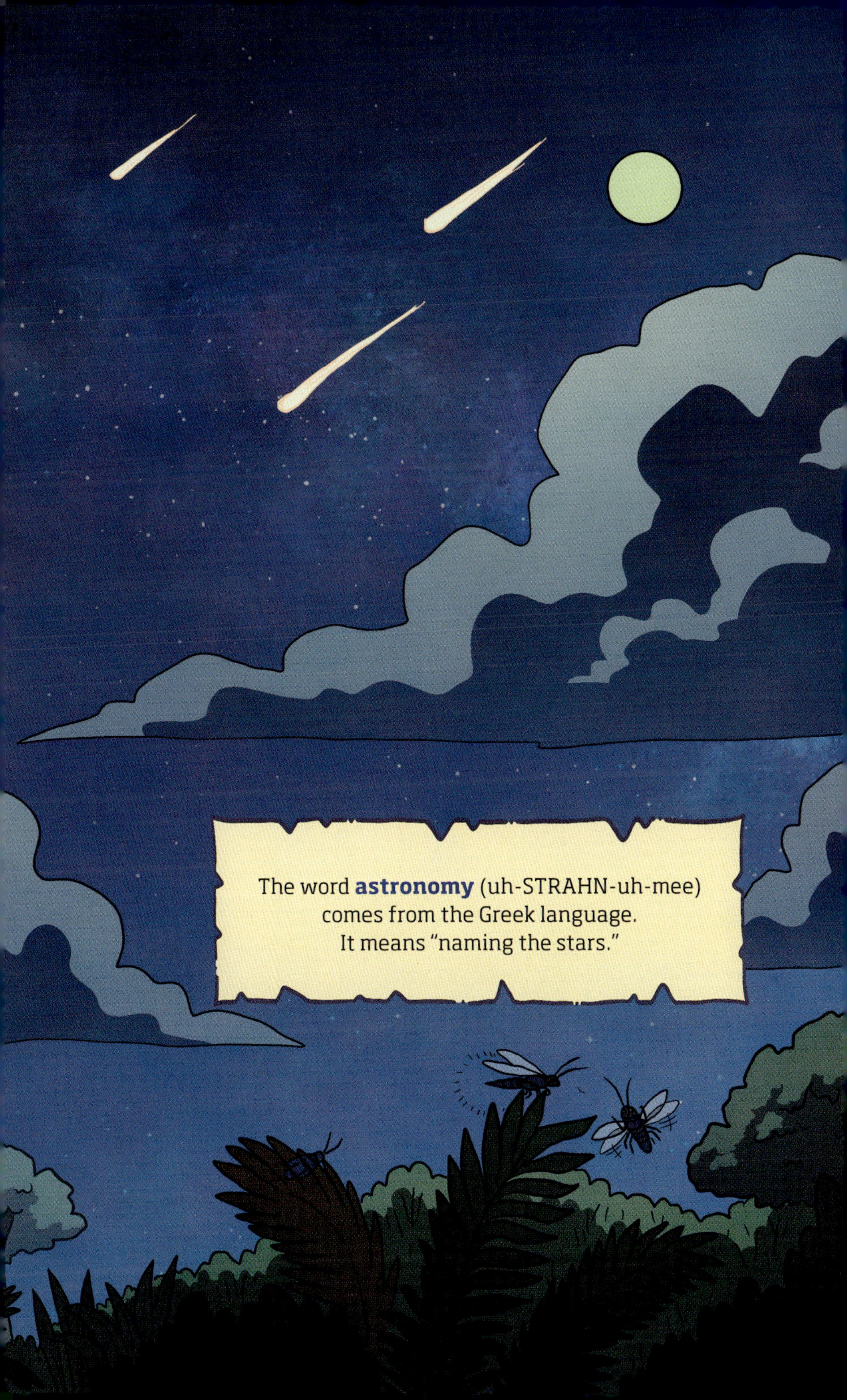
The word **astronomy** (uh-STRAHN-uh-mee) comes from the Greek language. It means "naming the stars."

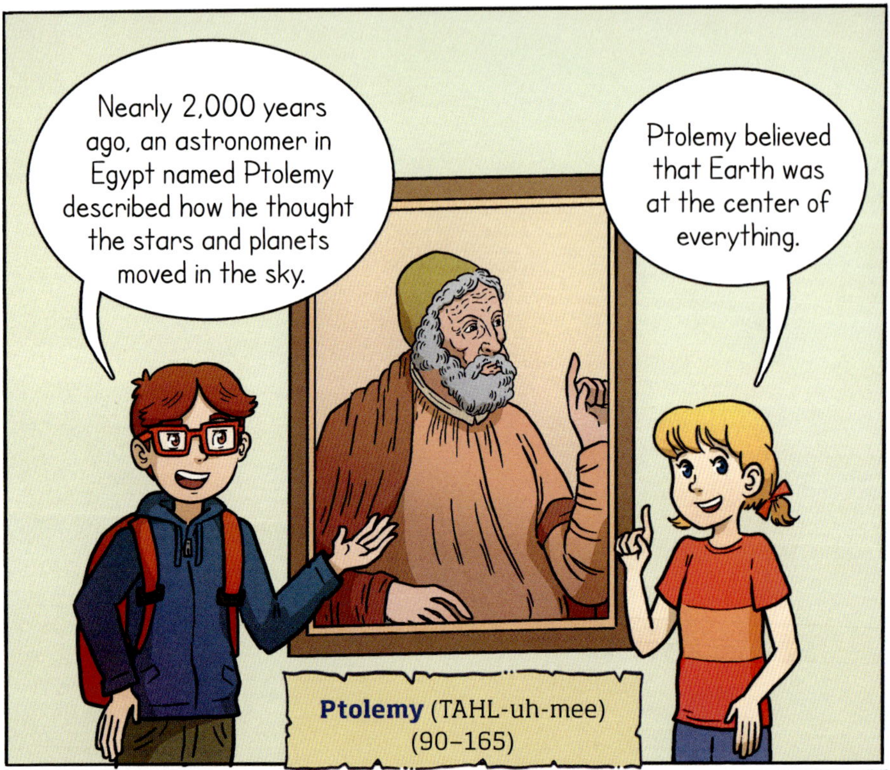
Nearly 2,000 years ago, an astronomer in Egypt named Ptolemy described how he thought the stars and planets moved in the sky.
Ptolemy believed that Earth was at the center of everything.
Ptolemy (TAHL-uh-mee)
(90–165)

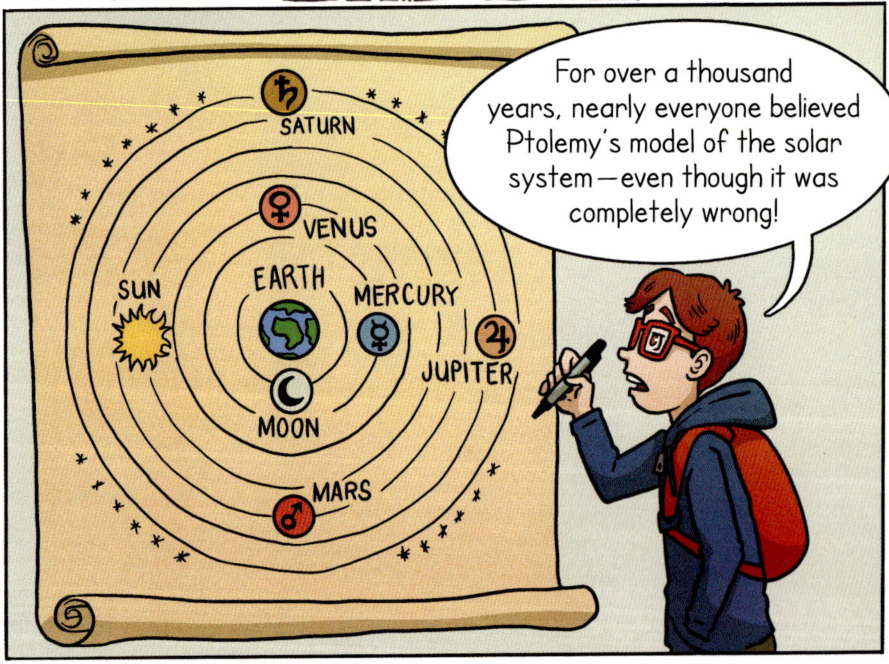
SATURN
VENUS
EARTH
MERCURY
SUN
JUPITER
MOON
MARS
For over a thousand years, nearly everyone believed Ptolemy's model of the solar system—even though it was completely wrong!

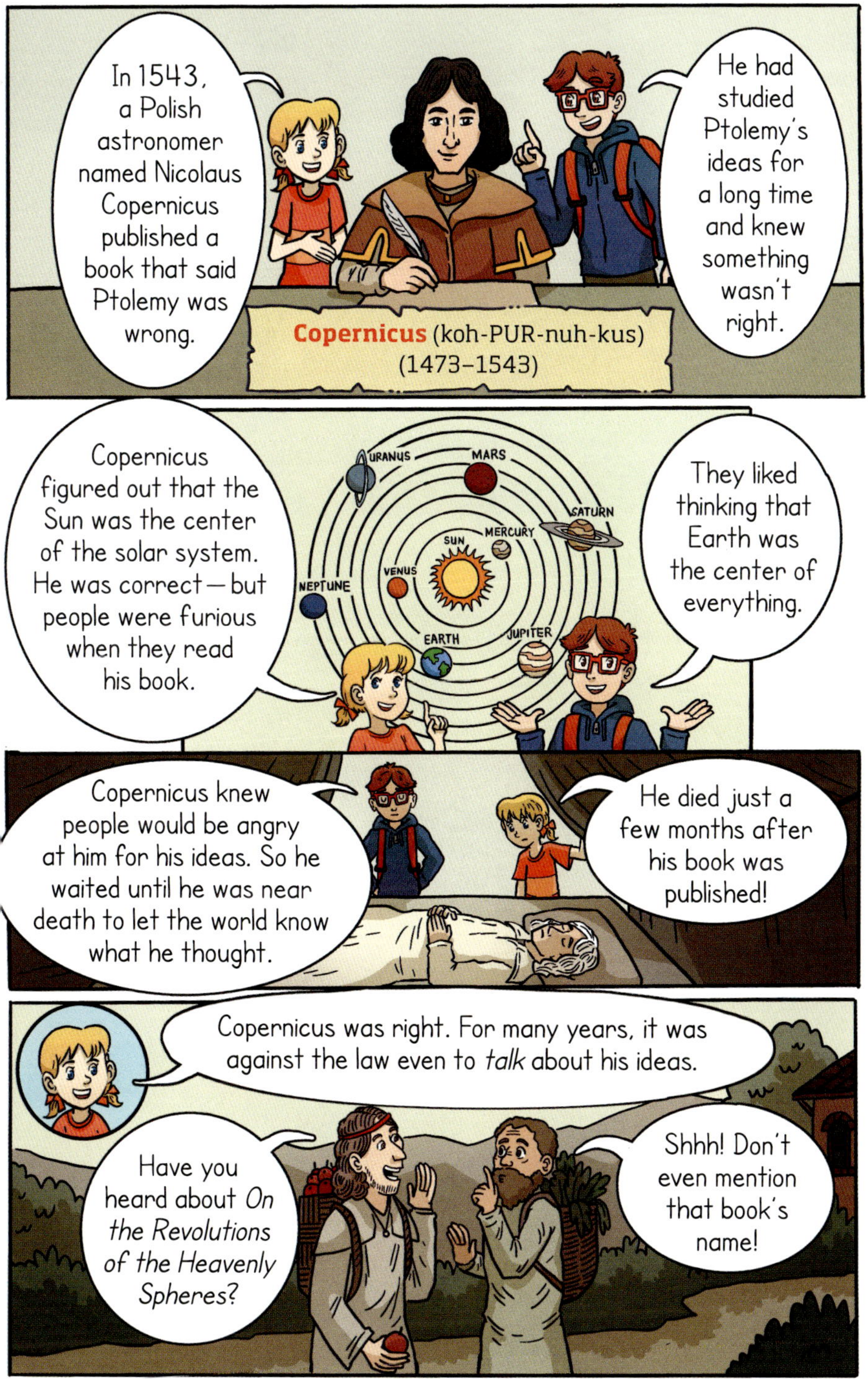
In 1543, a Polish astronomer named Nicolaus Copernicus published a book that said Ptolemy was wrong.
He had studied Ptolemy's ideas for a long time and knew something wasn't right.
Copernicus (koh-PUR-nuh-kus) (1473–1543)
Copernicus figured out that the Sun was the center of the solar system. He was correct—but people were furious when they read his book.
URANUS
MARS
SATURN
MERCURY
SUN
VENUS
NEPTUNE
EARTH
JUPITER
They liked thinking that Earth was the center of everything.
Copernicus knew people would be angry at him for his ideas. So he waited until he was near death to let the world know what he thought.
He died just a few months after his book was published!
Copernicus was right. For many years, it was against the law even to *talk* about his ideas.
Have you heard about *On the Revolutions of the Heavenly Spheres?*
Shhh! Don't even mention that book's name!

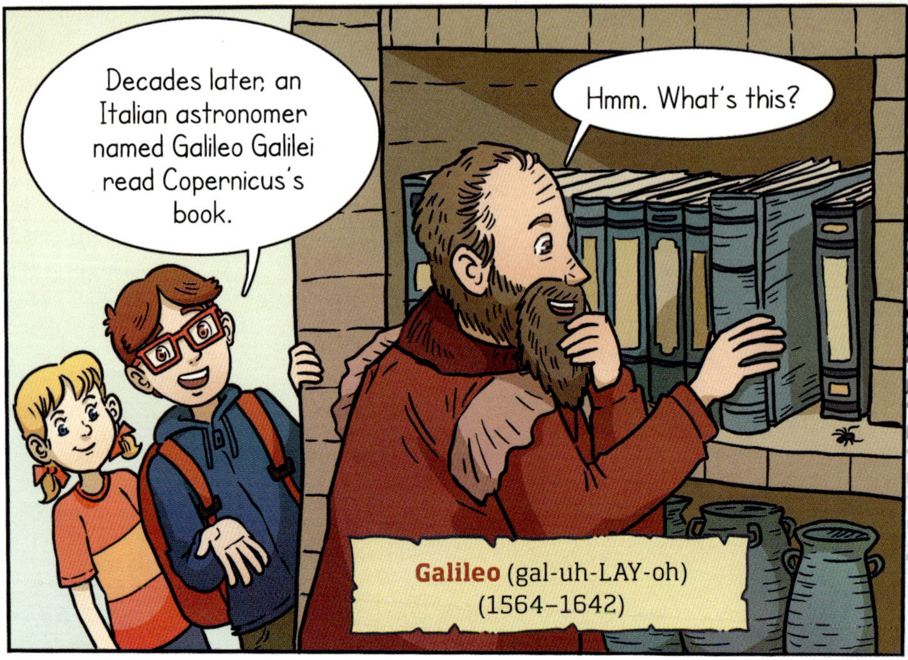
Decades later, an Italian astronomer named Galileo Galilei read Copernicus's book.
Hmm. What's this?
Galileo (gal-uh-LAY-oh) (1564–1642)

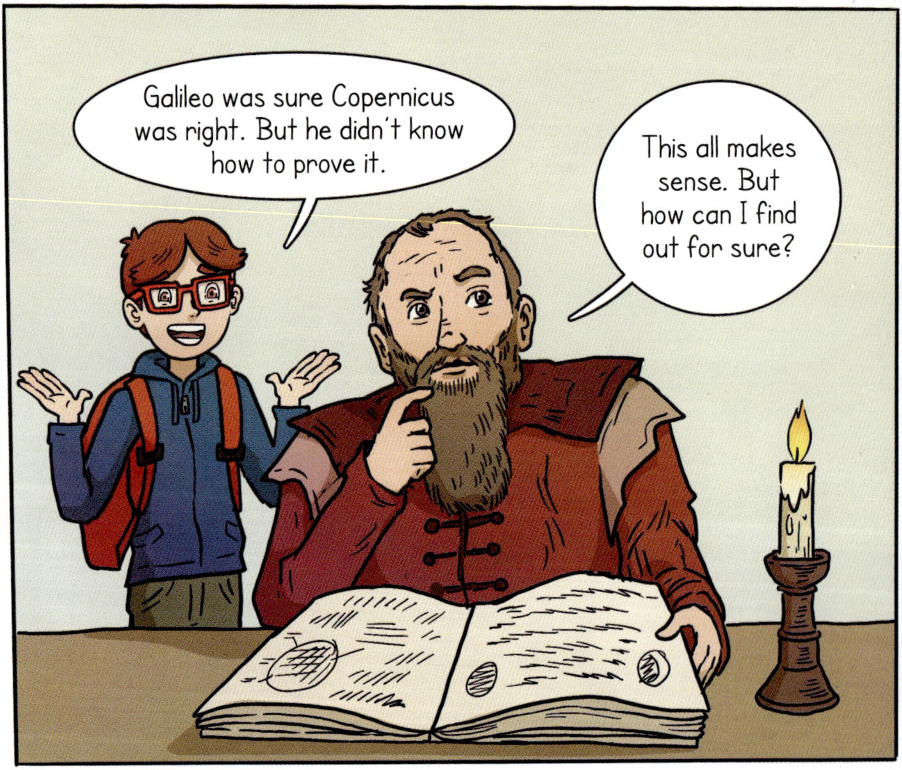
Galileo was sure Copernicus was right. But he didn't know how to prove it.
This all makes sense. But how can I find out for sure?

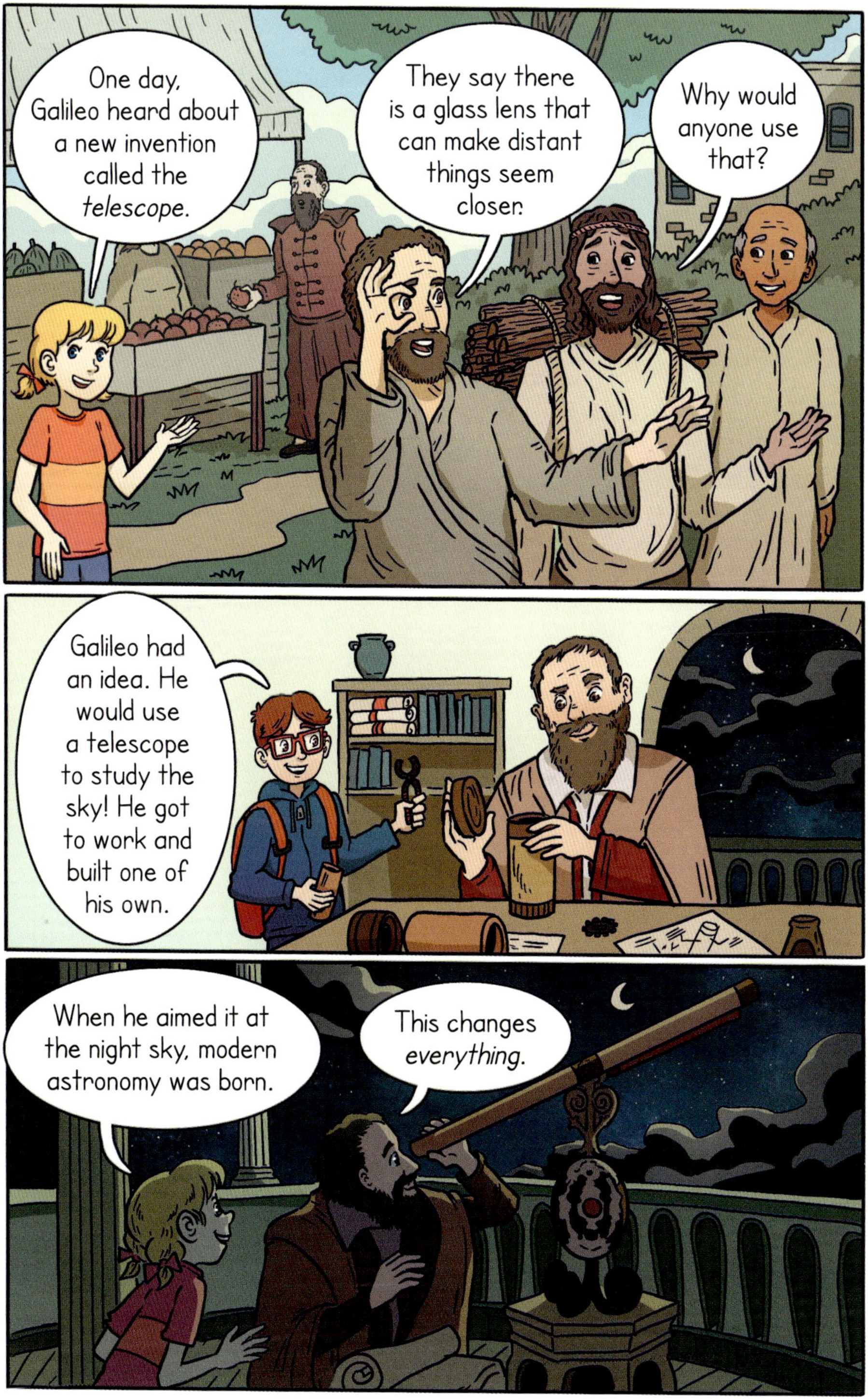
One day, Galileo heard about a new invention called the *telescope*.
They say there is a glass lens that can make distant things seem closer.
Why would anyone use that?
Galileo had an idea. He would use a telescope to study the sky! He got to work and built one of his own.
When he aimed it at the night sky, modern astronomy was born.
This changes *everything*.

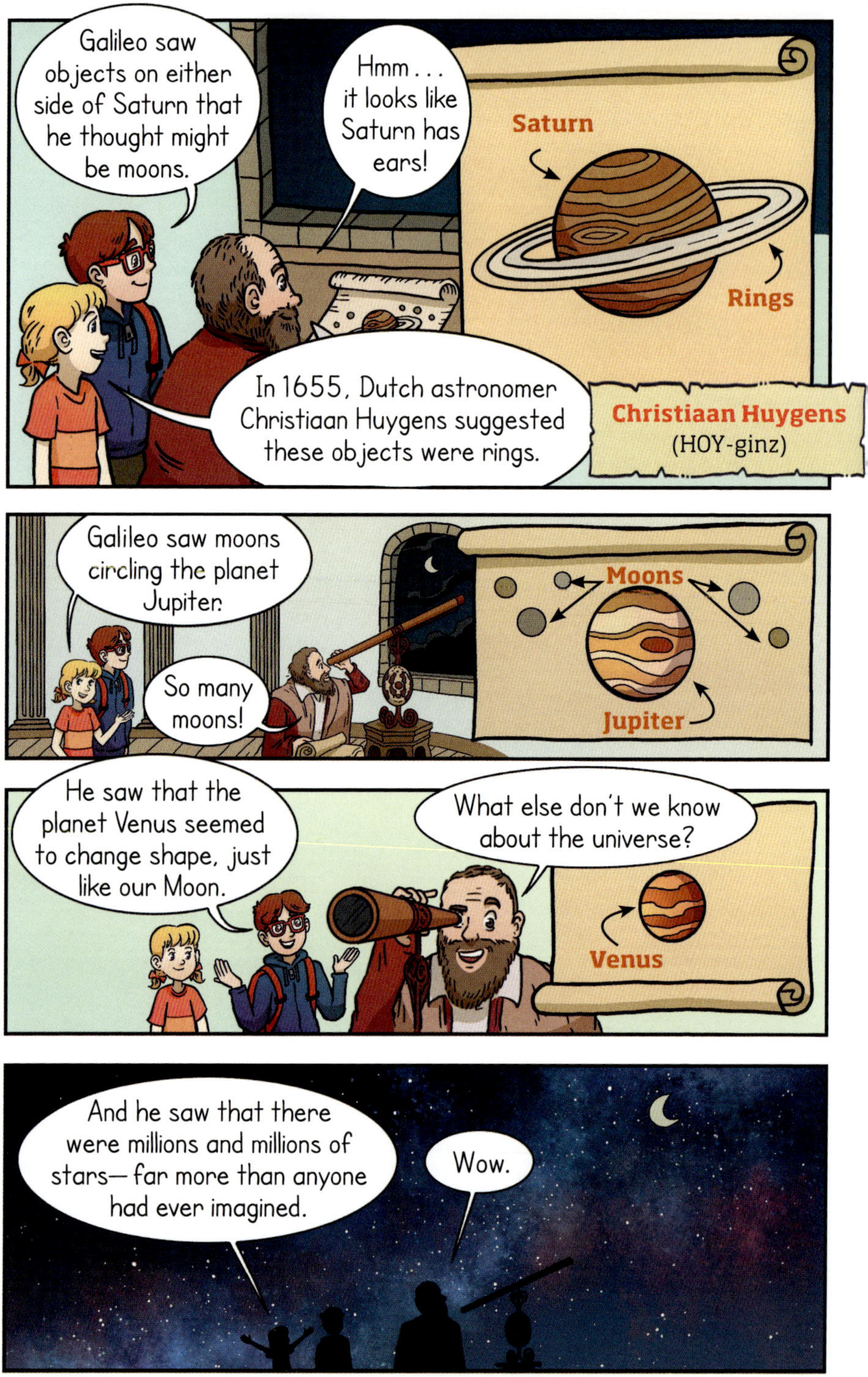
Galileo saw objects on either side of Saturn that he thought might be moons.
Hmm . . . it looks like Saturn has ears!
Saturn
Rings
In 1655, Dutch astronomer Christiaan Huygens suggested these objects were rings.
Christiaan Huygens
(HOY-ginz)
Galileo saw moons circling the planet Jupiter.
So many moons!
Moons
Jupiter
He saw that the planet Venus seemed to change shape, just like our Moon.
What else don't we know about the universe?
Venus
And he saw that there were millions and millions of stars—far more than anyone had ever imagined.
Wow.

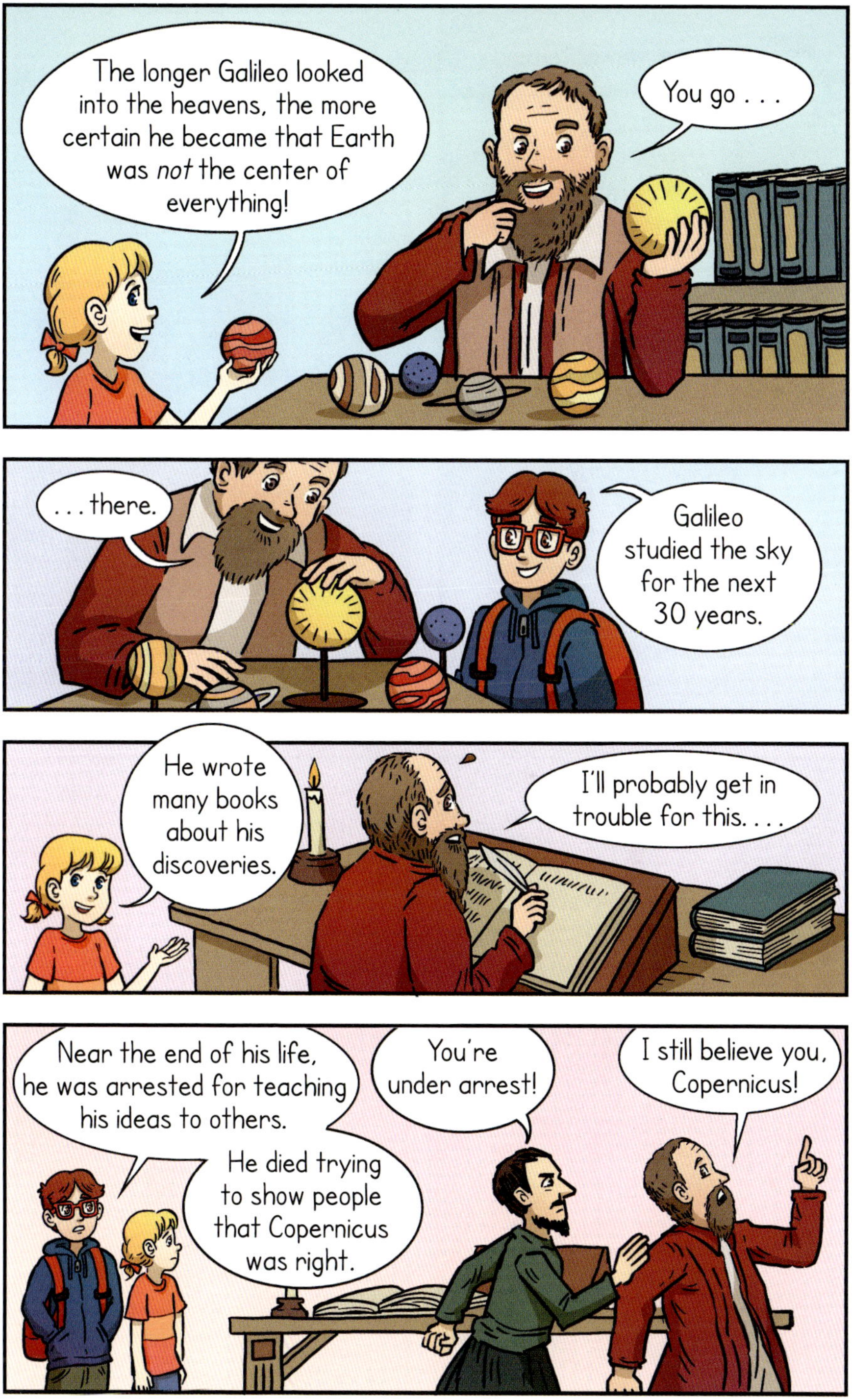
The longer Galileo looked into the heavens, the more certain he became that Earth was *not* the center of everything!
You go . . .
. . . there.
Galileo studied the sky for the next 30 years.
He wrote many books about his discoveries.
I'll probably get in trouble for this. . . .
Near the end of his life, he was arrested for teaching his ideas to others.
He died trying to show people that Copernicus was right.
You're under arrest!
I still believe you, Copernicus!

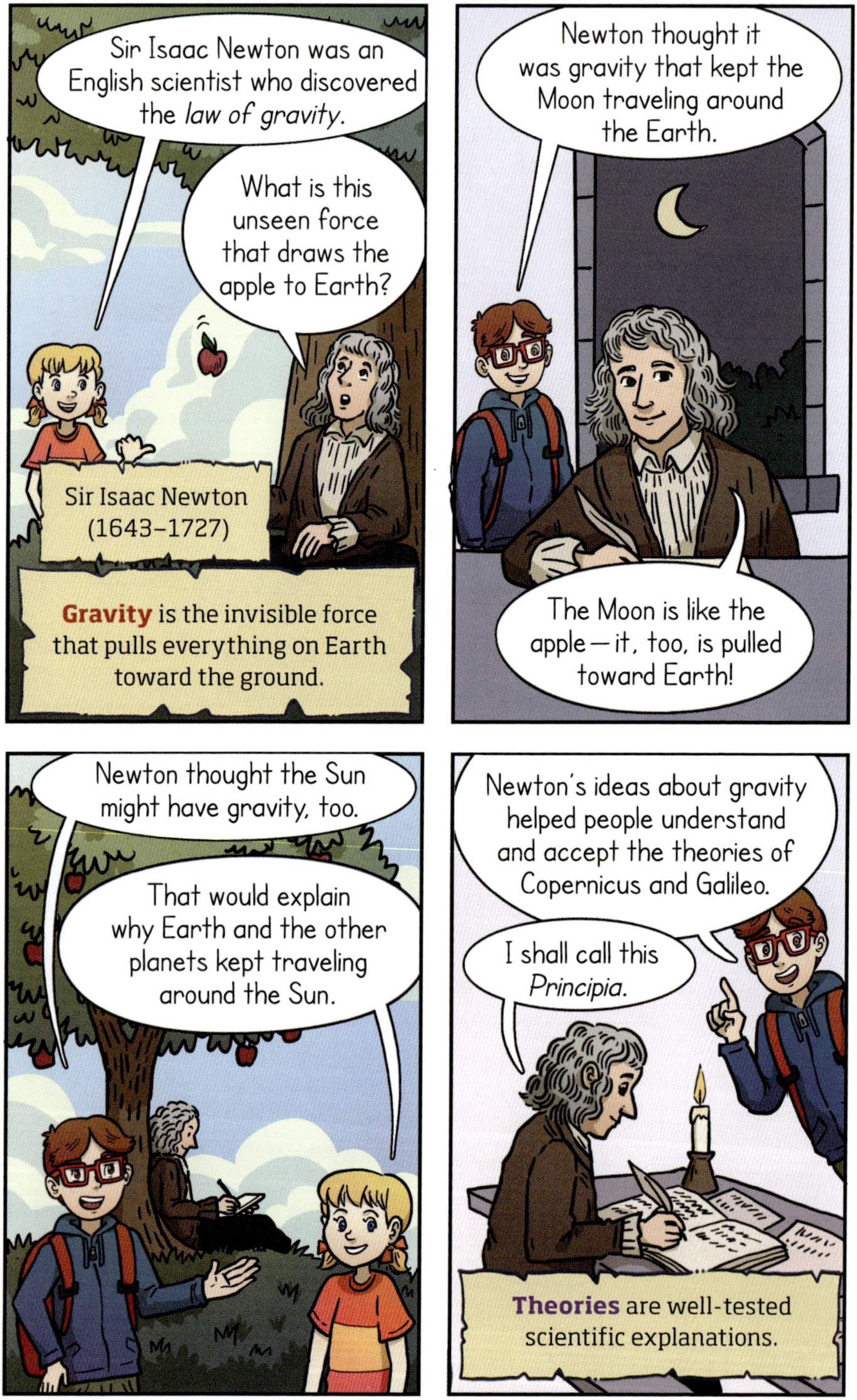
Sir Isaac Newton was an English scientist who discovered the *law of gravity*.
What is this unseen force that draws the apple to Earth?
Sir Isaac Newton (1643–1727)
Gravity is the invisible force that pulls everything on Earth toward the ground.
Newton thought it was gravity that kept the Moon traveling around the Earth.
The Moon is like the apple — it, too, is pulled toward Earth!
Newton thought the Sun might have gravity, too.
That would explain why Earth and the other planets kept traveling around the Sun.
Newton's ideas about gravity helped people understand and accept the theories of Copernicus and Galileo.
I shall call this *Principia*.
Theories are well-tested scientific explanations.

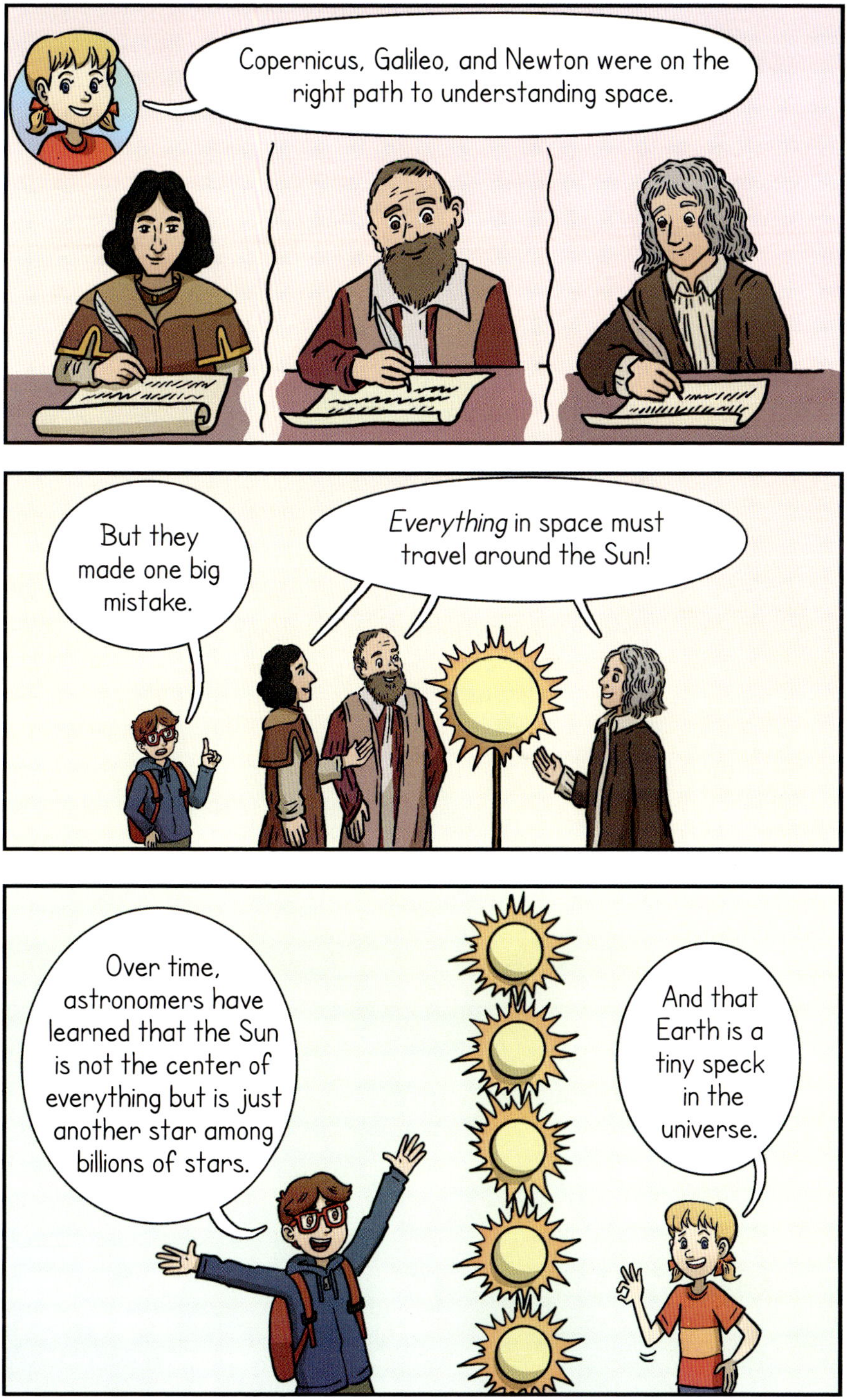
Copernicus, Galileo, and Newton were on the right path to understanding space.
But they made one big mistake.
Everything in space must travel around the Sun!
Over time, astronomers have learned that the Sun is not the center of everything but is just another star among billions of stars.
And that Earth is a tiny speck in the universe.

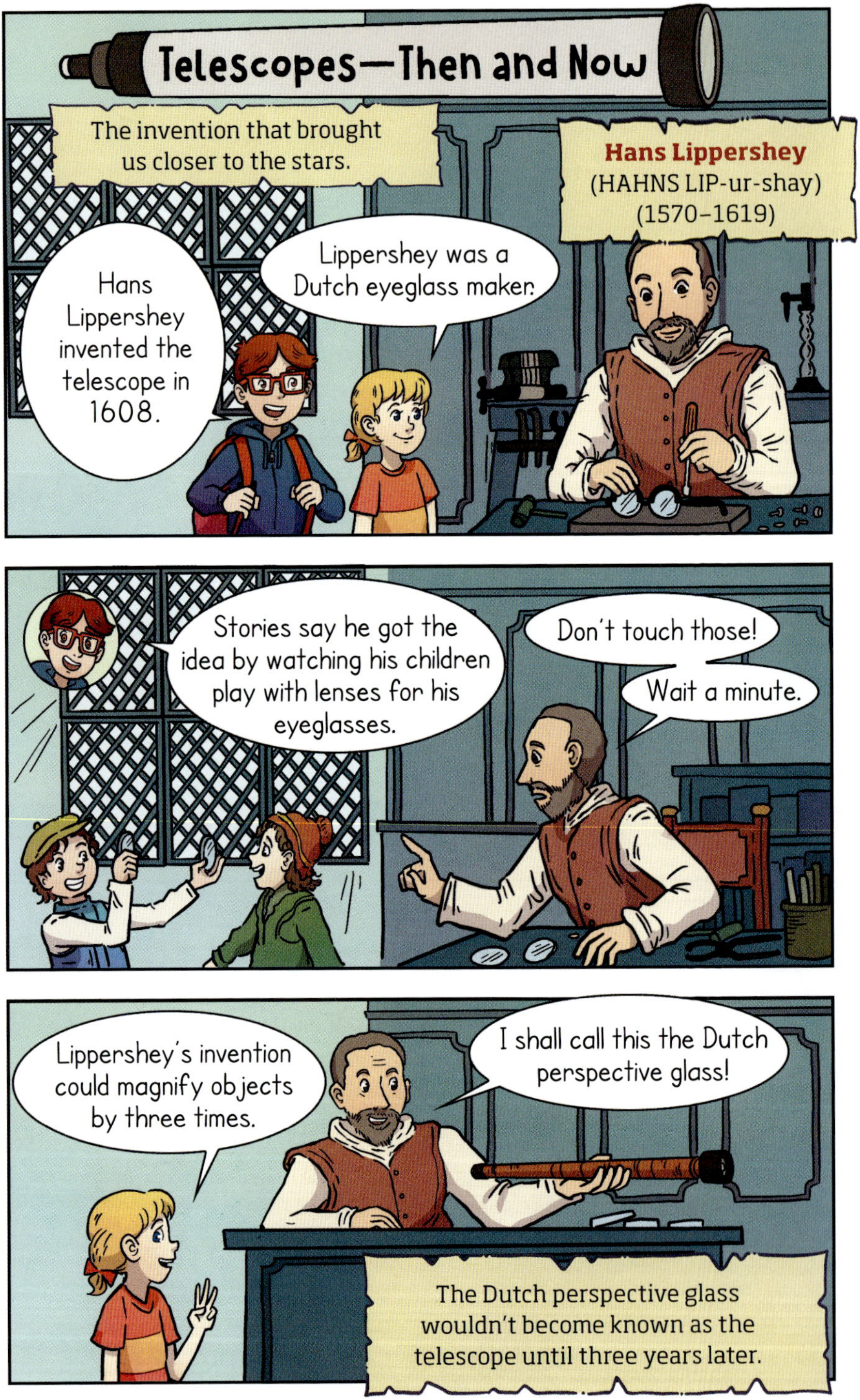
Telescopes—Then and Now
The invention that brought us closer to the stars.
Hans Lippershey (HAHNS LIP-ur-shay) (1570–1619)
Hans Lippershey invented the telescope in 1608.
Lippershey was a Dutch eyeglass maker.
Stories say he got the idea by watching his children play with lenses for his eyeglasses.
Don't touch those!
Wait a minute.
Lippershey's invention could magnify objects by three times.
I shall call this the Dutch perspective glass!
The Dutch perspective glass wouldn't become known as the telescope until three years later.

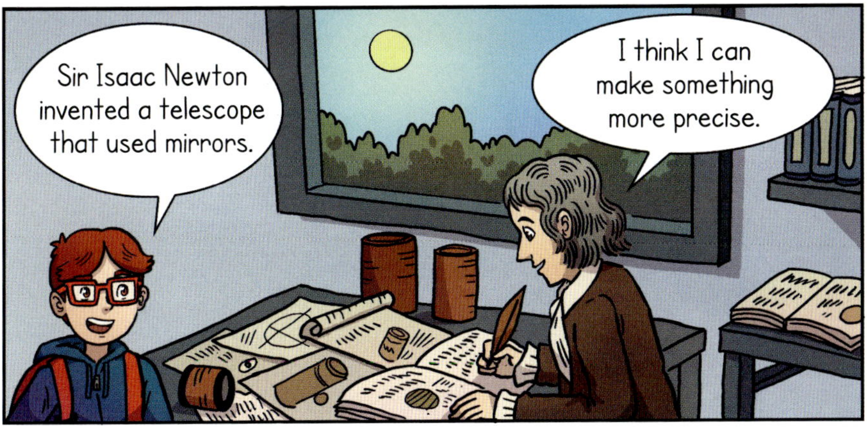
Sir Isaac Newton invented a telescope that used mirrors.
I think I can make something more precise.

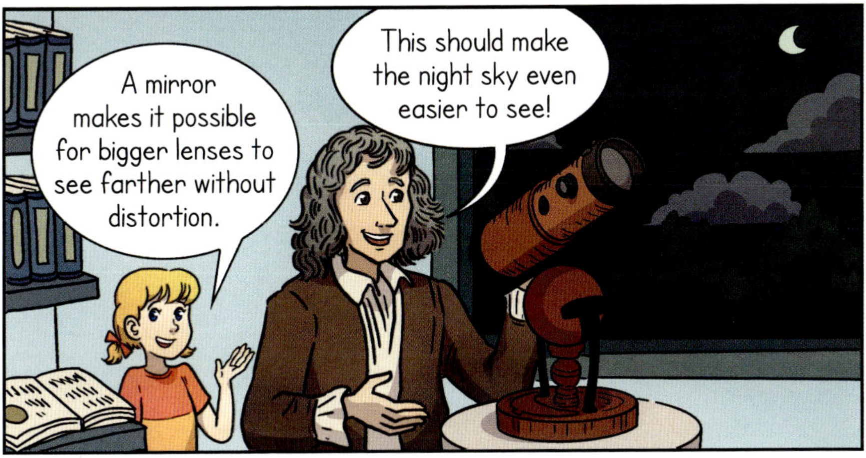
A mirror makes it possible for bigger lenses to see farther without distortion.
This should make the night sky even easier to see!

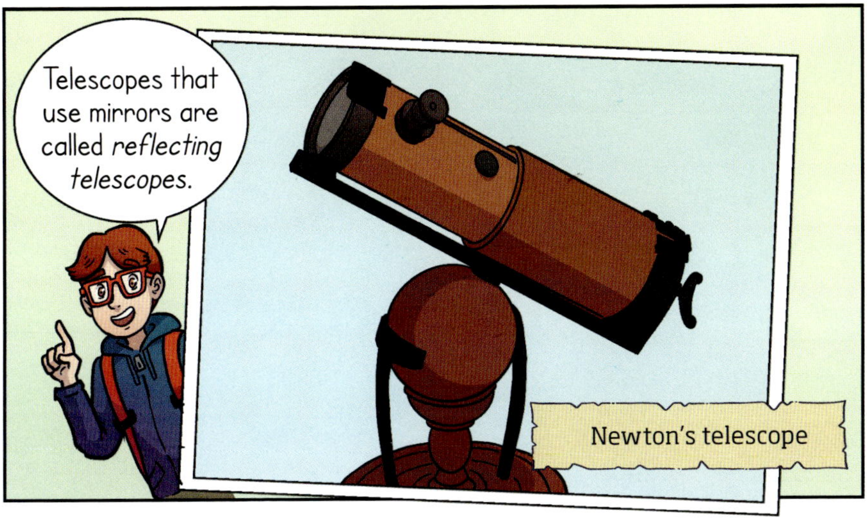
Telescopes that use mirrors are called *reflecting telescopes.*
Newton's telescope

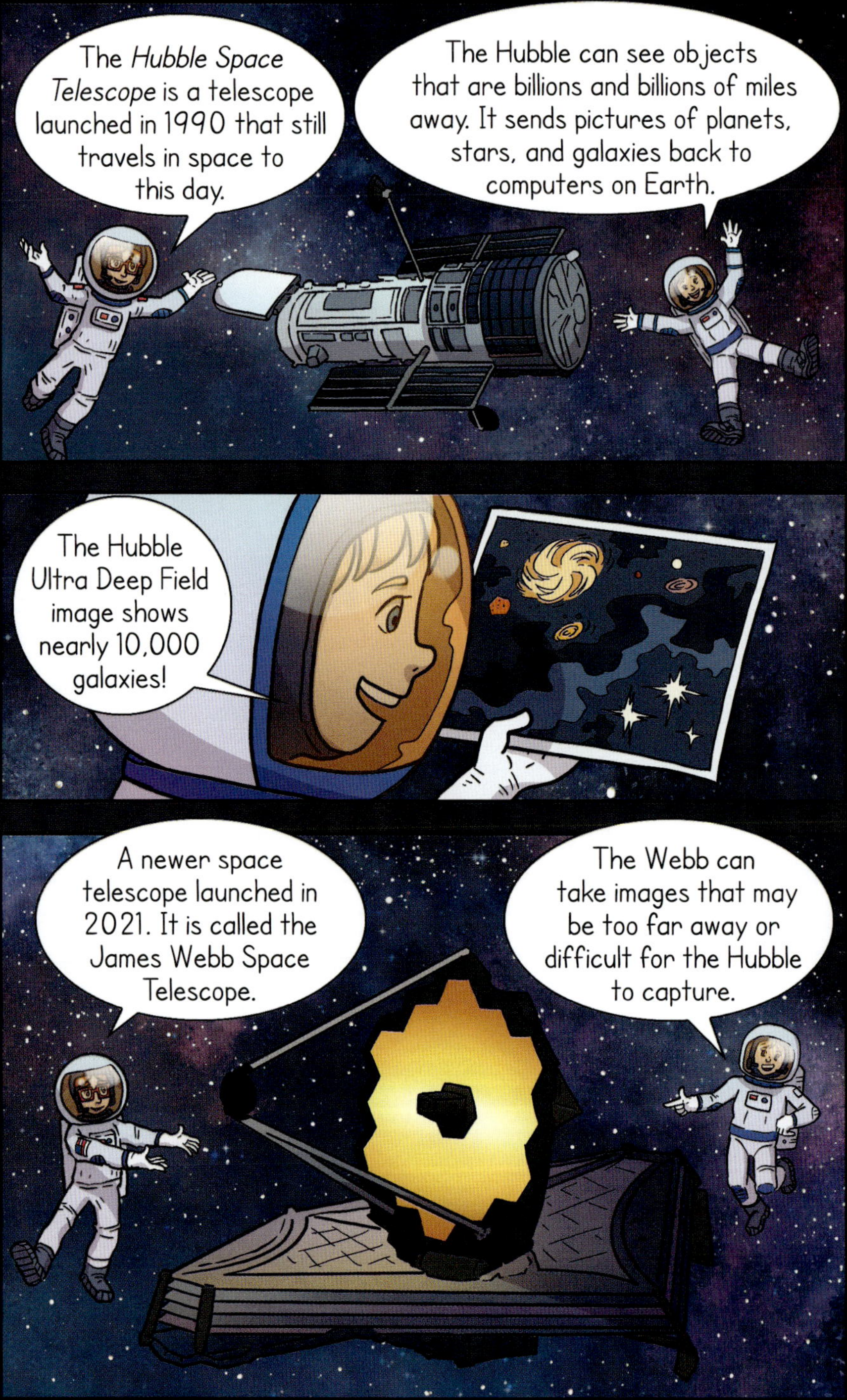
The *Hubble Space Telescope* is a telescope launched in 1990 that still travels in space to this day.
The Hubble can see objects that are billions and billions of miles away. It sends pictures of planets, stars, and galaxies back to computers on Earth.
The Hubble Ultra Deep Field image shows nearly 10,000 galaxies!
A newer space telescope launched in 2021. It is called the James Webb Space Telescope.
The Webb can take images that may be too far away or difficult for the Hubble to capture.

South Africa

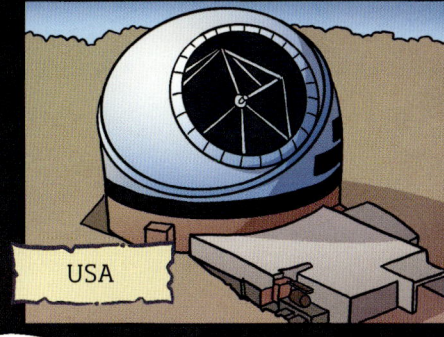
USA

Chile

There are lots of large optical telescopes all over the world, including ones in the USA, Spain, South Africa, Chile, Russia, Canada, China, India, and Iran.

One in Arizona is named the Large Binocular Telescope. At over 27 feet in diameter, it's a lot bigger and more powerful than my binoculars!

Spain

USA

Spain

Russia

CHAPTER TWO

The Universe

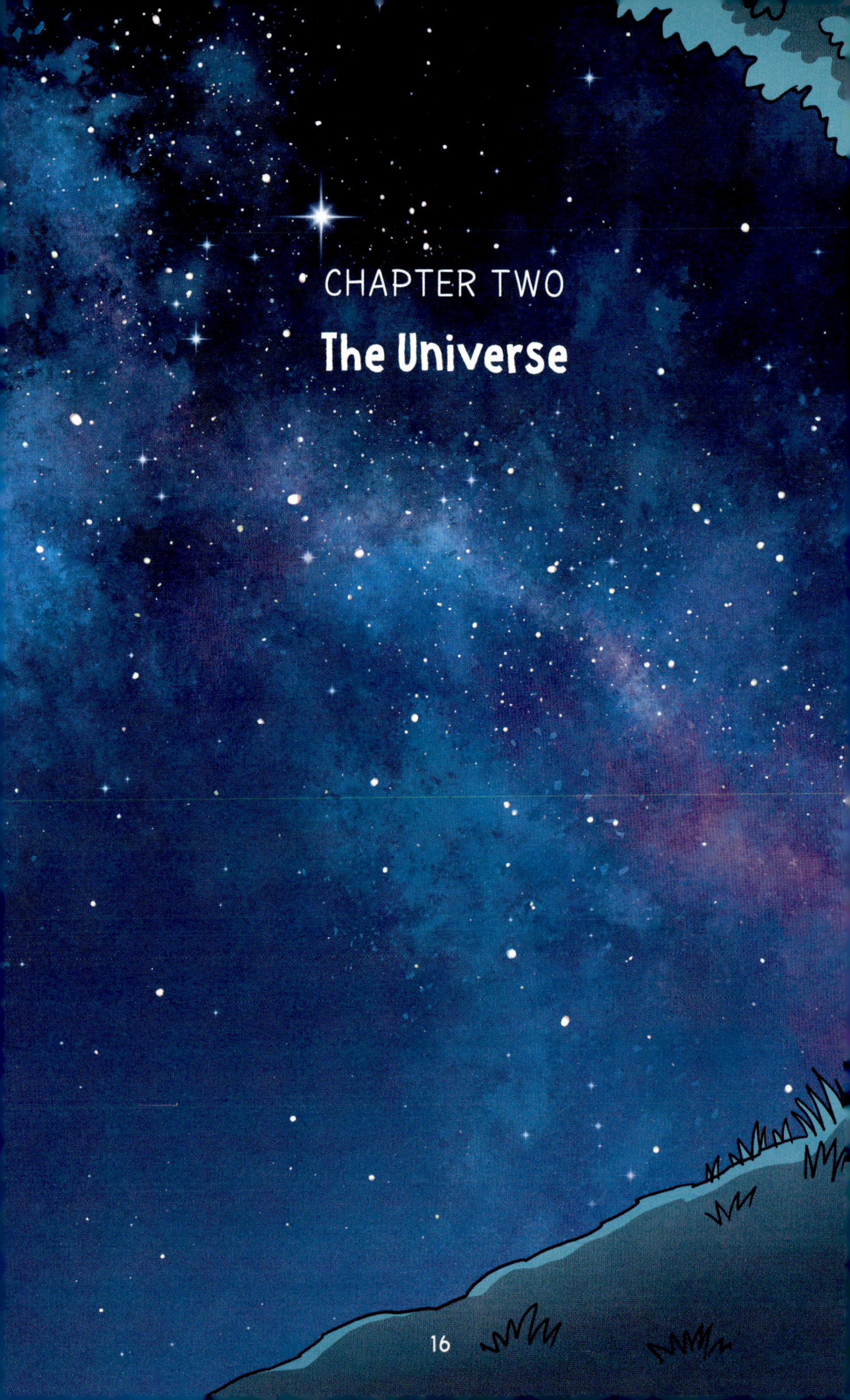

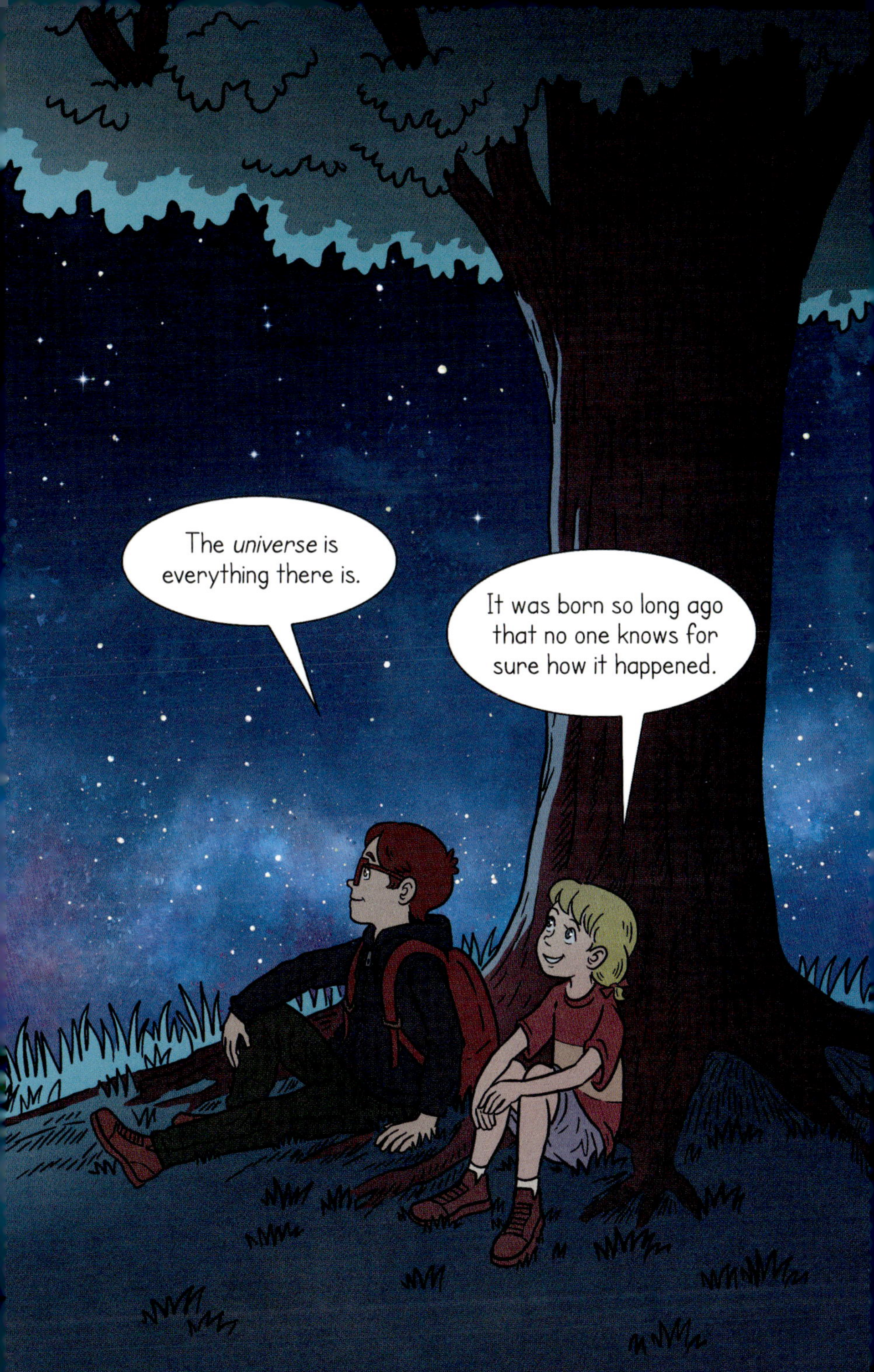
The *universe* is everything there is.
It was born so long ago that no one knows for sure how it happened.

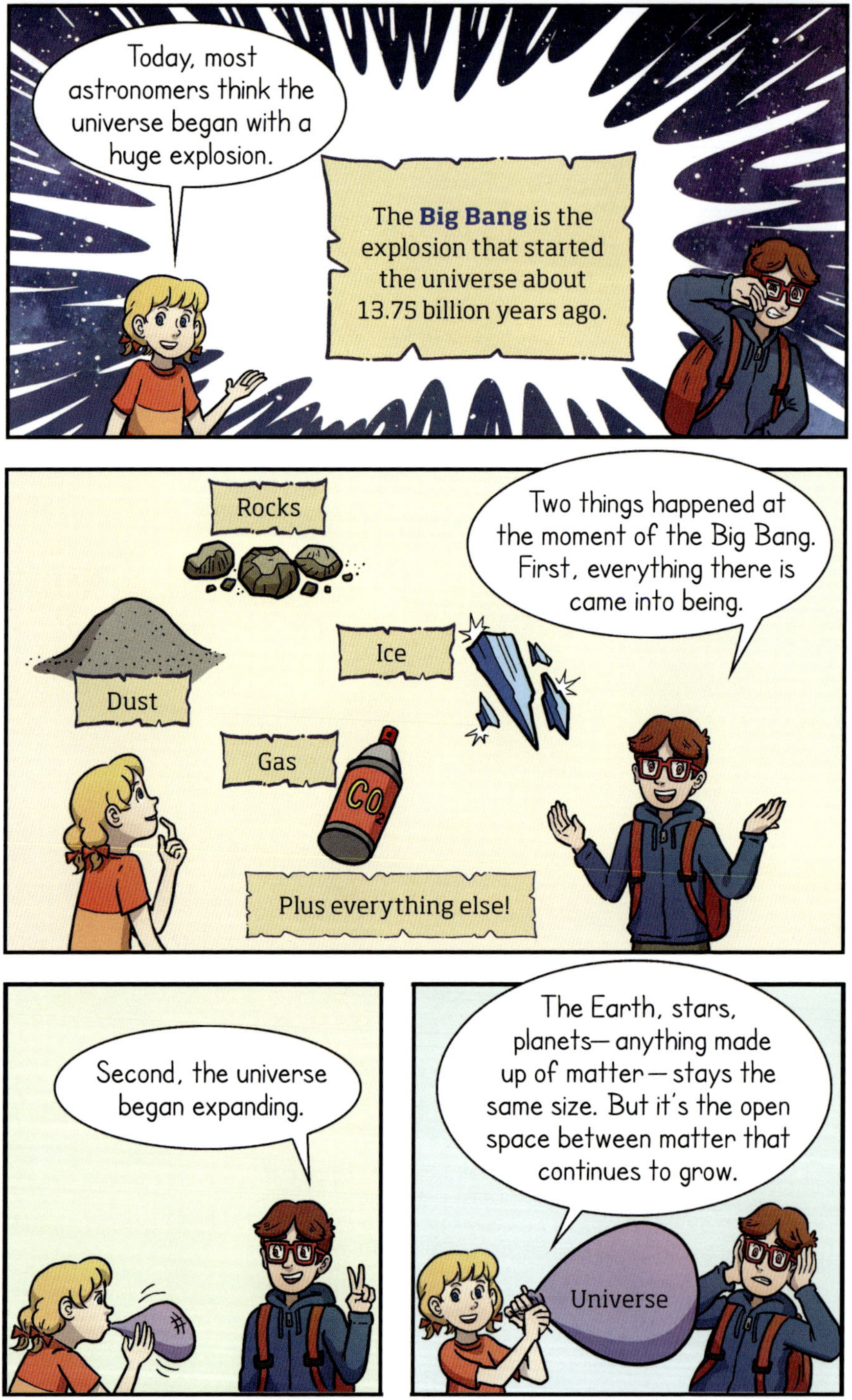
Today, most astronomers think the universe began with a huge explosion.
The **Big Bang** is the explosion that started the universe about 13.75 billion years ago.
Rocks
Two things happened at the moment of the Big Bang. First, everything there is came into being.
Dust
Ice
Gas
CO_2
Plus everything else!
Second, the universe began expanding.
The Earth, stars, planets— anything made up of matter— stays the same size. But it's the open space between matter that continues to grow.
Universe

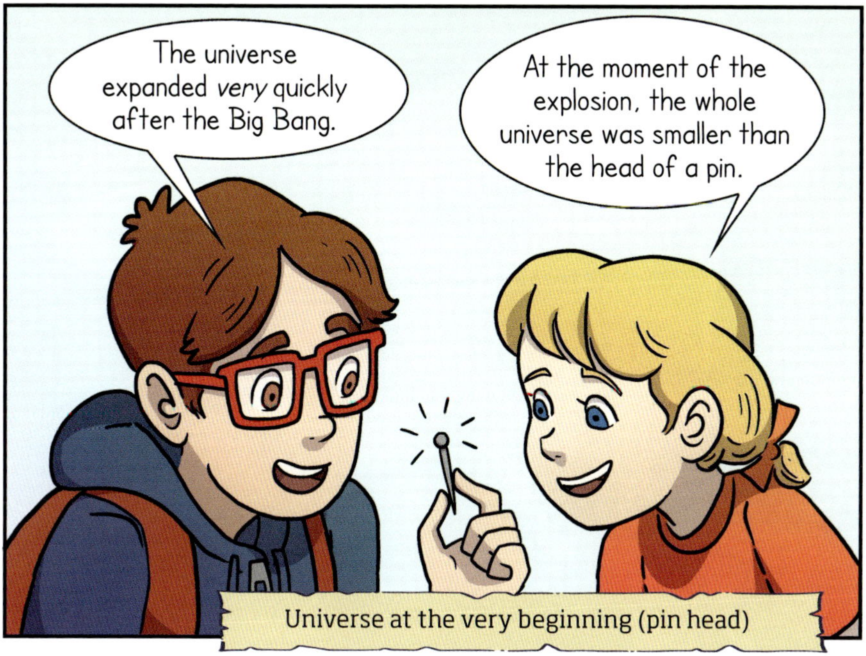
The universe expanded *very* quickly after the Big Bang.
At the moment of the explosion, the whole universe was smaller than the head of a pin.
Universe at the very beginning (pin head)

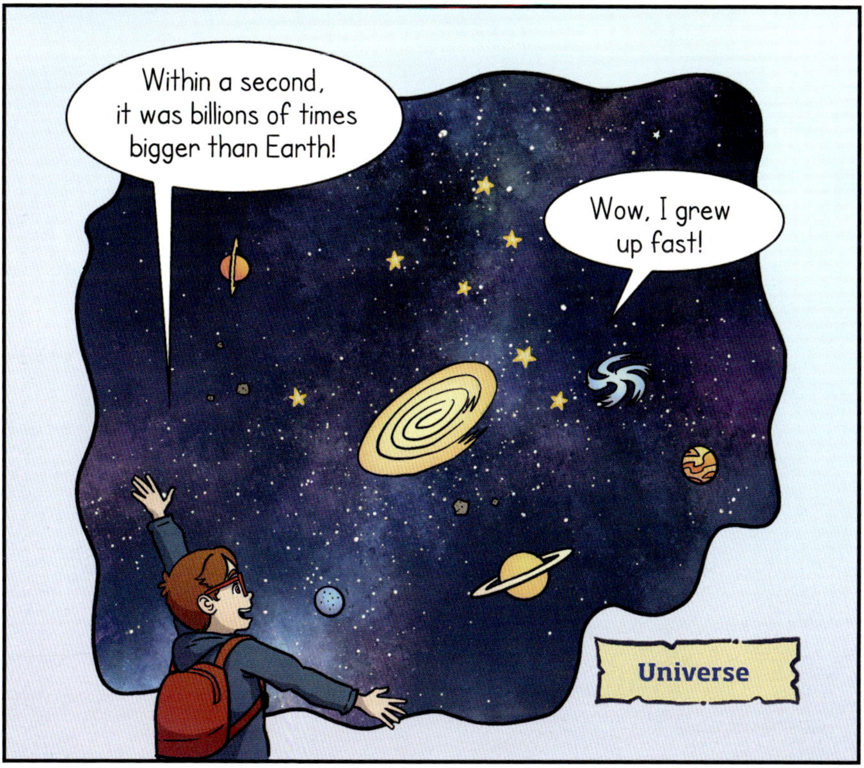
Within a second, it was billions of times bigger than Earth!
Wow, I grew up fast!
Universe

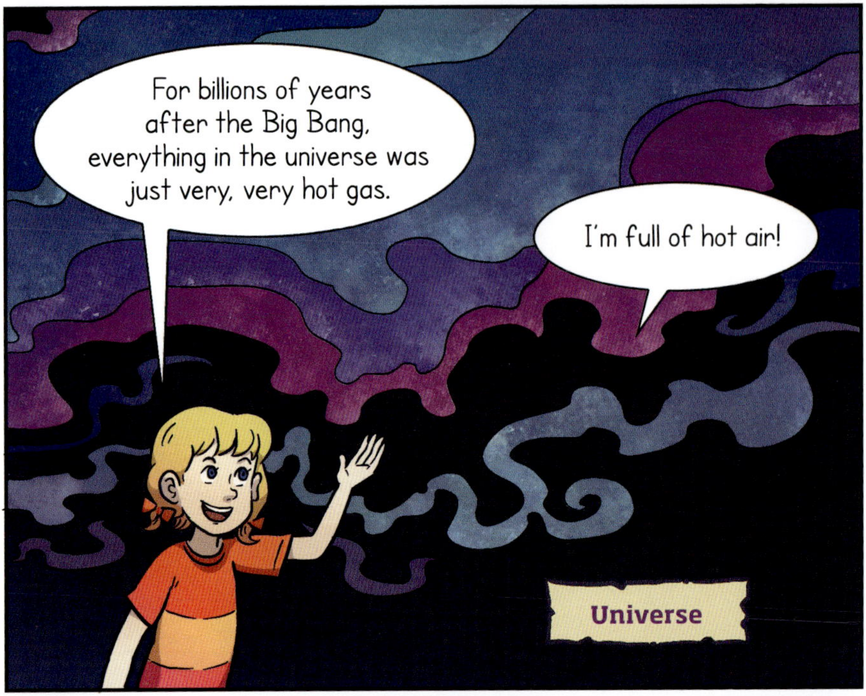
For billions of years after the Big Bang, everything in the universe was just very, very hot gas.
I'm full of hot air!
Universe

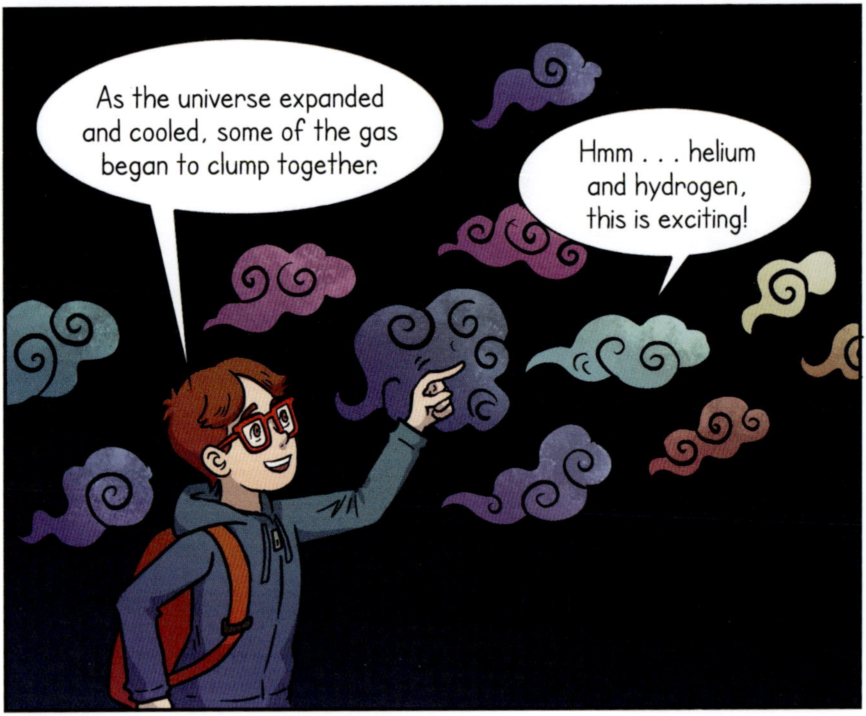
As the universe expanded and cooled, some of the gas began to clump together.
Hmm . . . helium and hydrogen, this is exciting!

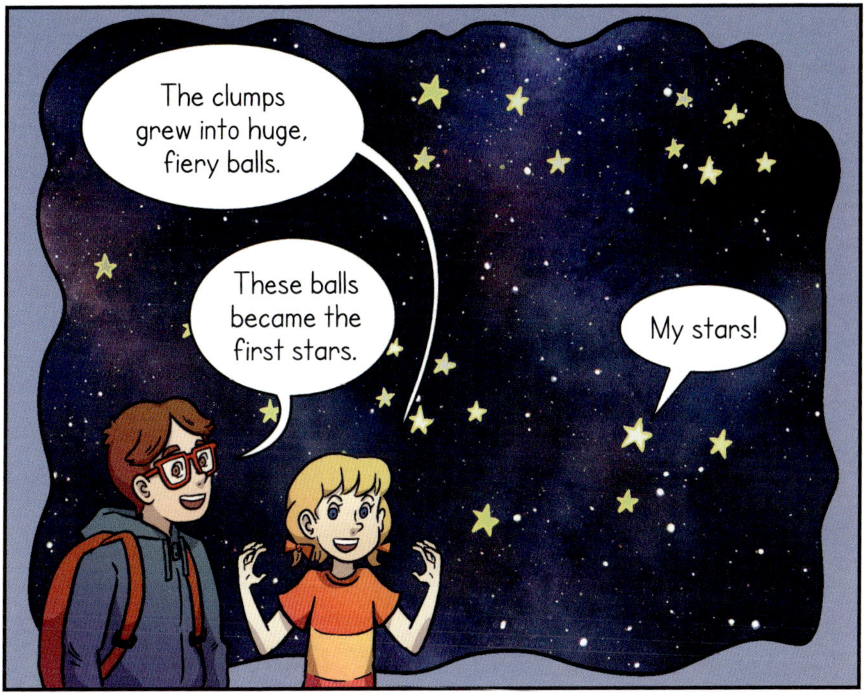

The clumps grew into huge, fiery balls.
These balls became the first stars.
My stars!

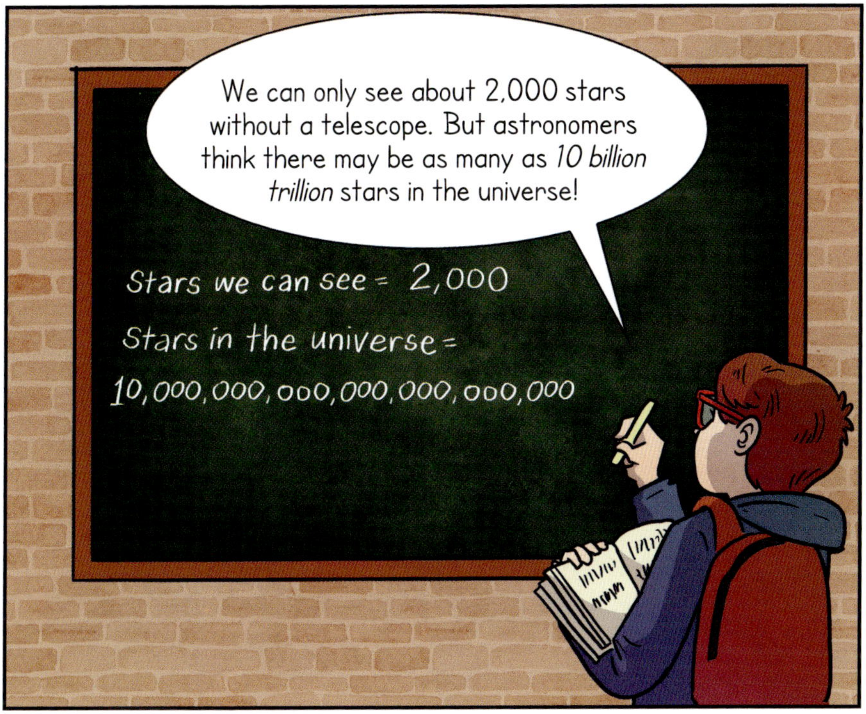

We can only see about 2,000 stars without a telescope. But astronomers think there may be as many as *10 billion trillion* stars in the universe!
Stars we can see = 2,000
Stars in the universe =
10,000,000,000,000,000,000,000

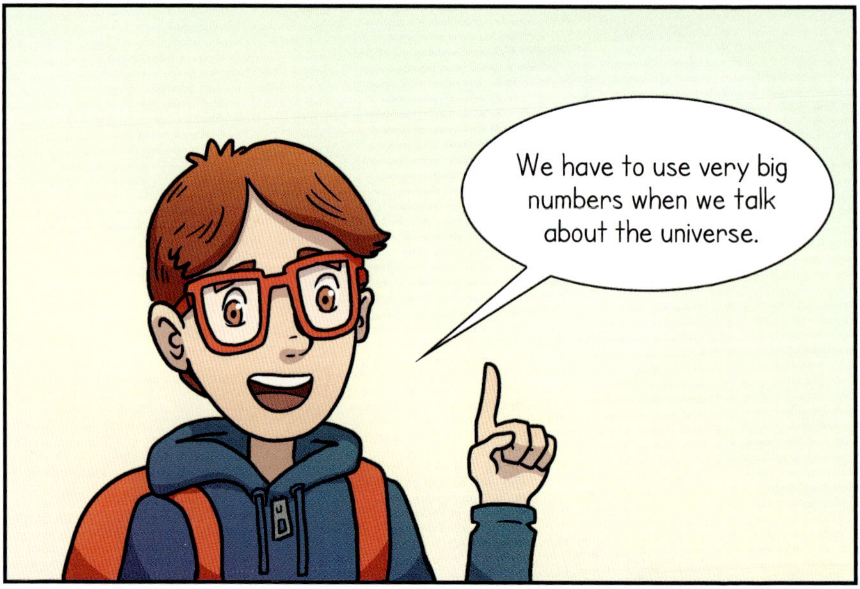
We have to use very big numbers when we talk about the universe.

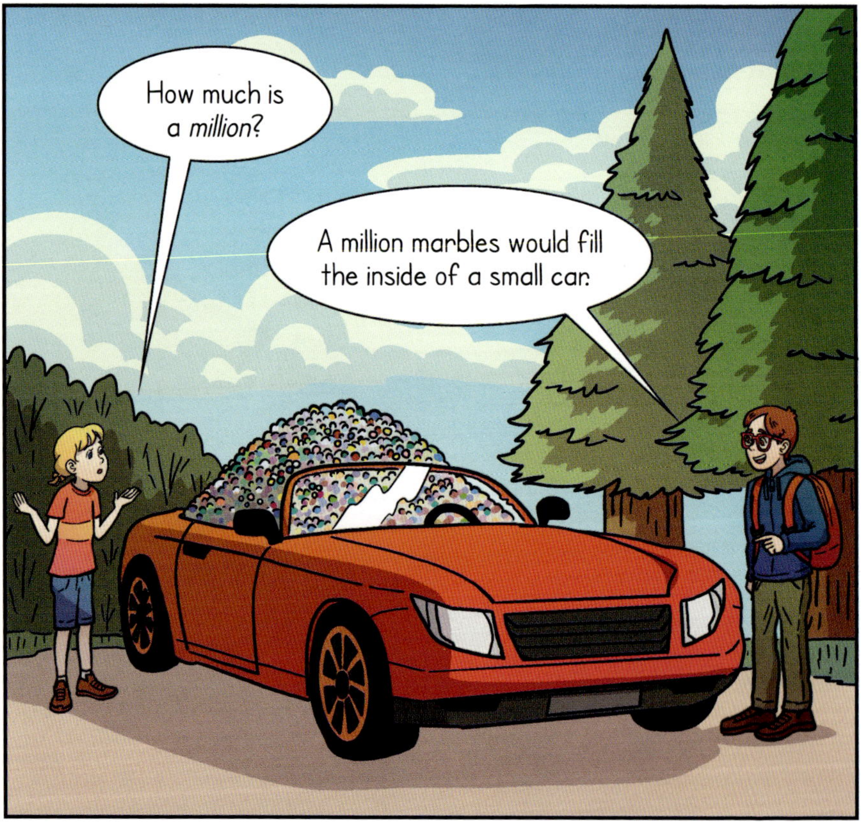
How much is a *million*?
A million marbles would fill the inside of a small car.

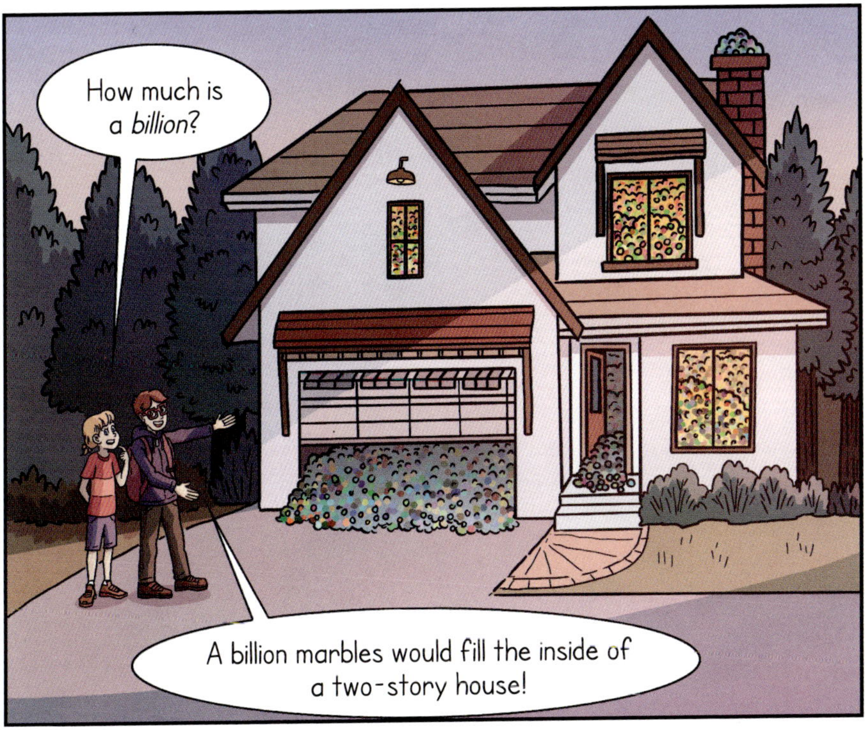
How much is a *billion*?
A billion marbles would fill the inside of a two-story house!

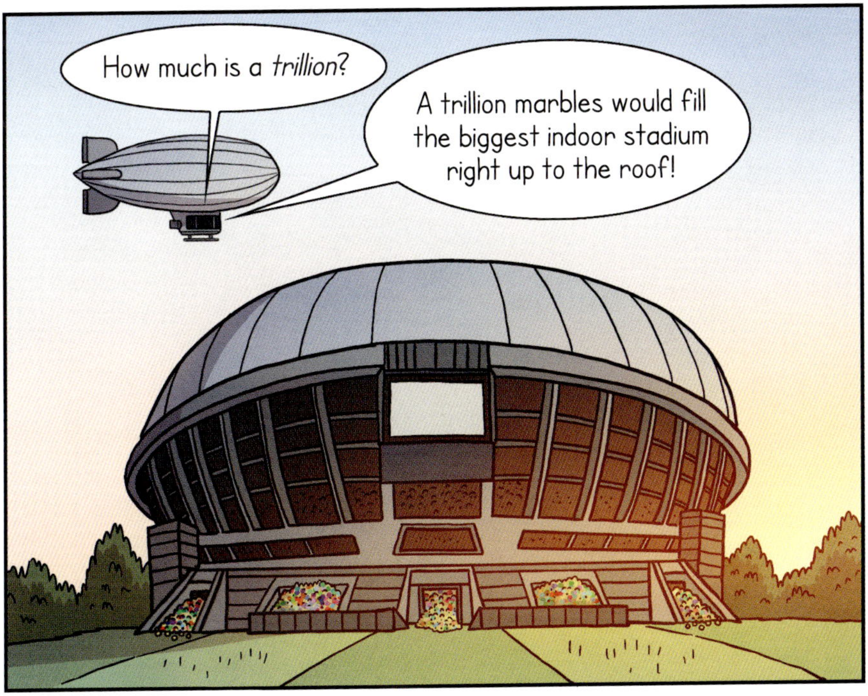
How much is a *trillion*?
A trillion marbles would fill the biggest indoor stadium right up to the roof!

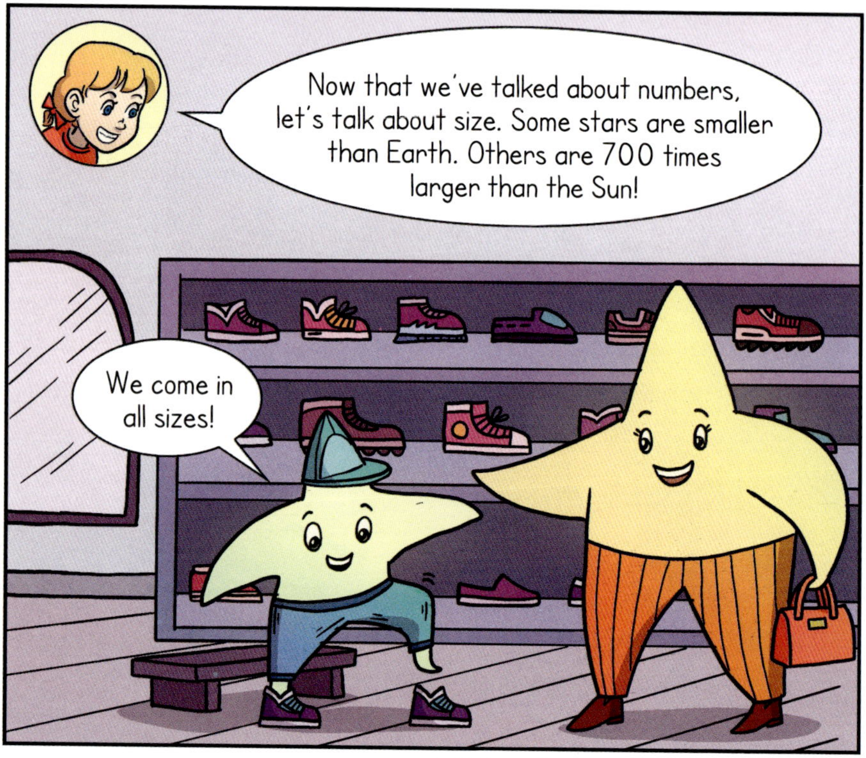
Now that we've talked about numbers, let's talk about size. Some stars are smaller than Earth. Others are 700 times larger than the Sun!
We come in all sizes!

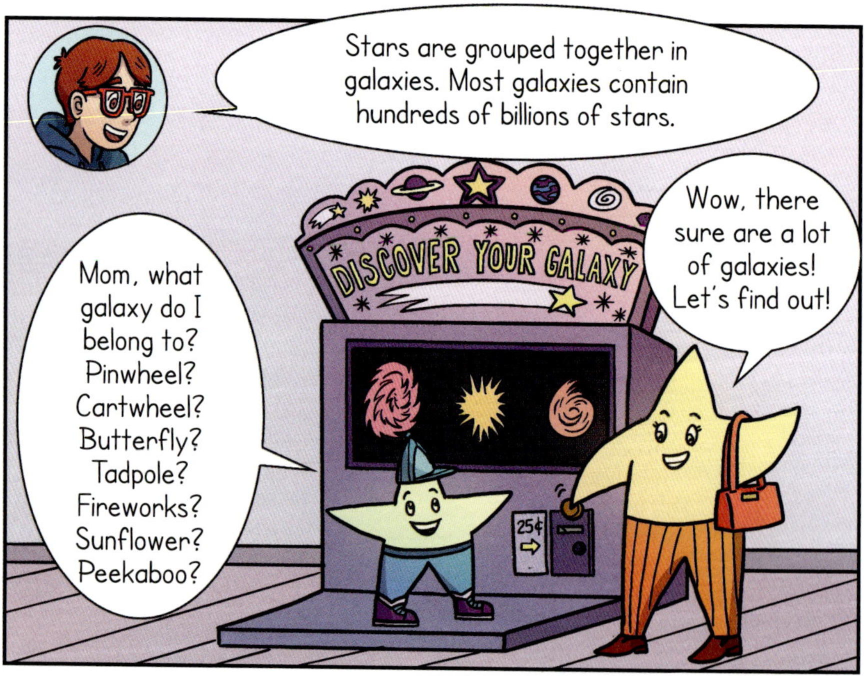
Stars are grouped together in galaxies. Most galaxies contain hundreds of billions of stars.
DISCOVER YOUR GALAXY
Wow, there sure are a lot of galaxies! Let's find out!
Mom, what galaxy do I belong to? Pinwheel? Cartwheel? Butterfly? Tadpole? Fireworks? Sunflower? Peekaboo?
25¢

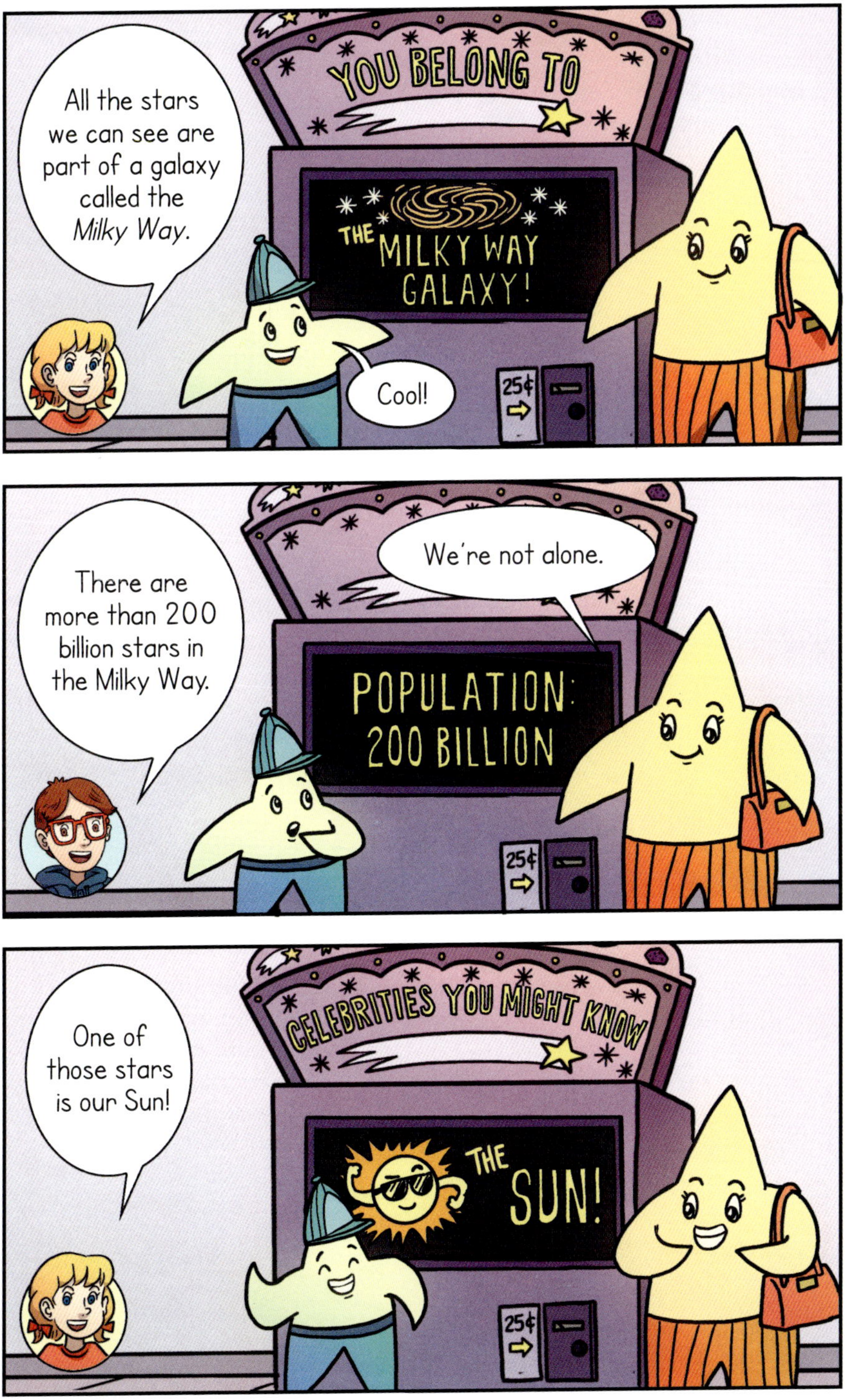
YOU BELONG TO
All the stars we can see are part of a galaxy called the *Milky Way*.
THE MILKY WAY GALAXY!
Cool!
25¢
There are more than 200 billion stars in the Milky Way.
We're not alone.
POPULATION: 200 BILLION
25¢
CELEBRITIES YOU MIGHT KNOW
One of those stars is our Sun!
THE SUN!
25¢

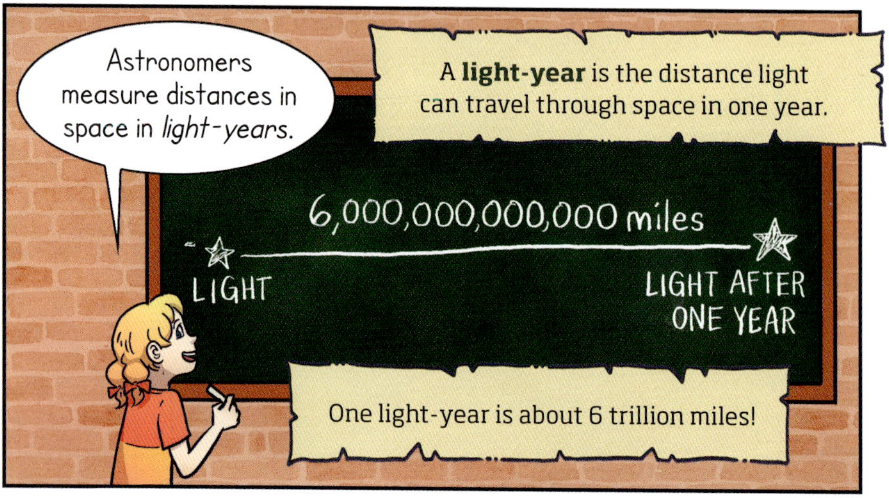
Astronomers measure distances in space in *light-years.*
A **light-year** is the distance light can travel through space in one year.
6,000,000,000,000 miles
LIGHT
LIGHT AFTER ONE YEAR
One light-year is about 6 trillion miles!

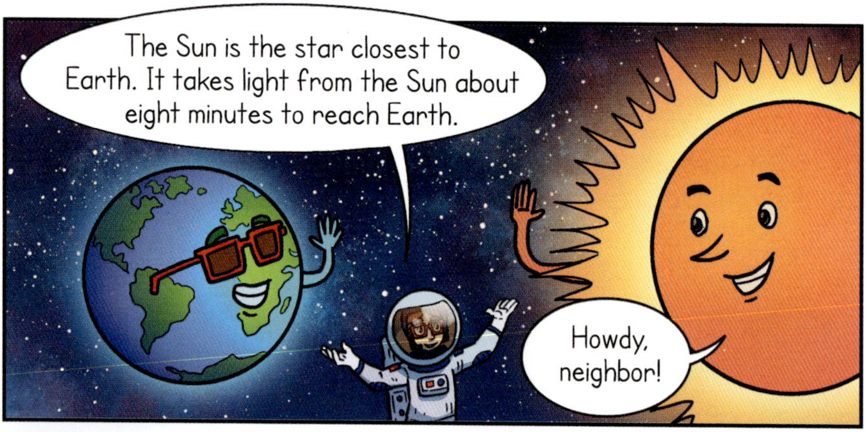
The Sun is the star closest to Earth. It takes light from the Sun about eight minutes to reach Earth.
Howdy, neighbor!

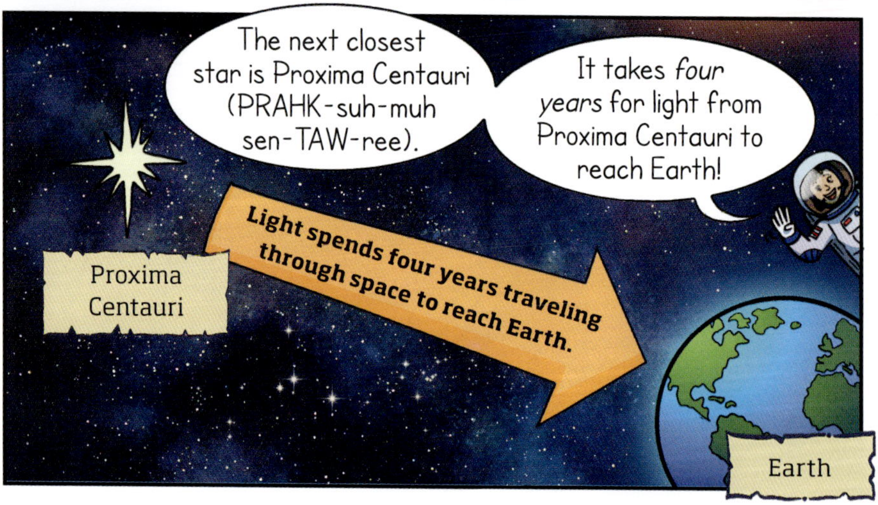
The next closest star is Proxima Centauri (PRAHK-suh-muh sen-TAW-ree).
It takes *four years* for light from Proxima Centauri to reach Earth!
Light spends four years traveling through space to reach Earth.
Proxima Centauri
Earth

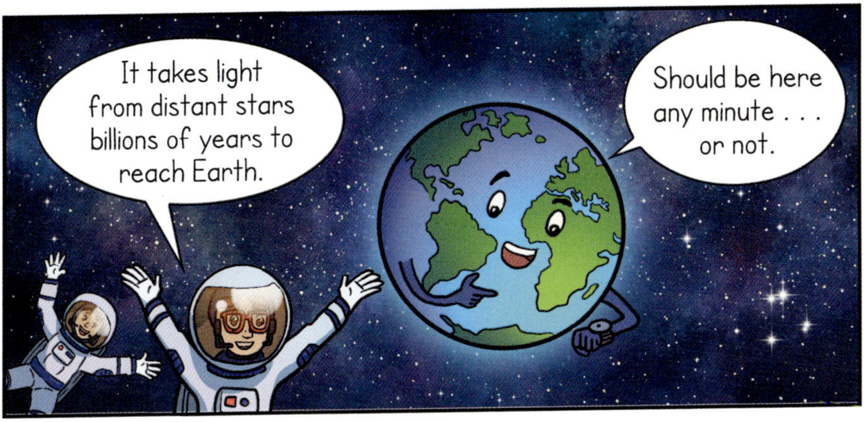
It takes light from distant stars billions of years to reach Earth.
Should be here any minute . . . or not.

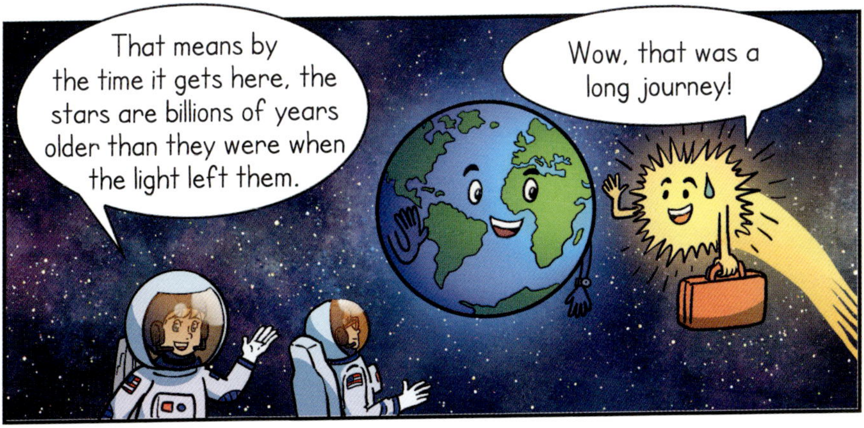
That means by the time it gets here, the stars are billions of years older than they were when the light left them.
Wow, that was a long journey!

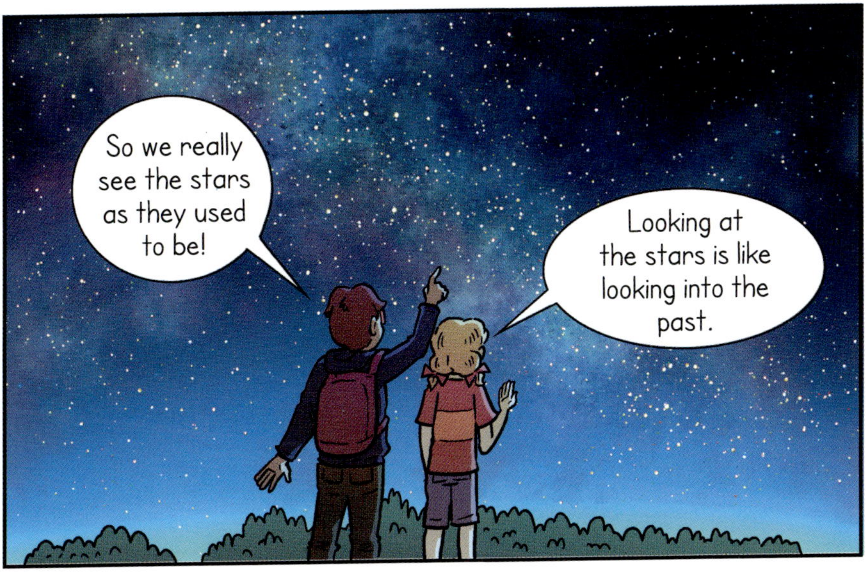
So we really see the stars as they used to be!
Looking at the stars is like looking into the past.

CHAPTER THREE

The Sun

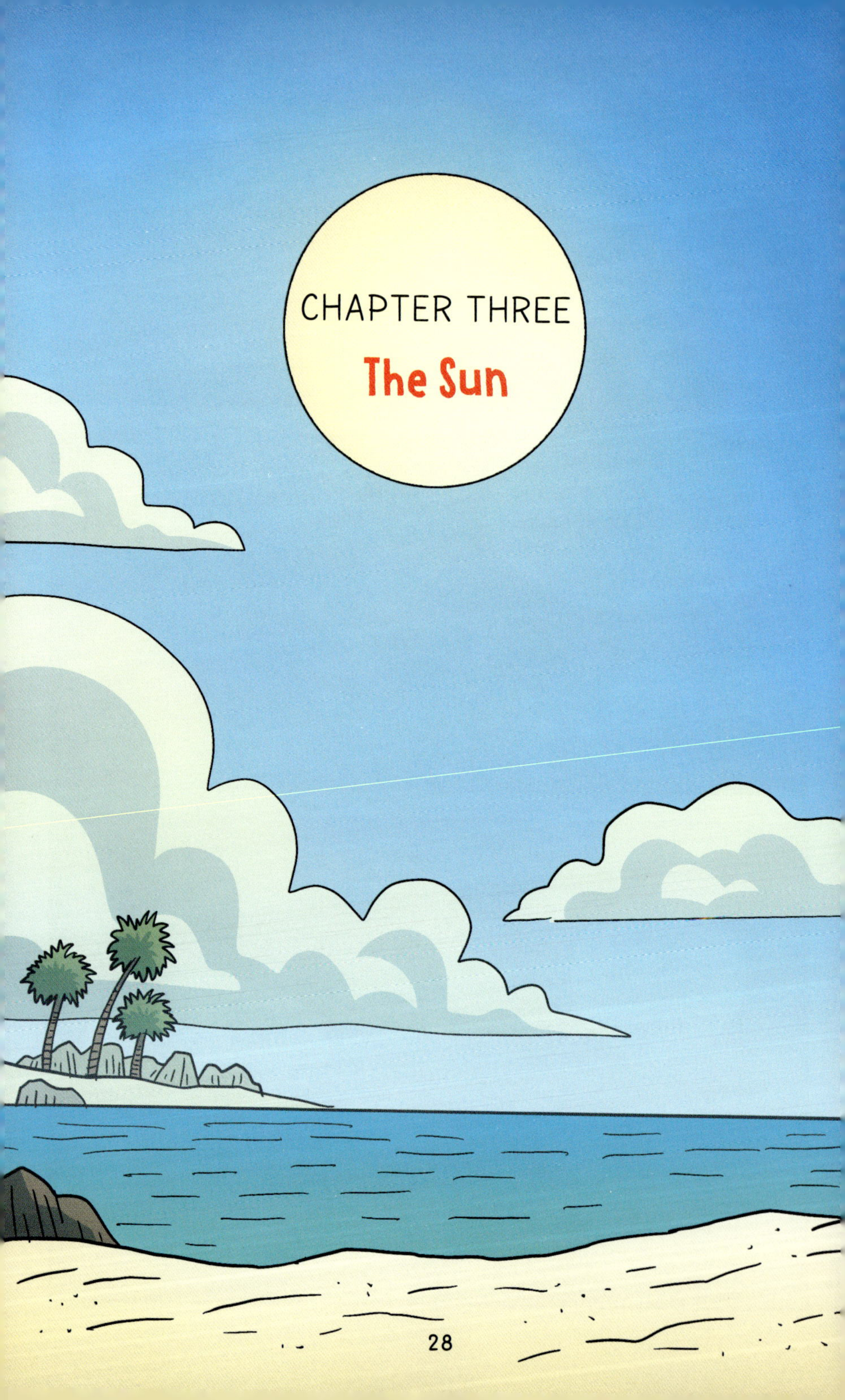

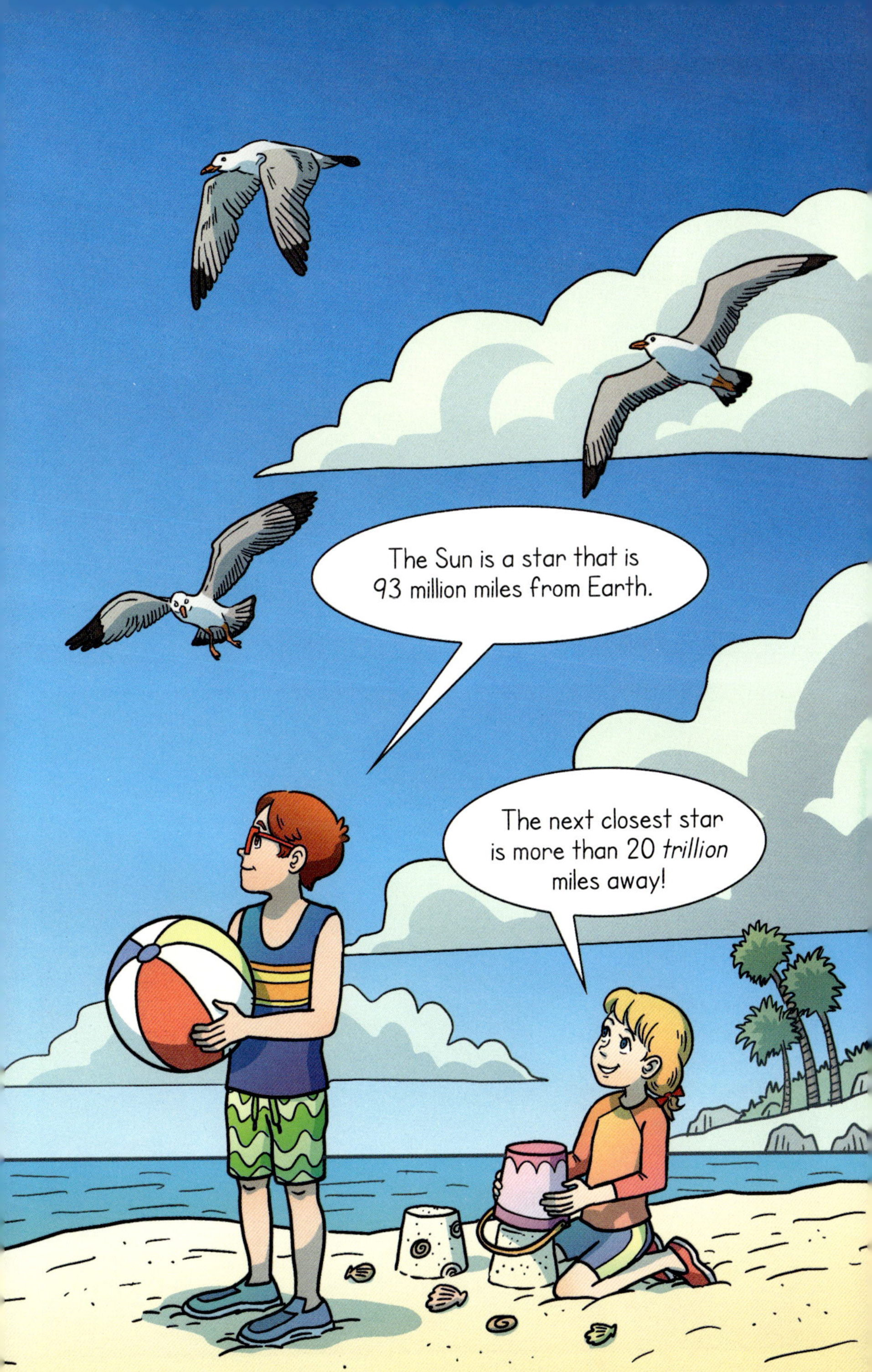
The Sun is a star that is 93 million miles from Earth.
The next closest star is more than 20 *trillion* miles away!

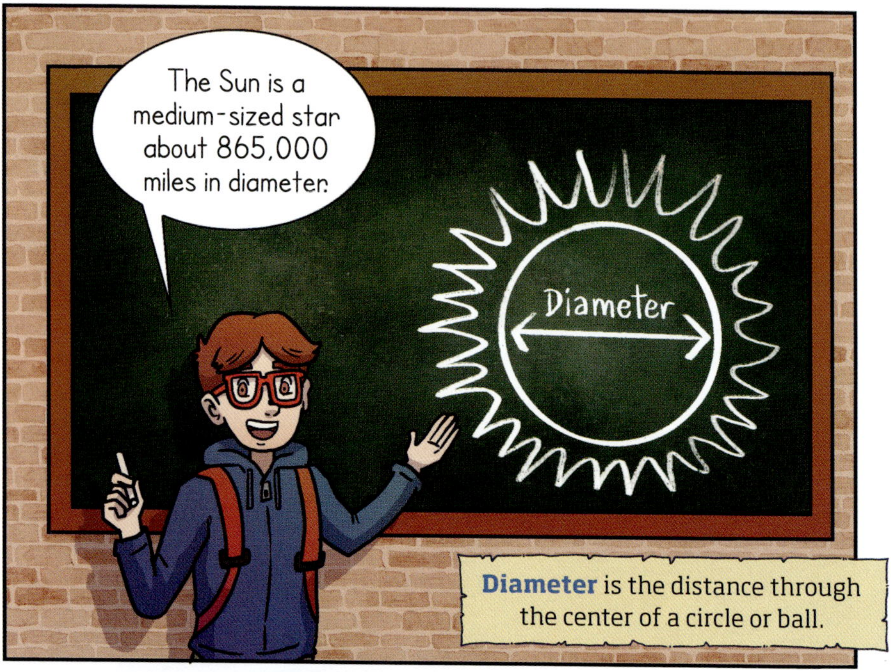
The Sun is a medium-sized star about 865,000 miles in diameter.
Diameter
Diameter is the distance through the center of a circle or ball.

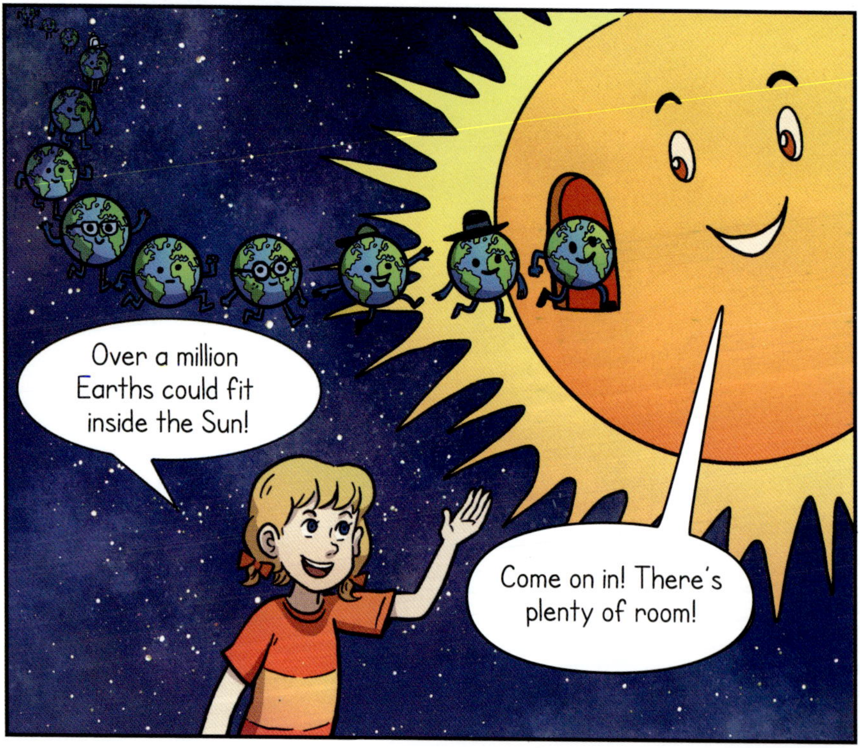
Over a million Earths could fit inside the Sun!
Come on in! There's plenty of room!

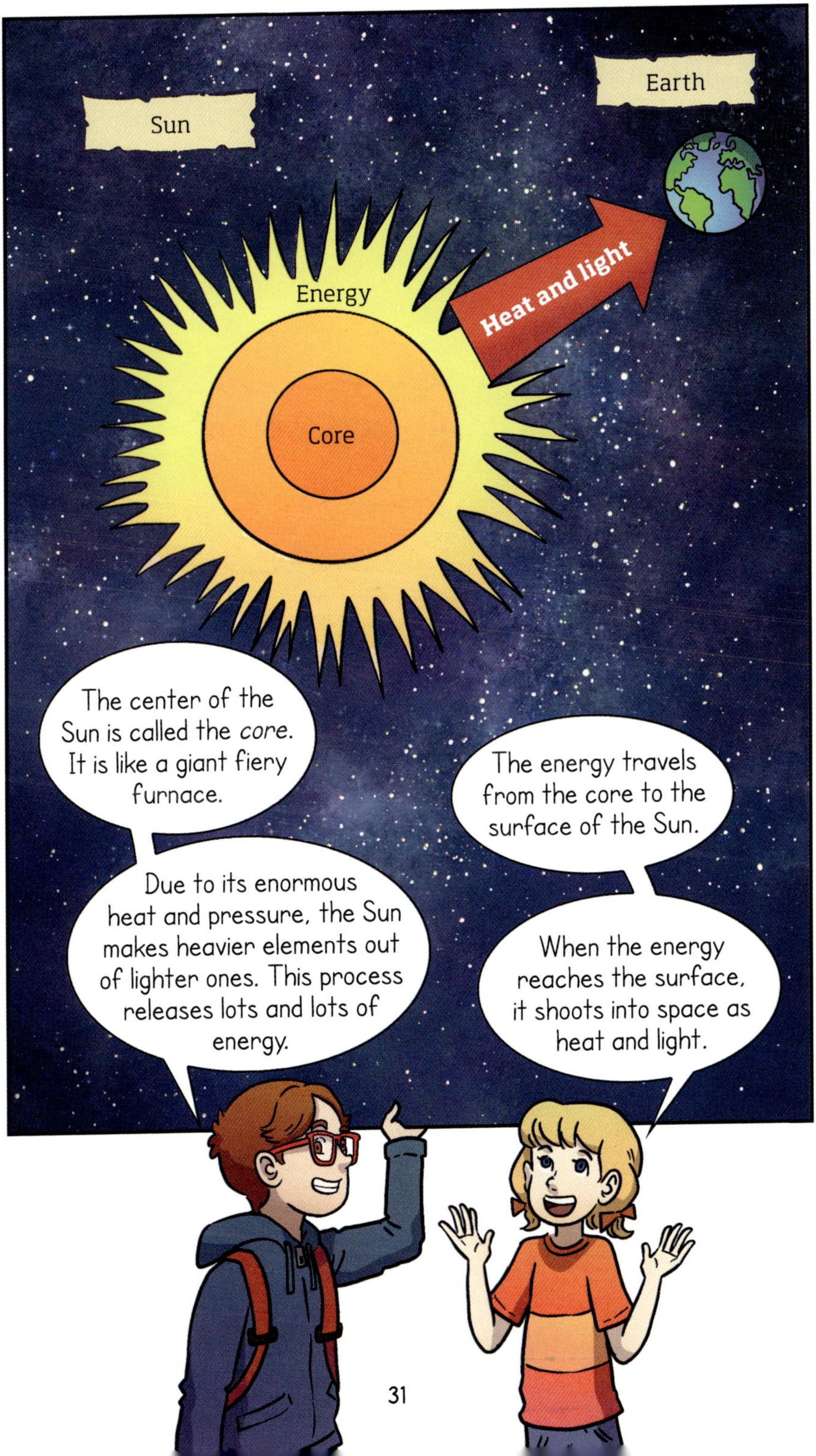
Sun
Earth
Energy
Core
Heat and light
The center of the Sun is called the *core*. It is like a giant fiery furnace.
Due to its enormous heat and pressure, the Sun makes heavier elements out of lighter ones. This process releases lots and lots of energy.
The energy travels from the core to the surface of the Sun.
When the energy reaches the surface, it shoots into space as heat and light.

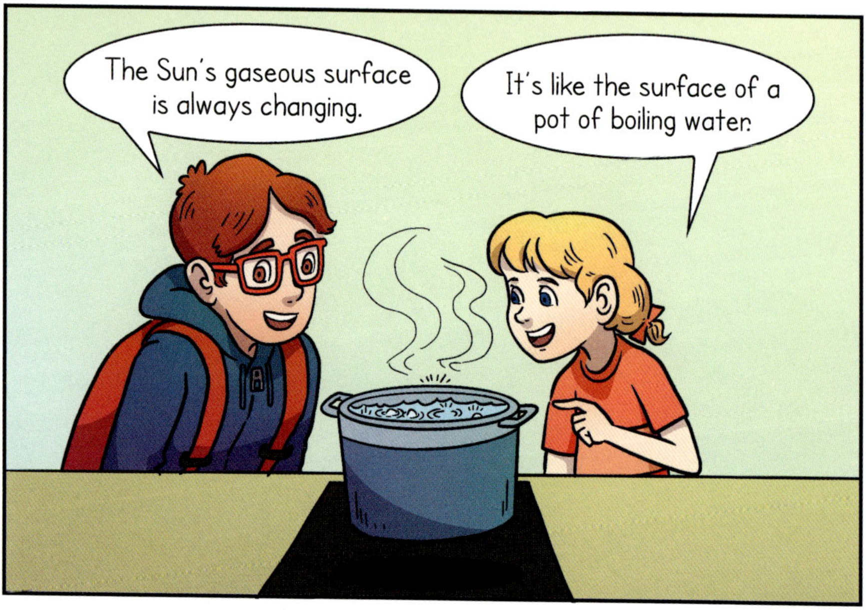
The Sun's gaseous surface is always changing.
It's like the surface of a pot of boiling water.

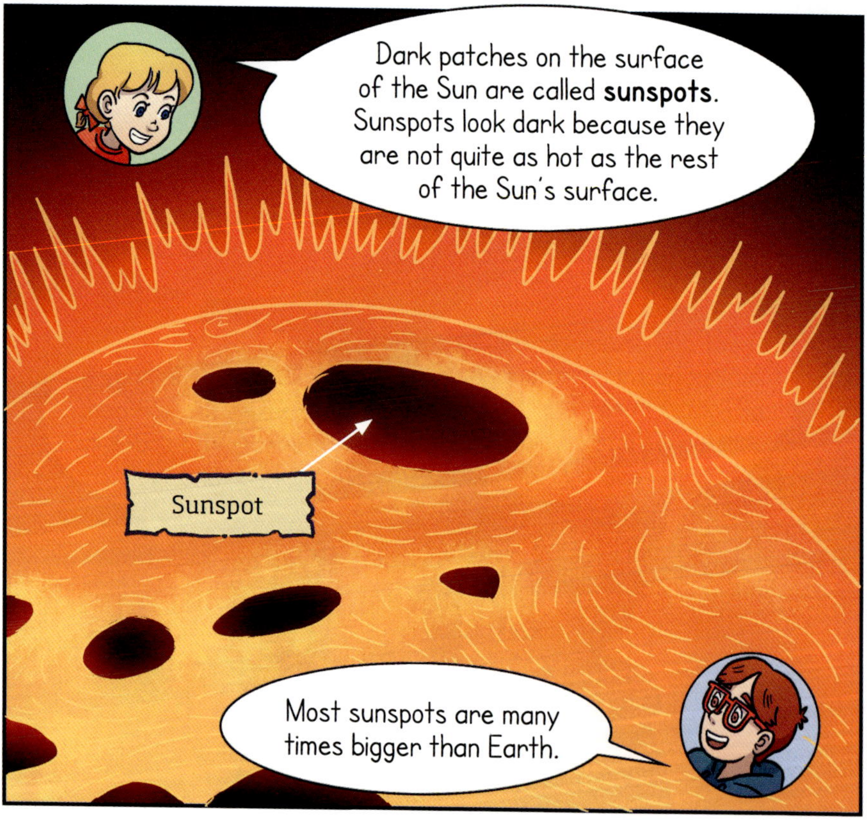
Dark patches on the surface of the Sun are called **sunspots**. Sunspots look dark because they are not quite as hot as the rest of the Sun's surface.
Sunspot
Most sunspots are many times bigger than Earth.

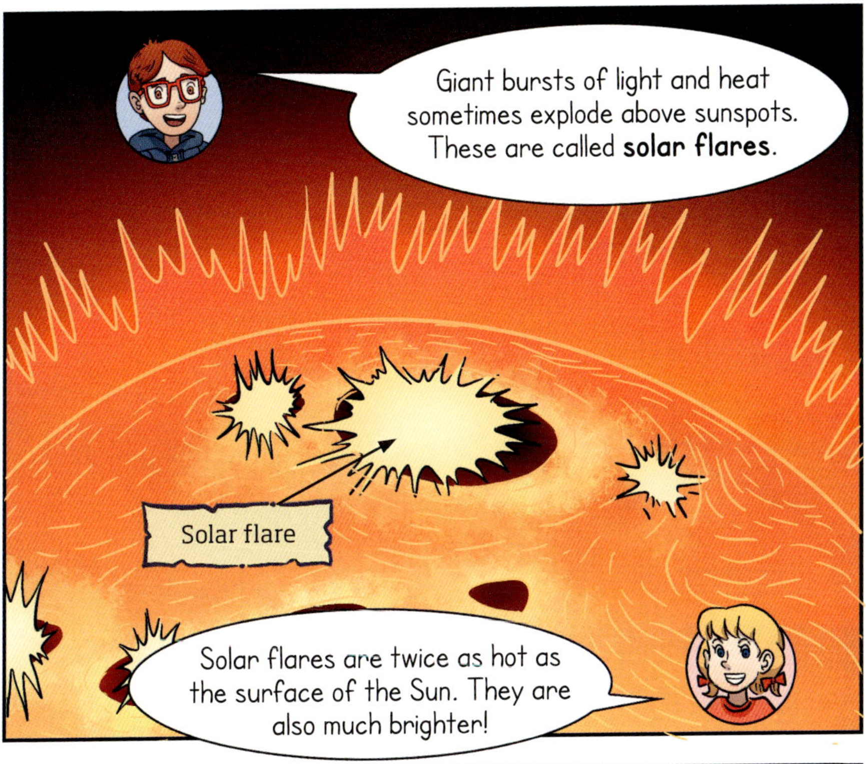
Giant bursts of light and heat sometimes explode above sunspots. These are called **solar flares**.
Solar flare
Solar flares are twice as hot as the surface of the Sun. They are also much brighter!

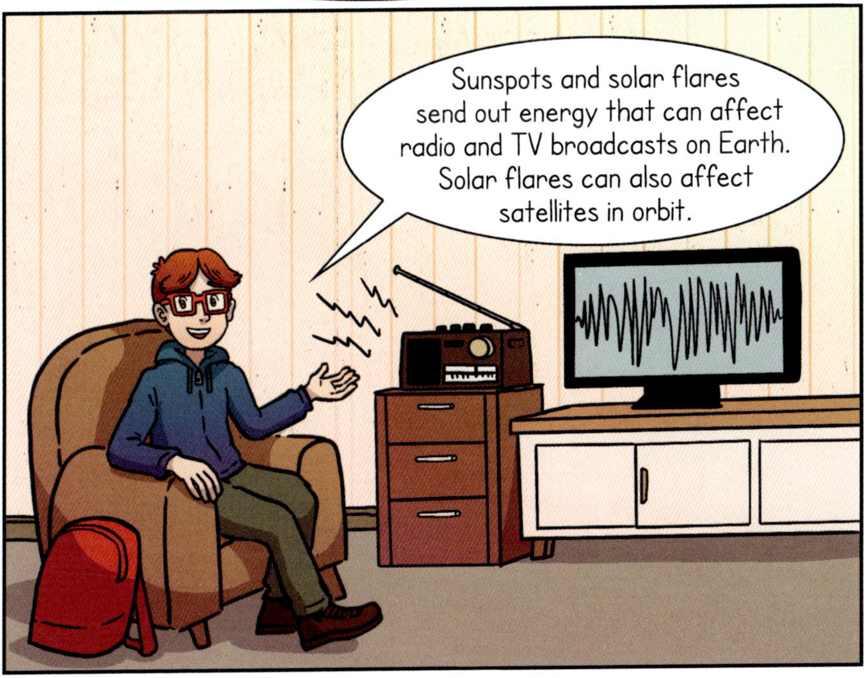
Sunspots and solar flares send out energy that can affect radio and TV broadcasts on Earth. Solar flares can also affect satellites in orbit.

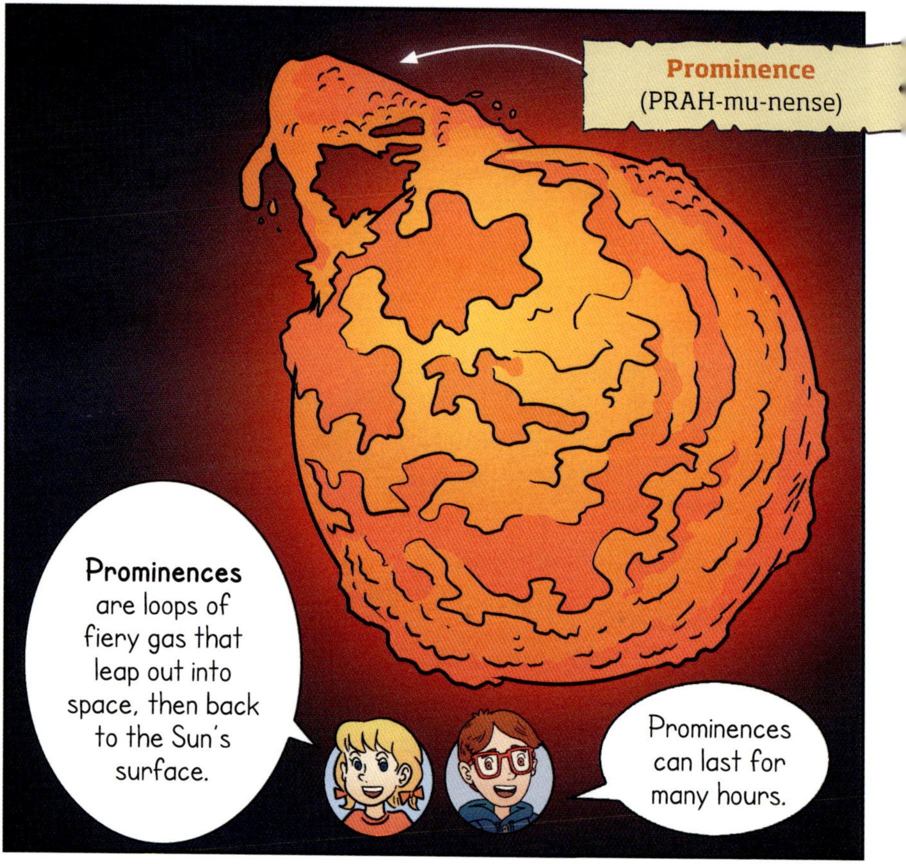
Prominence
(PRAH-mu-nense)
Prominences are loops of fiery gas that leap out into space, then back to the Sun's surface.
Prominences can last for many hours.

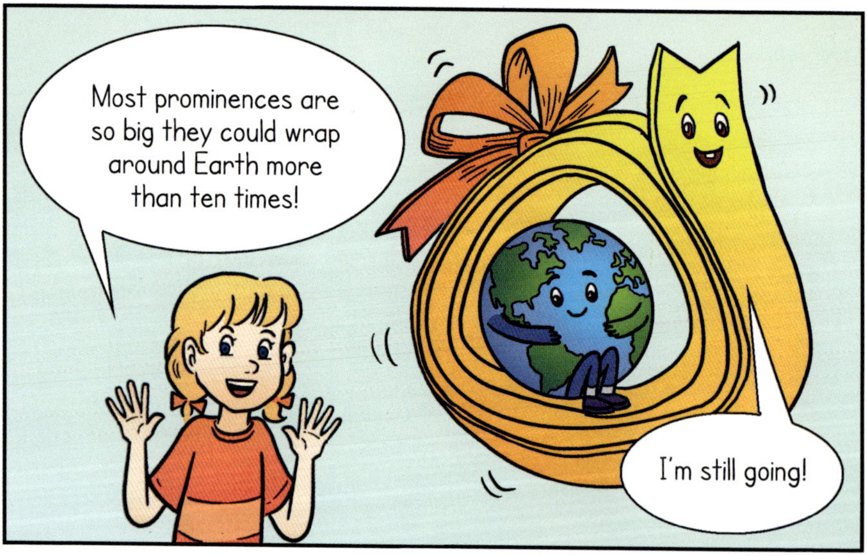
Most prominences are so big they could wrap around Earth more than ten times!
I'm still going!

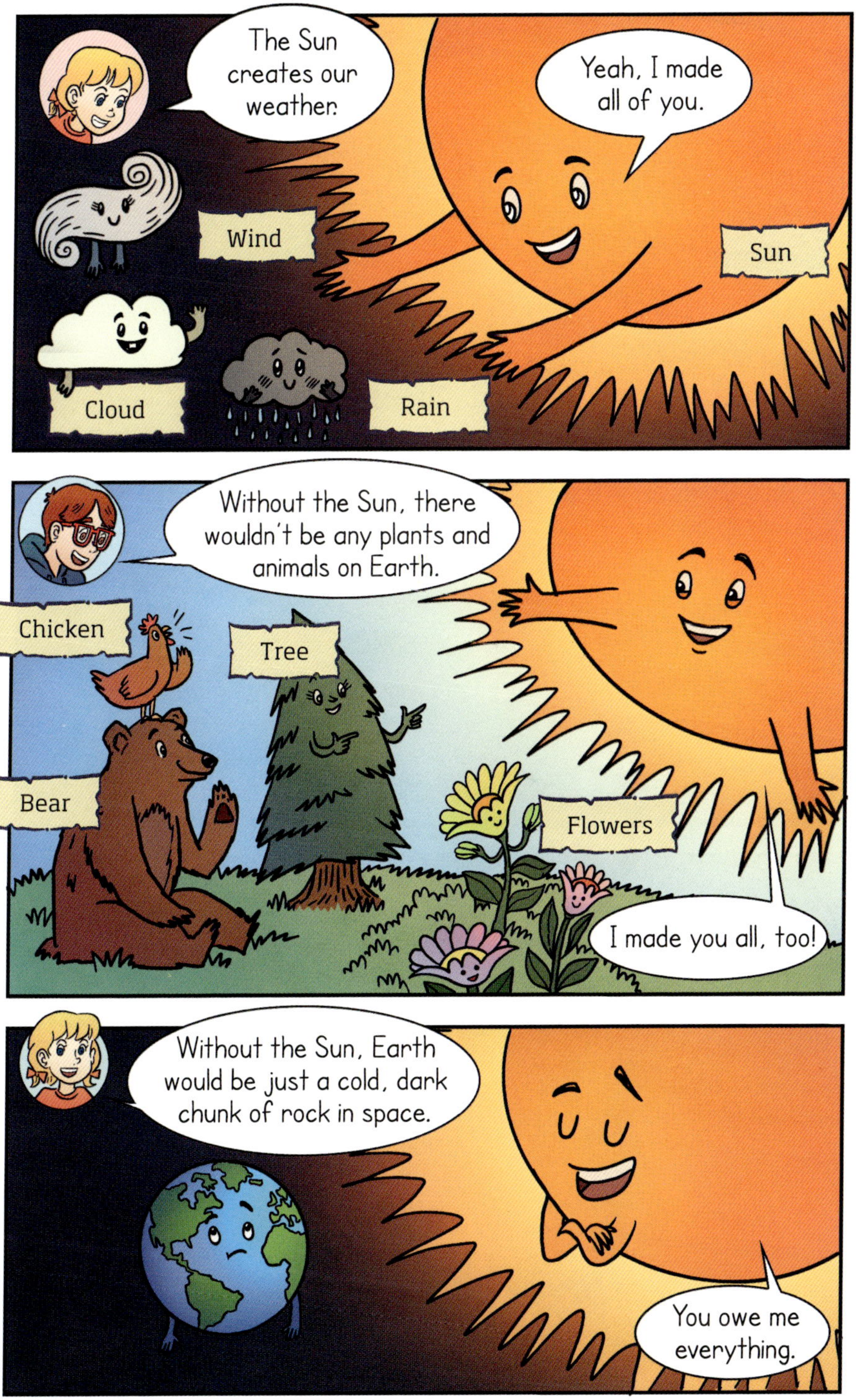
The Sun creates our weather.
Yeah, I made all of you.
Wind
Sun
Cloud
Rain
Without the Sun, there wouldn't be any plants and animals on Earth.
Chicken
Tree
Bear
Flowers
I made you all, too!
Without the Sun, Earth would be just a cold, dark chunk of rock in space.
You owe me everything.

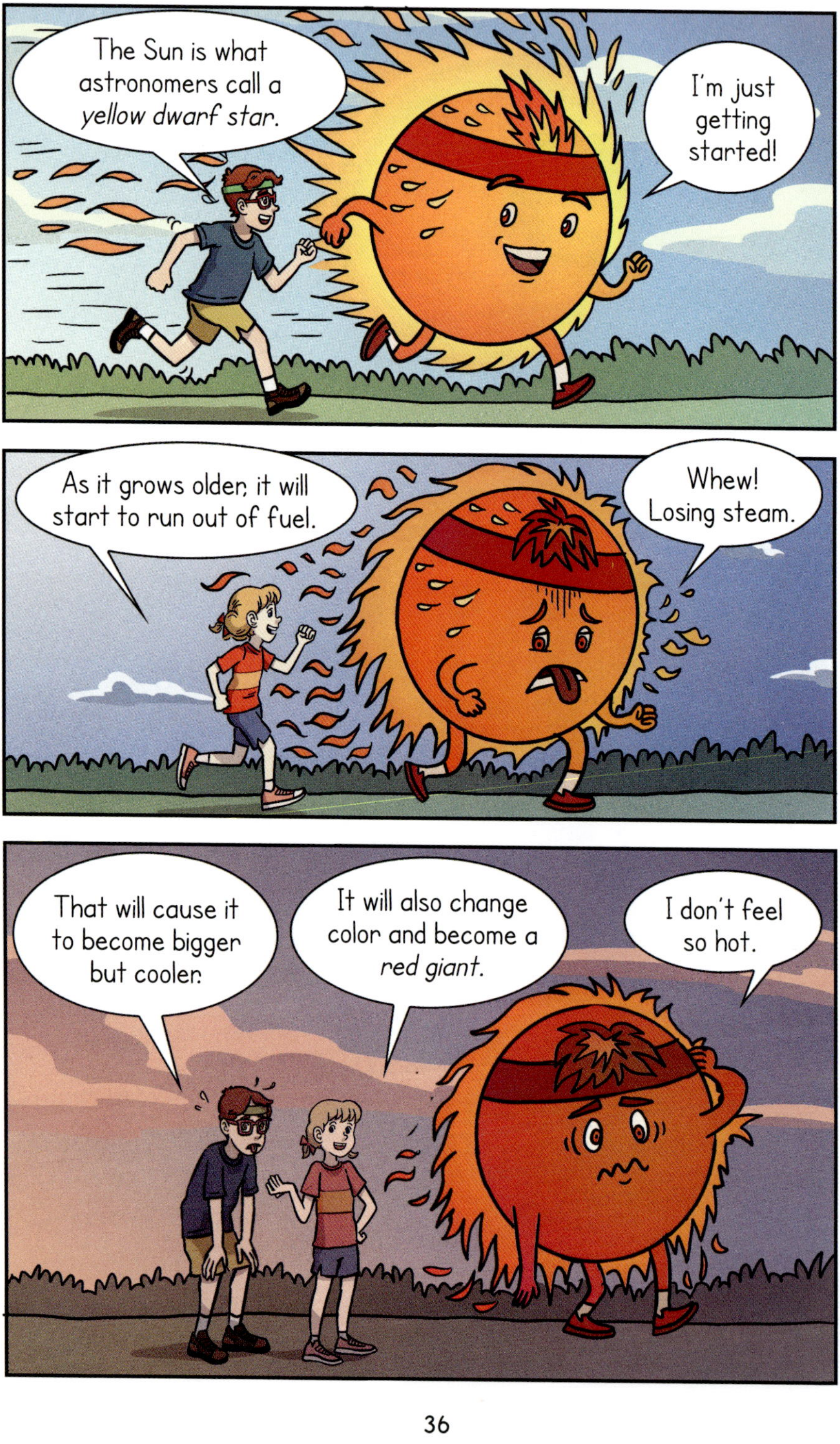
The Sun is what astronomers call a *yellow dwarf star*.
I'm just getting started!
As it grows older, it will start to run out of fuel.
Whew! Losing steam.
That will cause it to become bigger but cooler.
It will also change color and become a *red giant*.
I don't feel so hot.

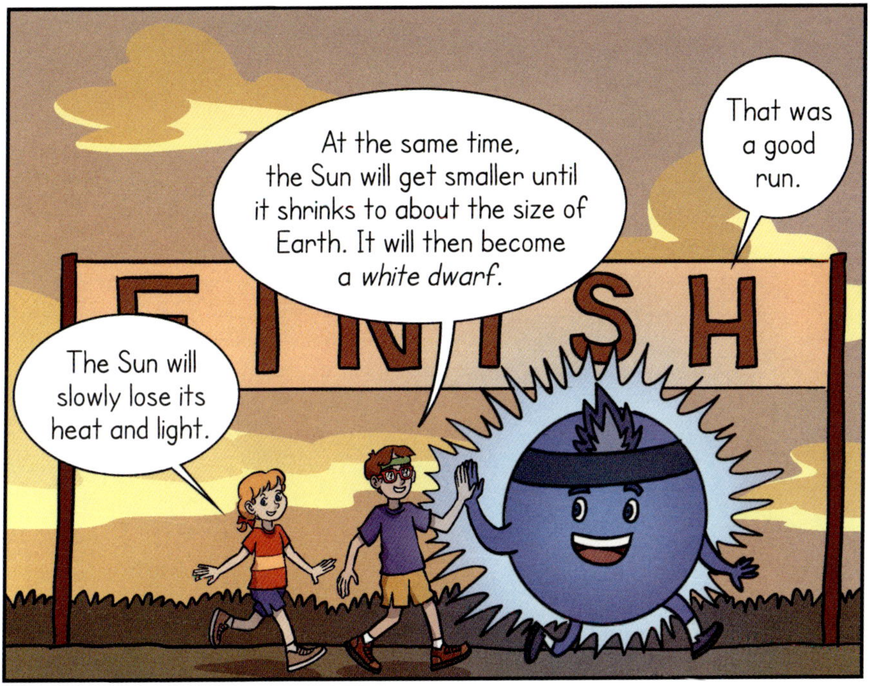
The Sun will slowly lose its heat and light.
At the same time, the Sun will get smaller until it shrinks to about the size of Earth. It will then become a *white dwarf*.
That was a good run.
FINISH

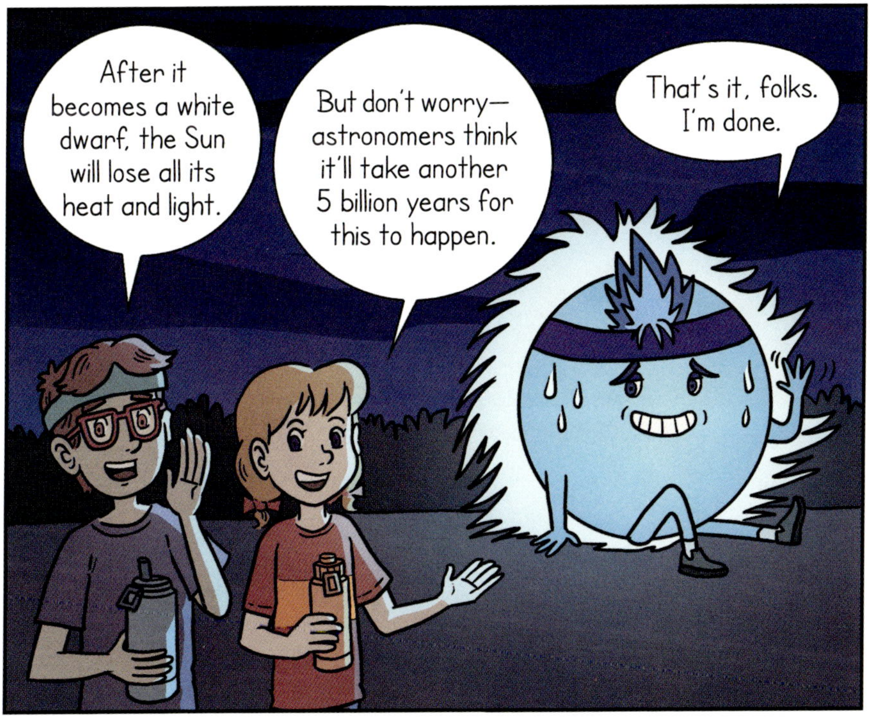
After it becomes a white dwarf, the Sun will lose all its heat and light.
But don't worry—astronomers think it'll take another 5 billion years for this to happen.
That's it, folks. I'm done.

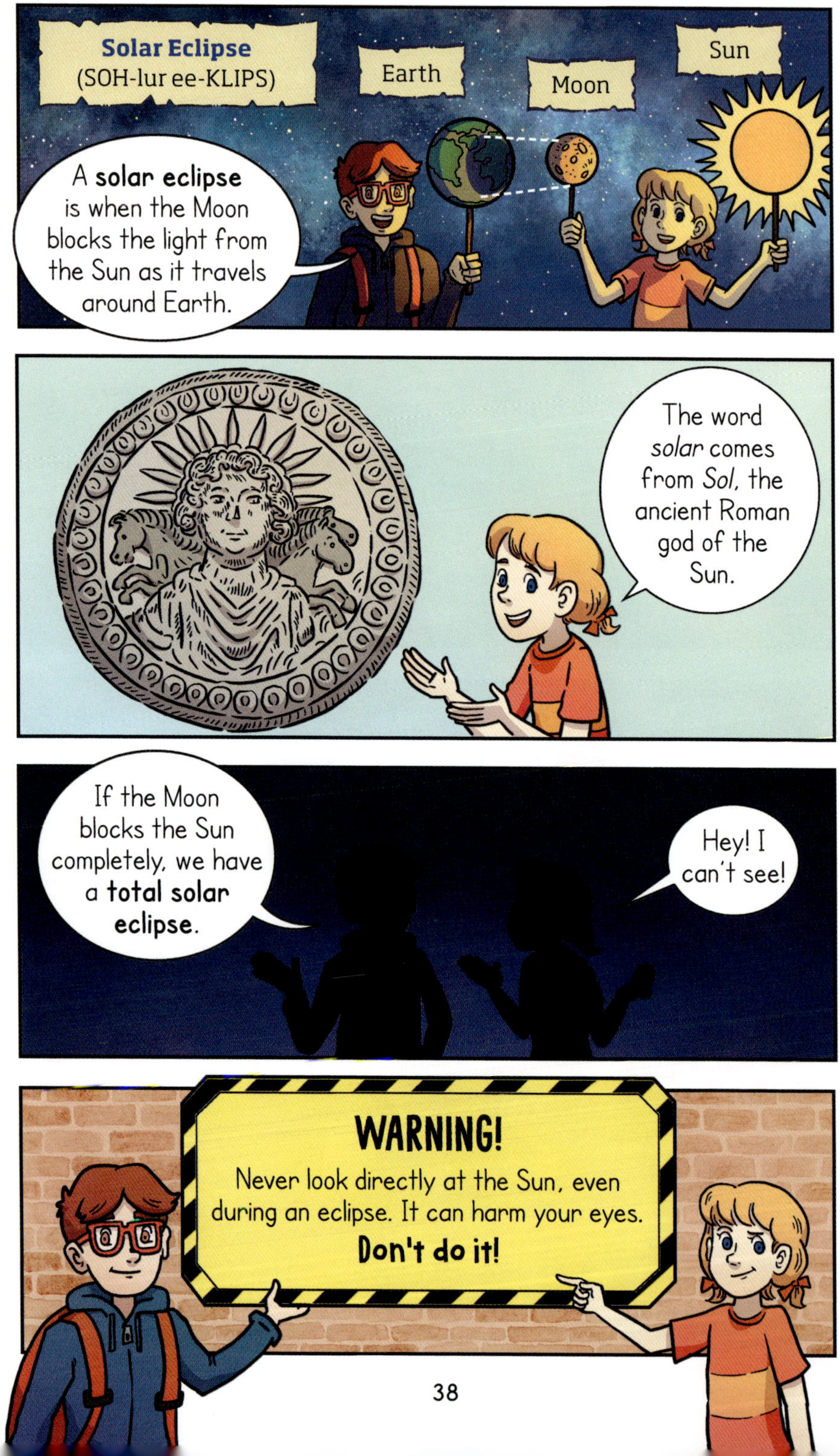

Solar Eclipse (SOH-lur ee-KLIPS)
Earth
Moon
Sun
A **solar eclipse** is when the Moon blocks the light from the Sun as it travels around Earth.
The word *solar* comes from *Sol*, the ancient Roman god of the Sun.
If the Moon blocks the Sun completely, we have a **total solar eclipse**.
Hey! I can't see!
WARNING!
Never look directly at the Sun, even during an eclipse. It can harm your eyes.
Don't do it!

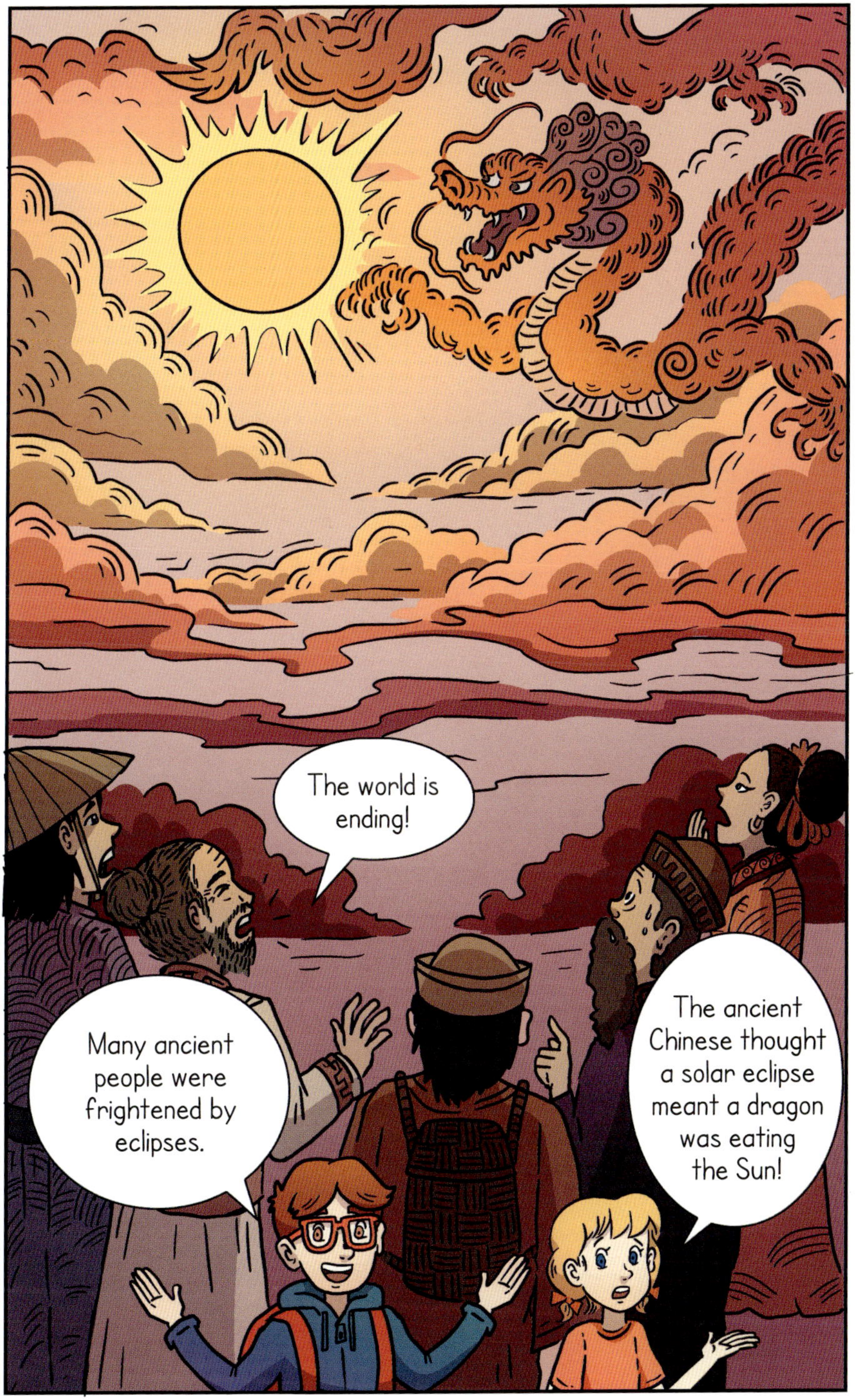
The world is ending!
Many ancient people were frightened by eclipses.
The ancient Chinese thought a solar eclipse meant a dragon was eating the Sun!

CHAPTER FOUR

Our Solar System

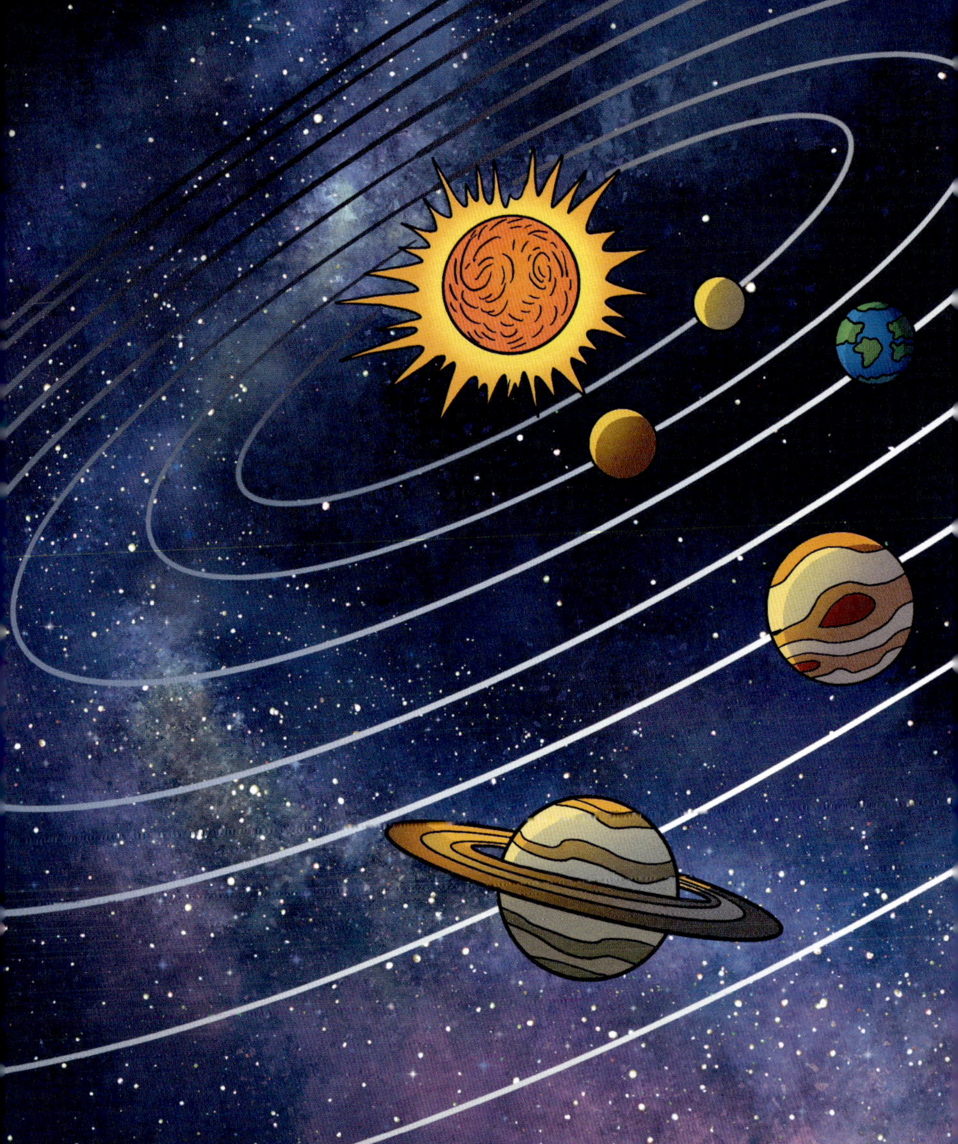

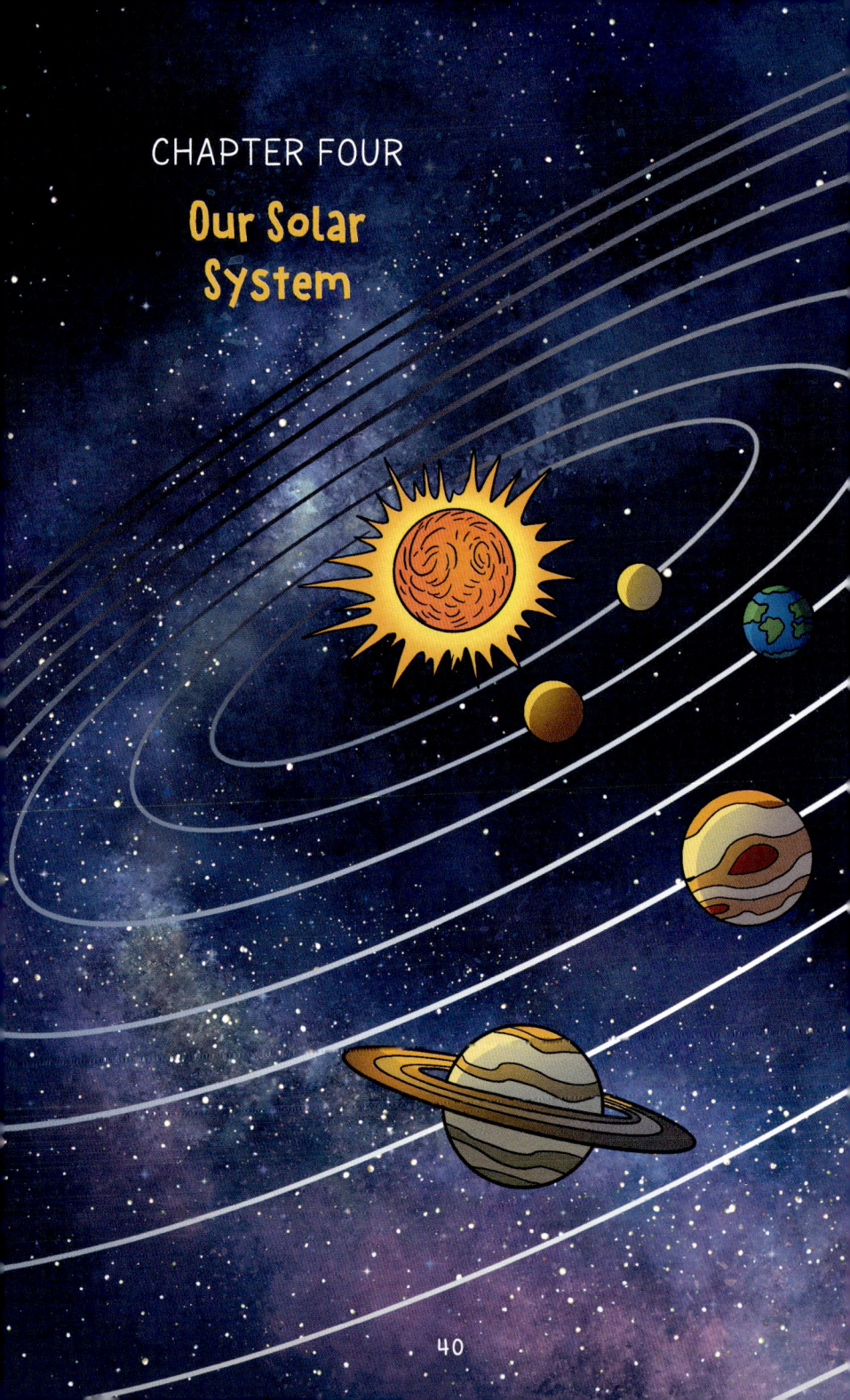

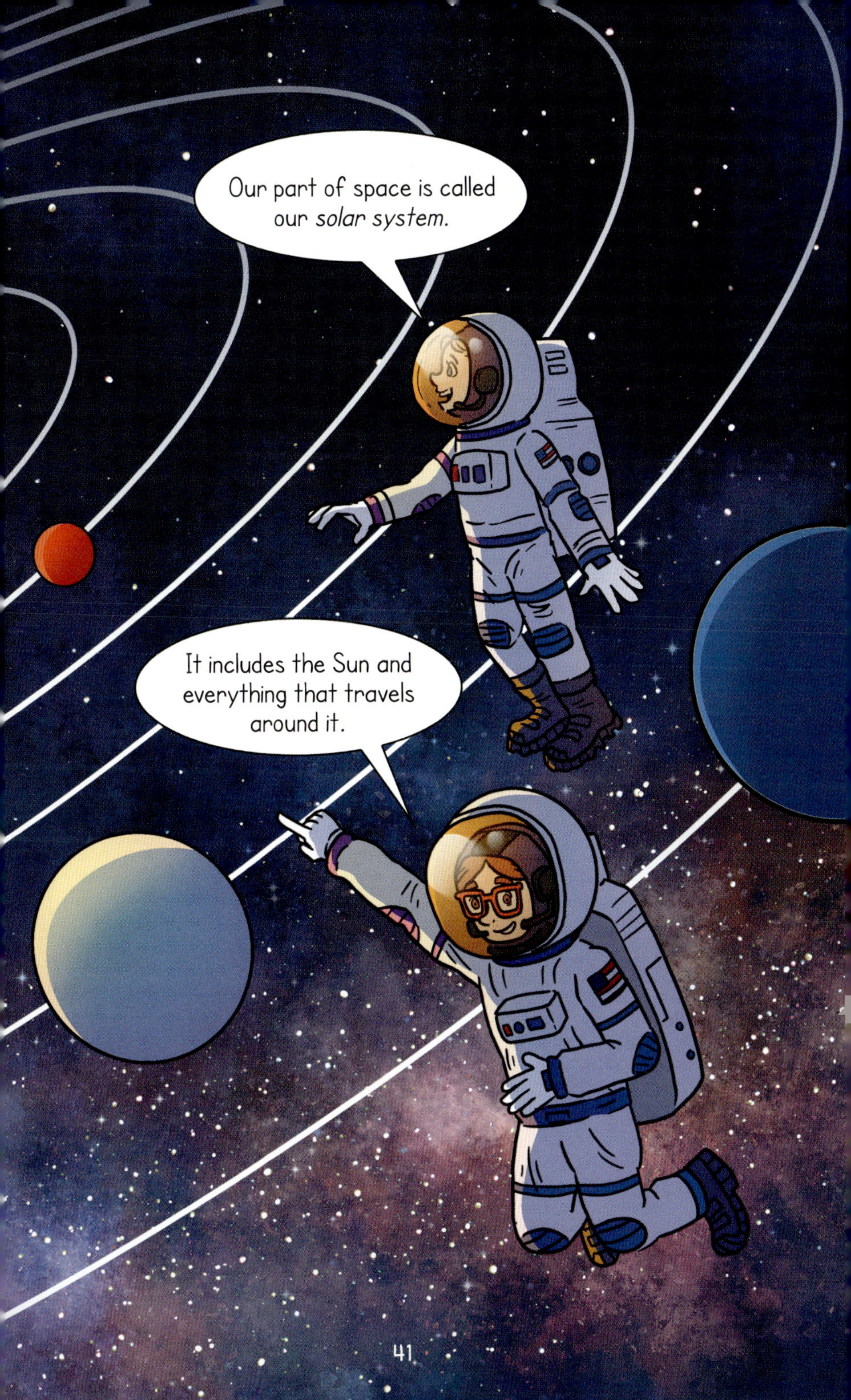

Our part of space is called our *solar system.*
It includes the Sun and everything that travels around it.

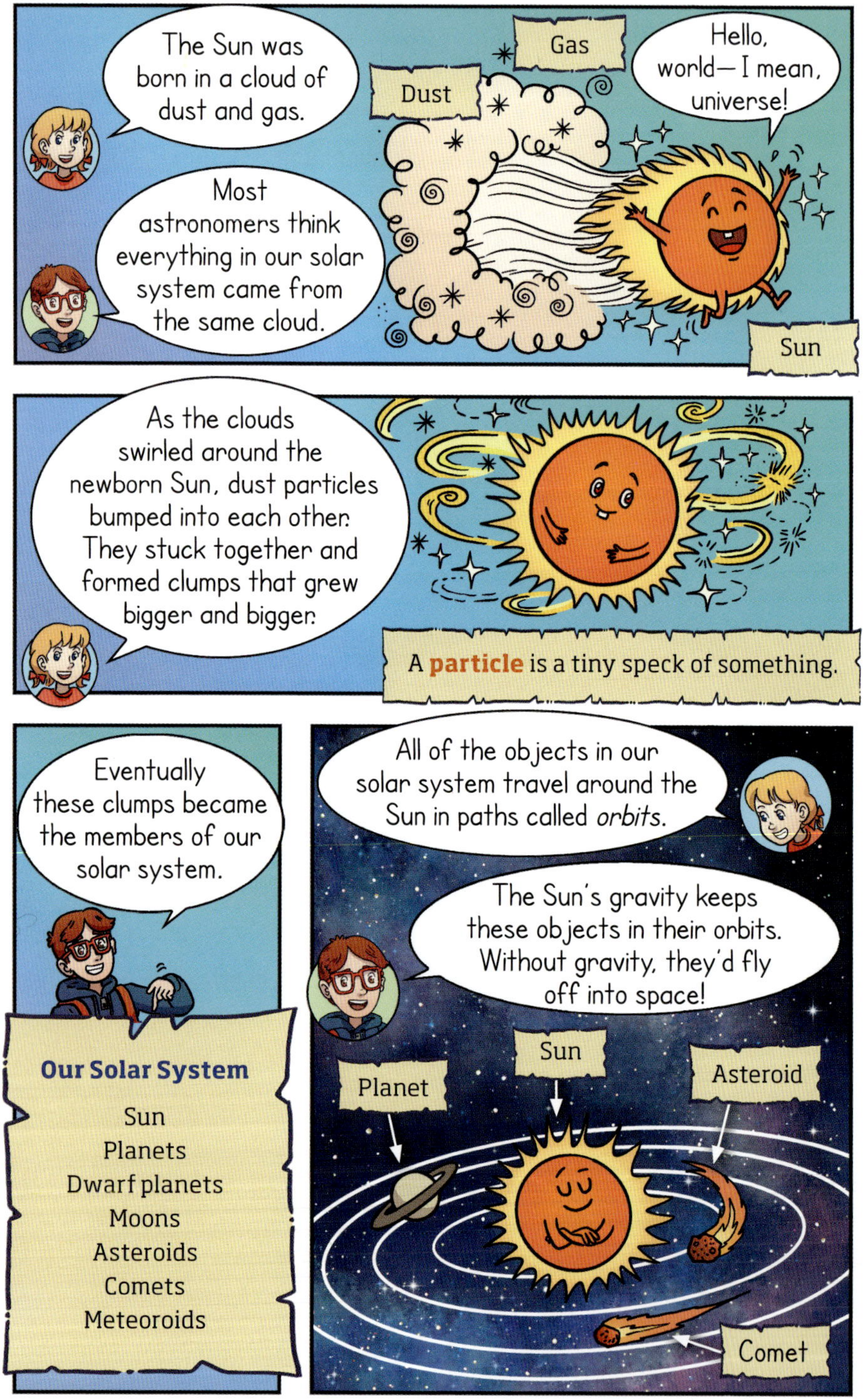
The Sun was born in a cloud of dust and gas.
Most astronomers think everything in our solar system came from the same cloud.
Gas
Dust
Hello, world—I mean, universe!
Sun
As the clouds swirled around the newborn Sun, dust particles bumped into each other. They stuck together and formed clumps that grew bigger and bigger.
A **particle** is a tiny speck of something.
Eventually these clumps became the members of our solar system.
Our Solar System
Sun
Planets
Dwarf planets
Moons
Asteroids
Comets
Meteoroids
All of the objects in our solar system travel around the Sun in paths called *orbits*.
The Sun's gravity keeps these objects in their orbits. Without gravity, they'd fly off into space!
Sun
Planet
Asteroid
Comet

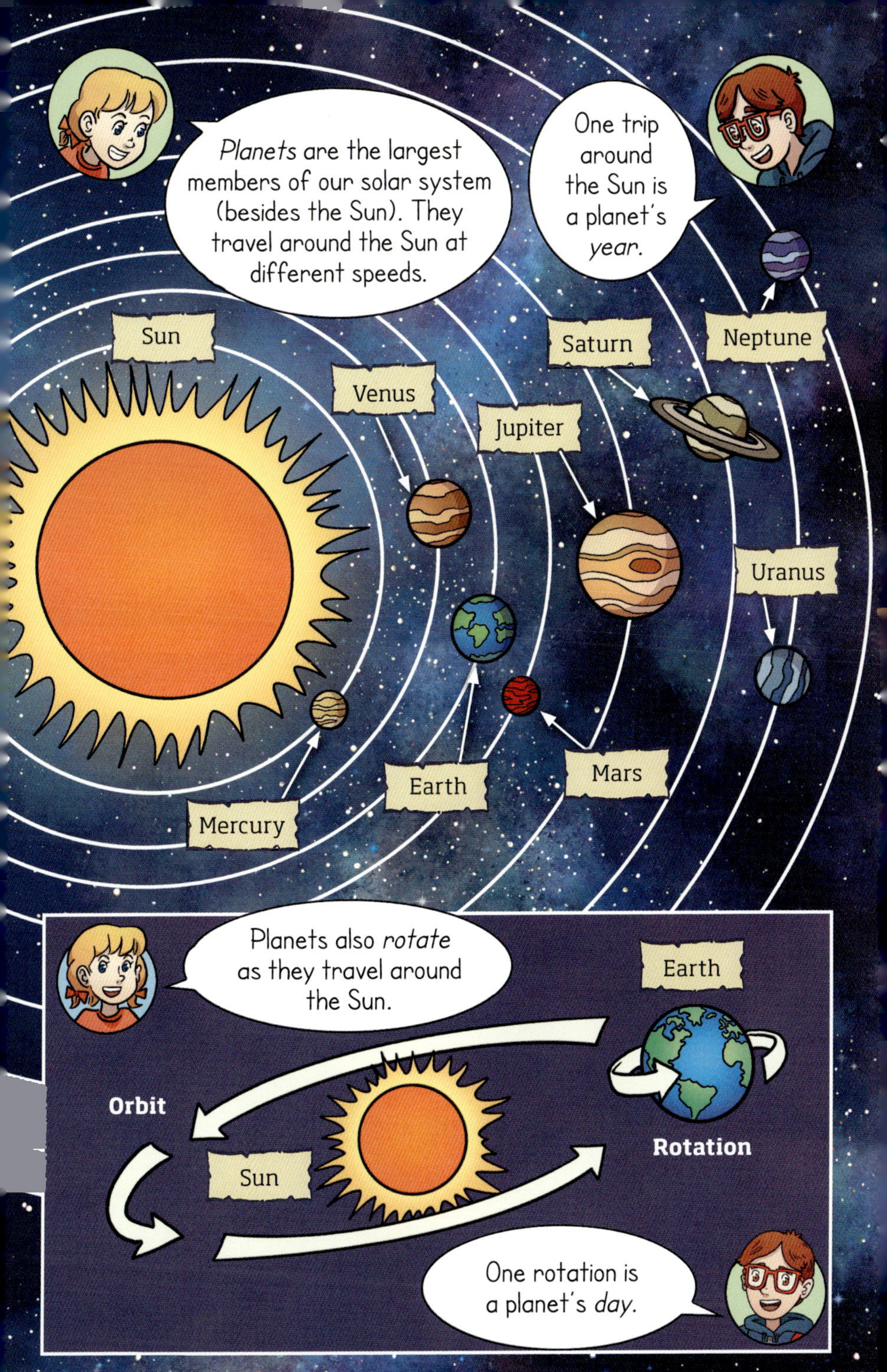
Planets are the largest members of our solar system (besides the Sun). They travel around the Sun at different speeds.
One trip around the Sun is a planet's year.
Sun
Venus
Jupiter
Saturn
Neptune
Uranus
Mars
Earth
Mercury
Planets also rotate as they travel around the Sun.
Earth
Orbit
Sun
Rotation
One rotation is a planet's day.

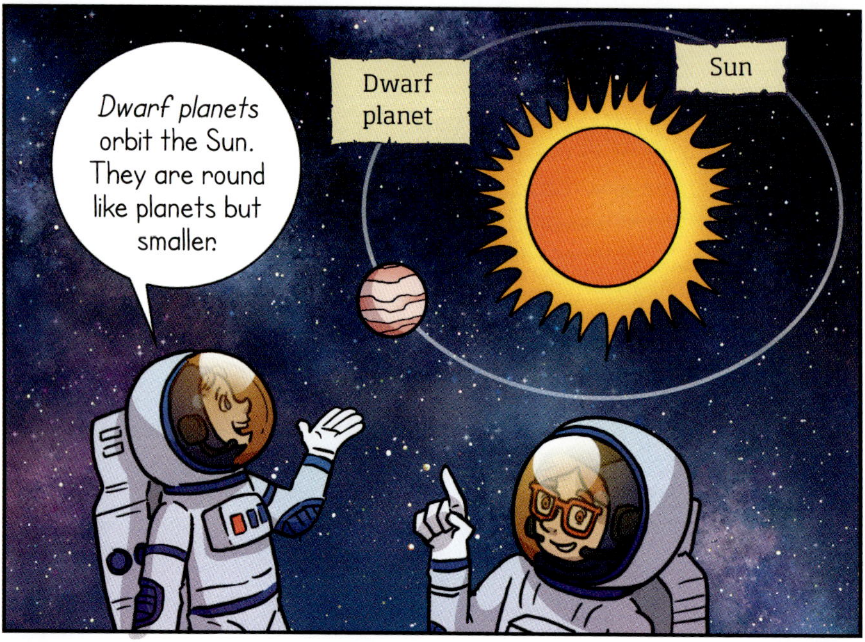
Dwarf planets orbit the Sun. They are round like planets but smaller.
Dwarf planet
Sun

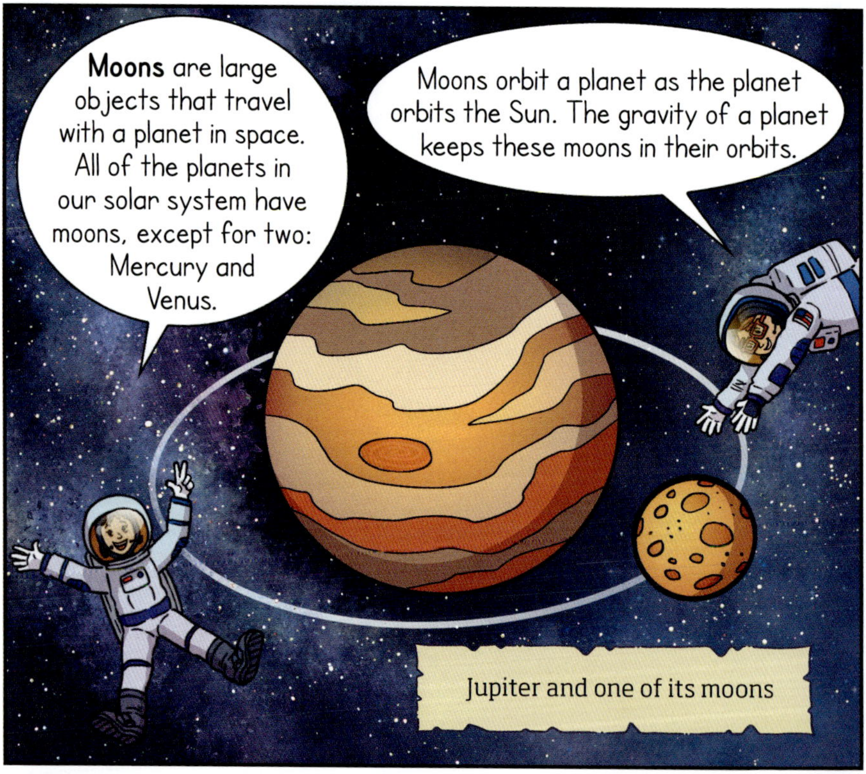
Moons are large objects that travel with a planet in space. All of the planets in our solar system have moons, except for two: Mercury and Venus.
Moons orbit a planet as the planet orbits the Sun. The gravity of a planet keeps these moons in their orbits.
Jupiter and one of its moons

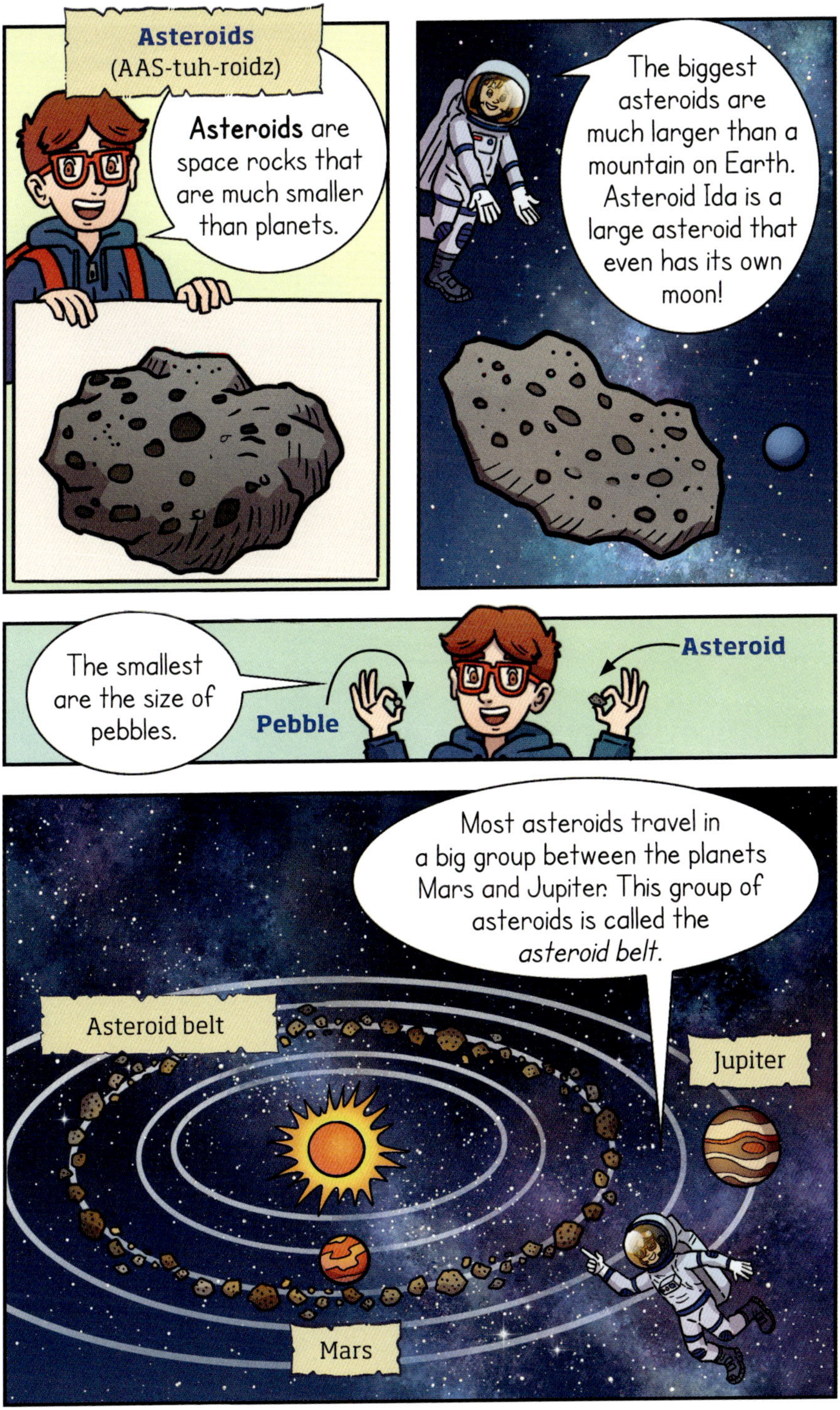
Asteroids
(AAS-tuh-roidz)
Asteroids are space rocks that are much smaller than planets.
The biggest asteroids are much larger than a mountain on Earth. Asteroid Ida is a large asteroid that even has its own moon!
The smallest are the size of pebbles.
Pebble
Asteroid
Most asteroids travel in a big group between the planets Mars and Jupiter. This group of asteroids is called the *asteroid belt*.
Asteroid belt
Jupiter
Mars

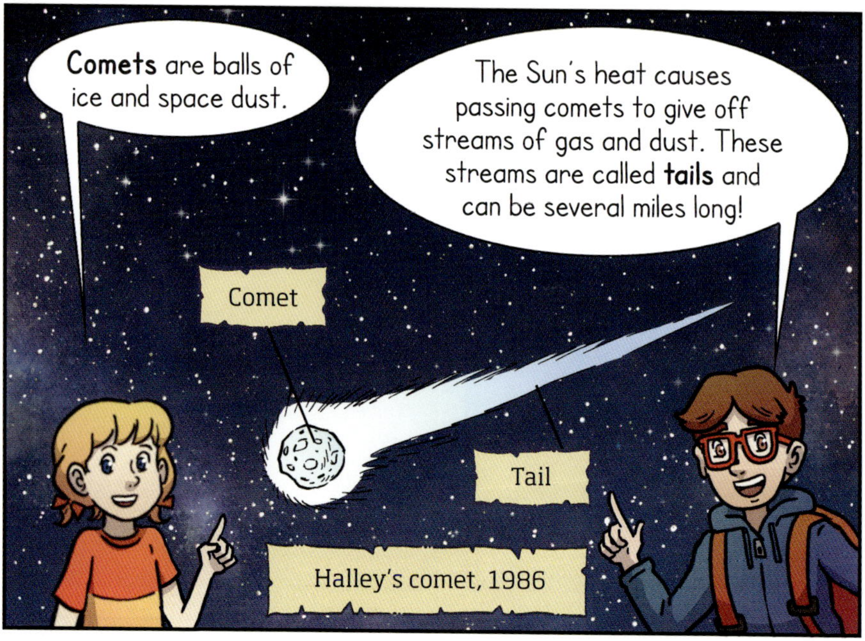
Comets are balls of ice and space dust.
The Sun's heat causes passing comets to give off streams of gas and dust. These streams are called **tails** and can be several miles long!
Comet
Tail
Halley's comet, 1986

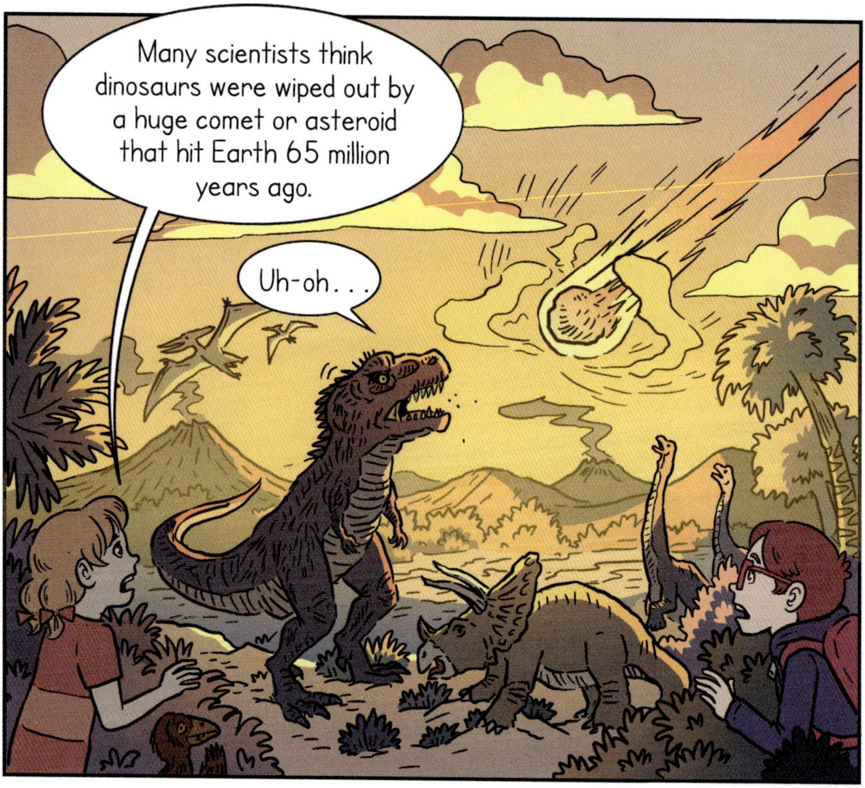
Many scientists think dinosaurs were wiped out by a huge comet or asteroid that hit Earth 65 million years ago.
Uh-oh. . .

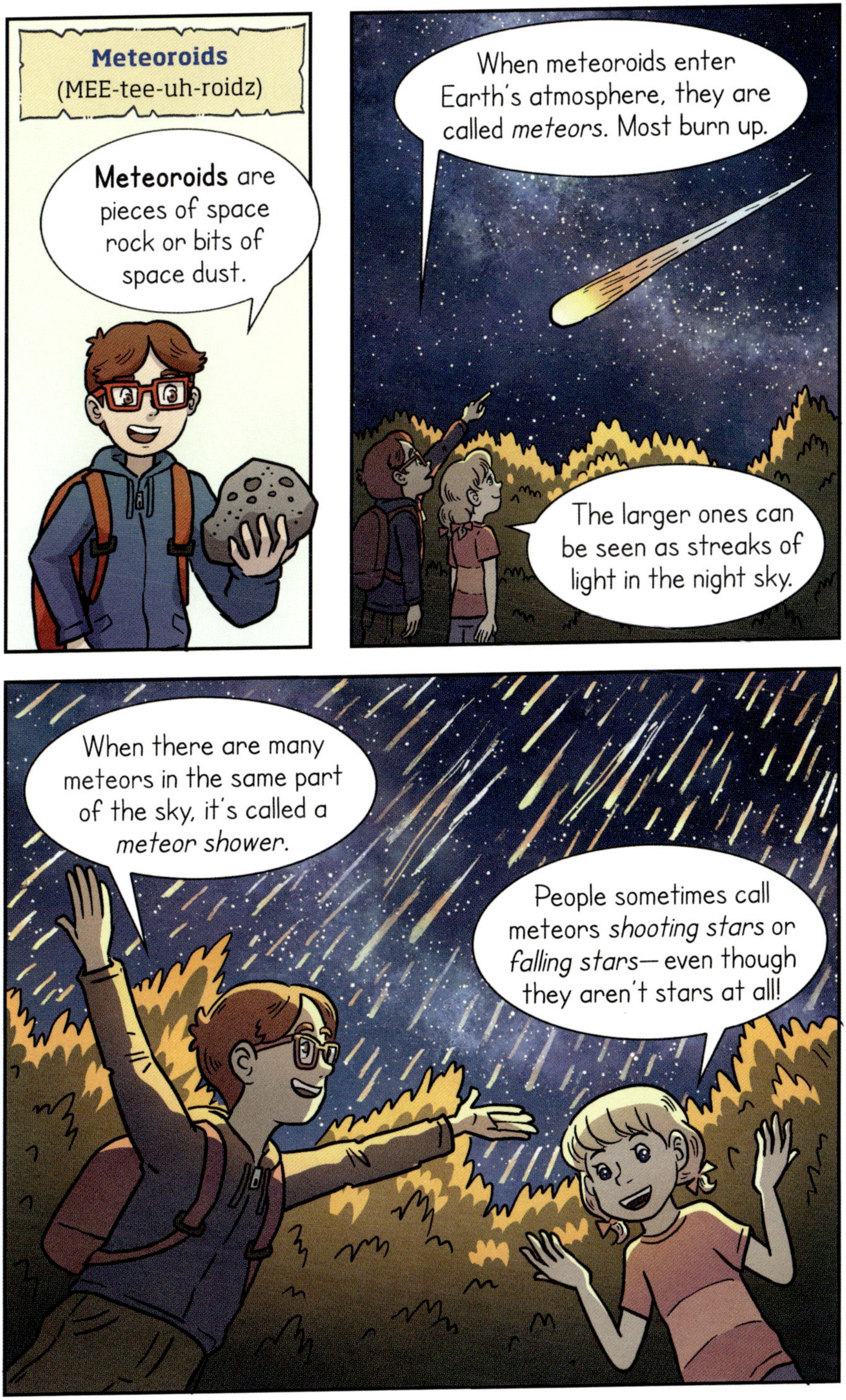
Meteoroids
(MEE-tee-uh-roidz)
Meteoroids are pieces of space rock or bits of space dust.
When meteoroids enter Earth's atmosphere, they are called *meteors*. Most burn up.
The larger ones can be seen as streaks of light in the night sky.
When there are many meteors in the same part of the sky, it's called a *meteor shower*.
People sometimes call meteors *shooting stars* or *falling stars*— even though they aren't stars at all!

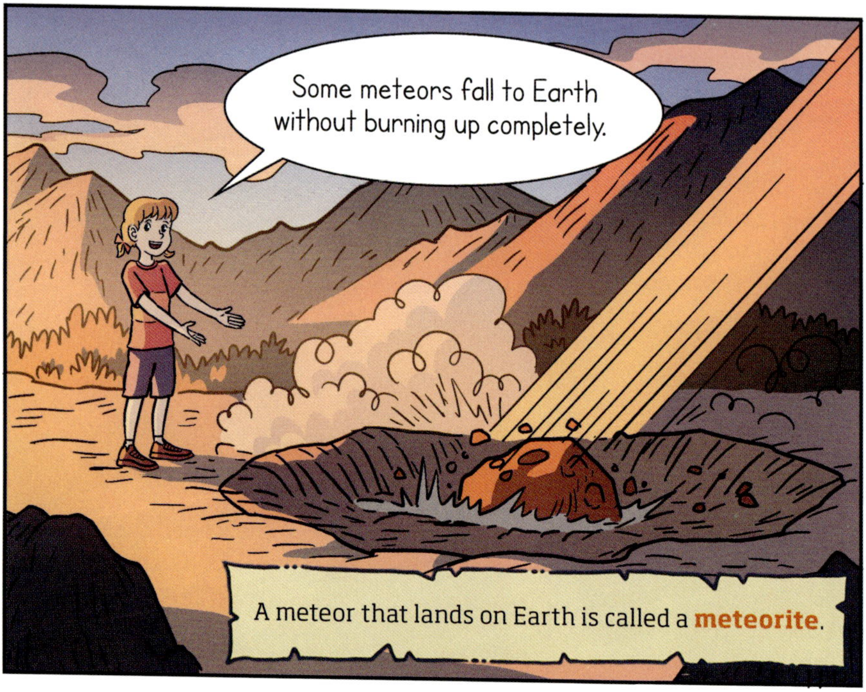
Some meteors fall to Earth without burning up completely.
A meteor that lands on Earth is called a **meteorite**.

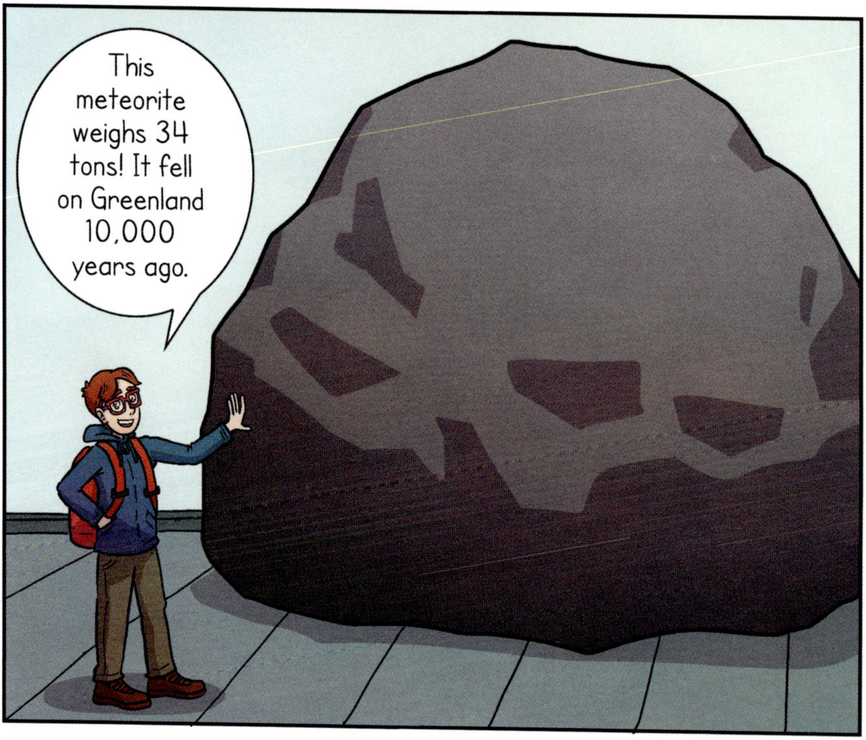
This meteorite weighs 34 tons! It fell on Greenland 10,000 years ago.

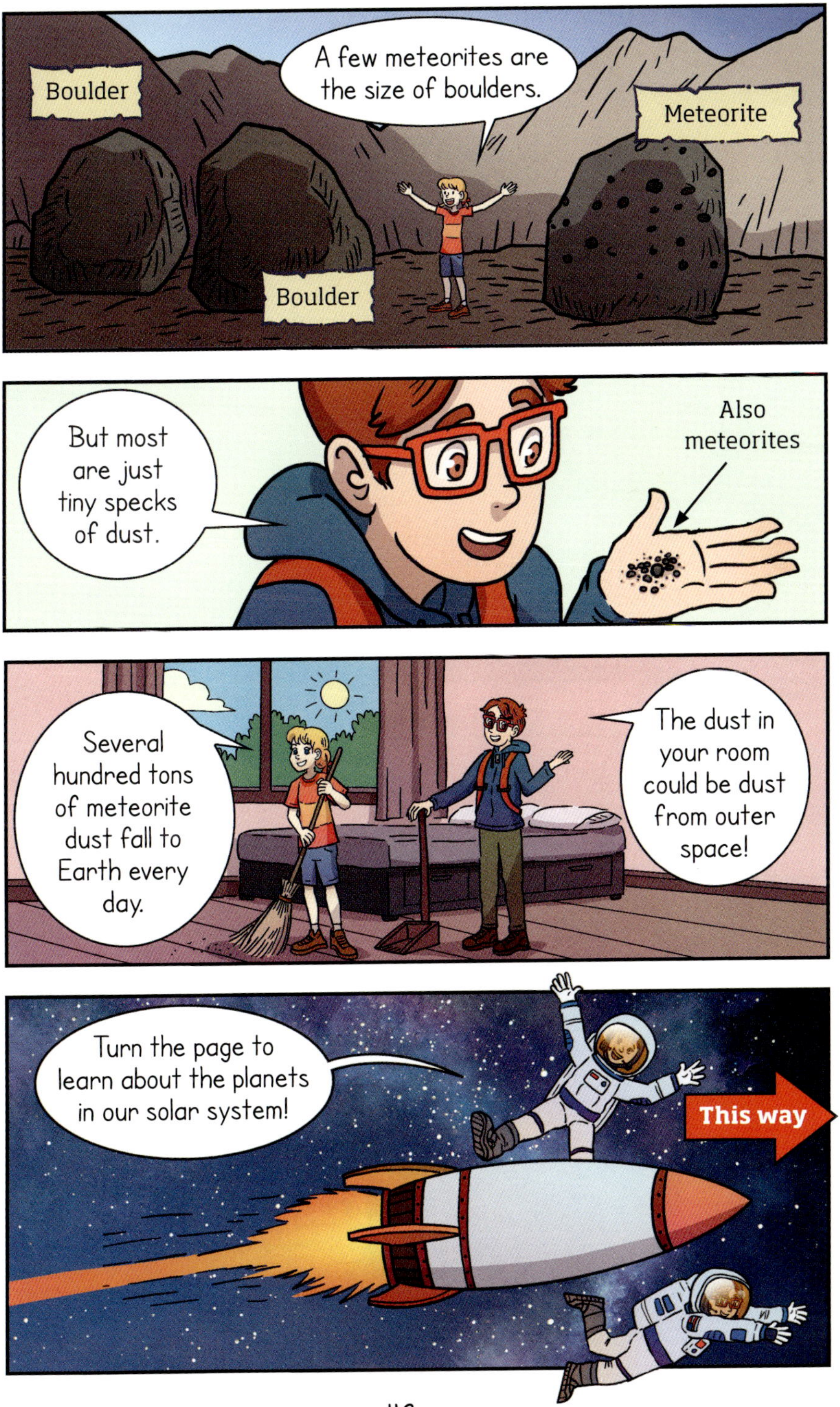
Boulder
A few meteorites are the size of boulders.
Meteorite
Boulder
But most are just tiny specks of dust.
Also meteorites
Several hundred tons of meteorite dust fall to Earth every day.
The dust in your room could be dust from outer space!
Turn the page to learn about the planets in our solar system!
This way

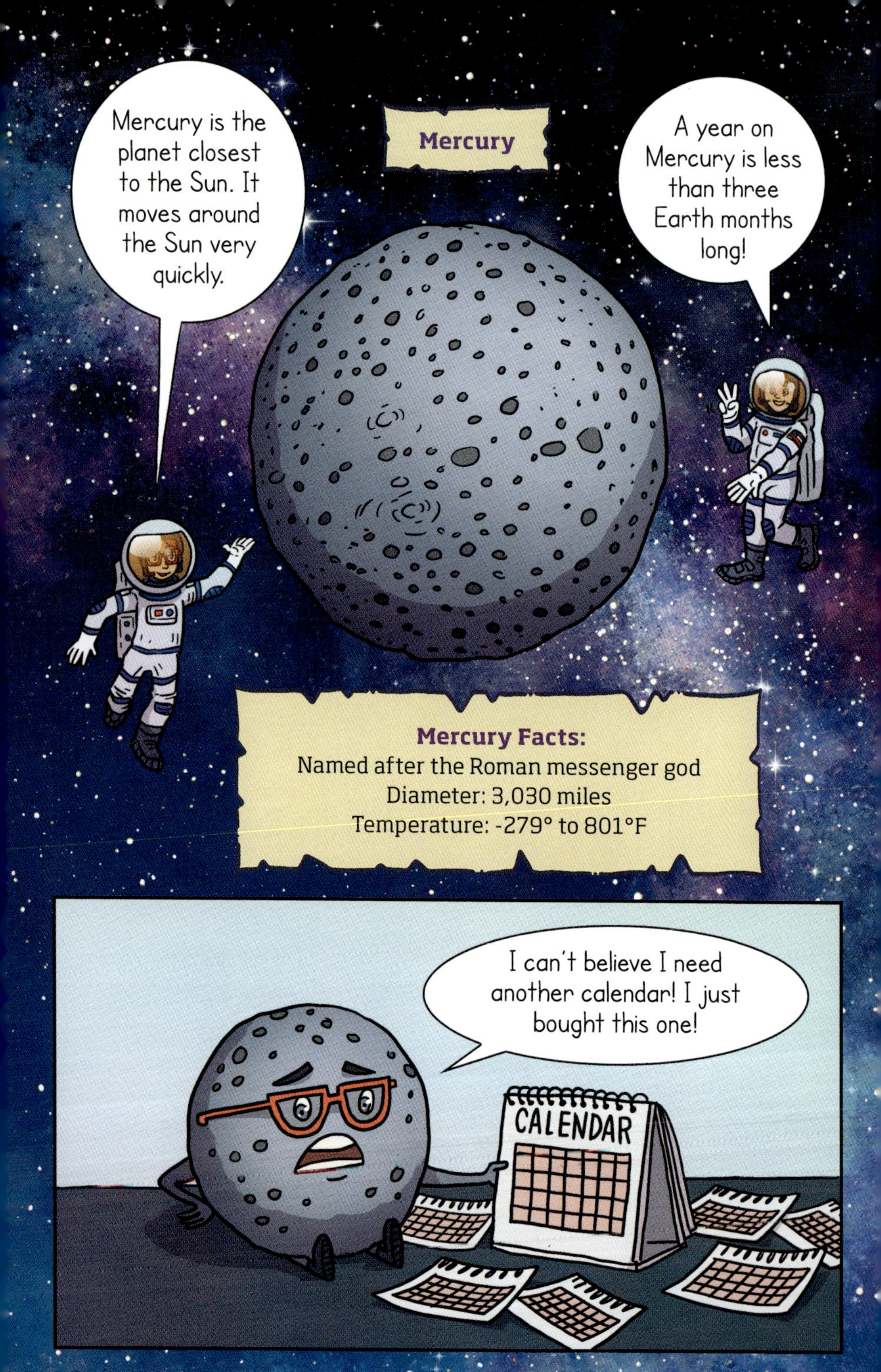
Mercury
Mercury is the planet closest to the Sun. It moves around the Sun very quickly.
A year on Mercury is less than three Earth months long!
Mercury Facts:
Named after the Roman messenger god
Diameter: 3,030 miles
Temperature: -279° to 801°F
I can't believe I need another calendar! I just bought this one!
CALENDAR

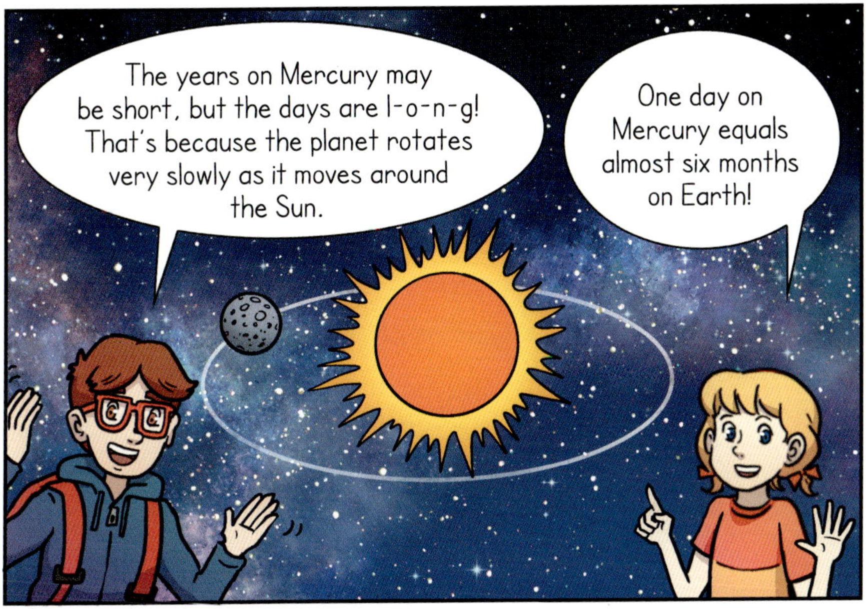
The years on Mercury may be short, but the days are l-o-n-g! That's because the planet rotates very slowly as it moves around the Sun.
One day on Mercury equals almost six months on Earth!

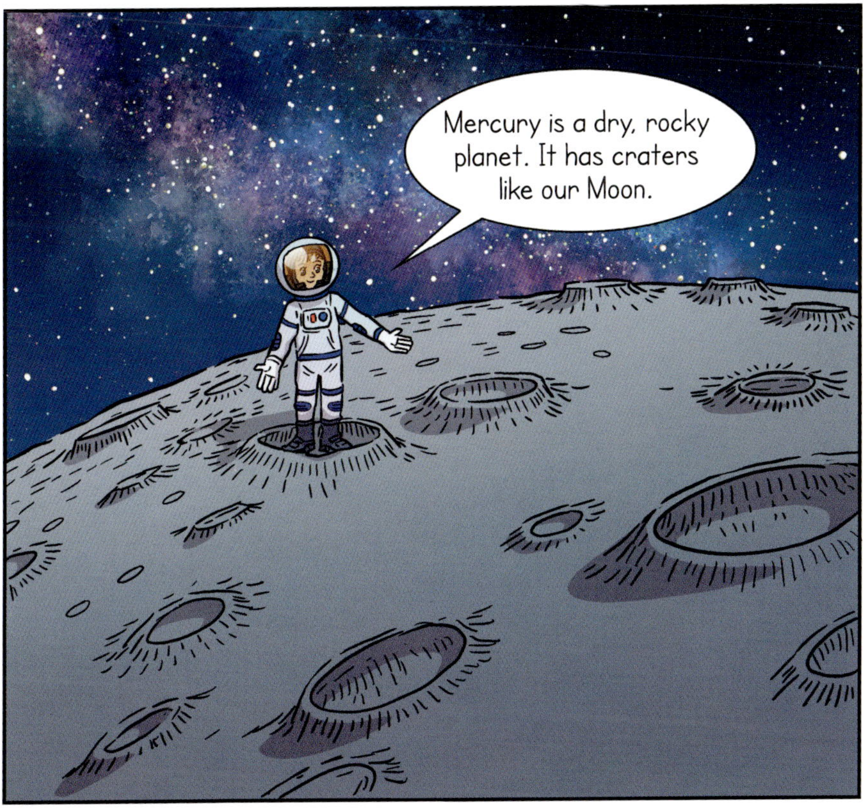
Mercury is a dry, rocky planet. It has craters like our Moon.

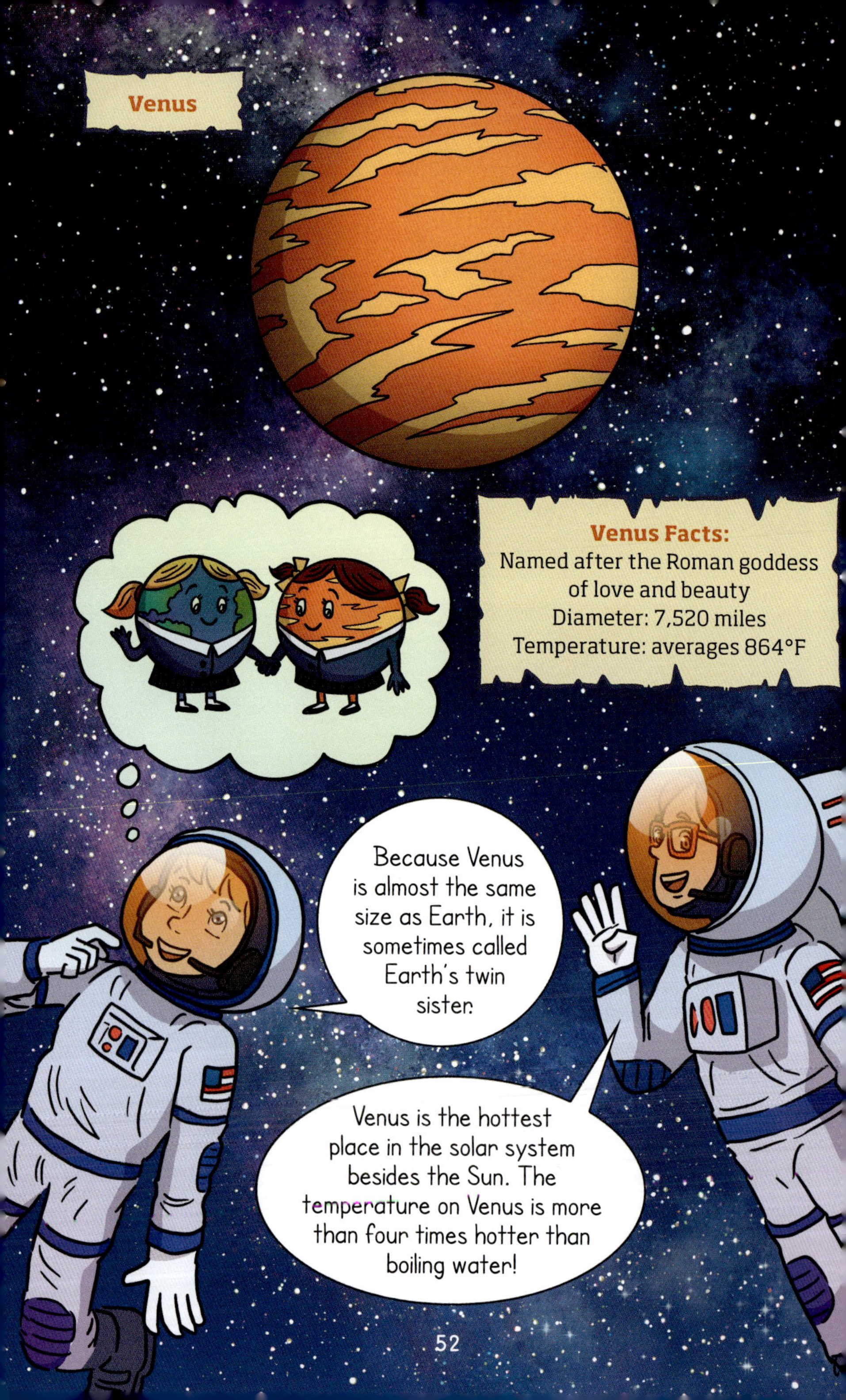
Venus
Venus Facts:
Named after the Roman goddess of love and beauty
Diameter: 7,520 miles
Temperature: averages 864°F
Because Venus is almost the same size as Earth, it is sometimes called Earth's twin sister.
Venus is the hottest place in the solar system besides the Sun. The temperature on Venus is more than four times hotter than boiling water!

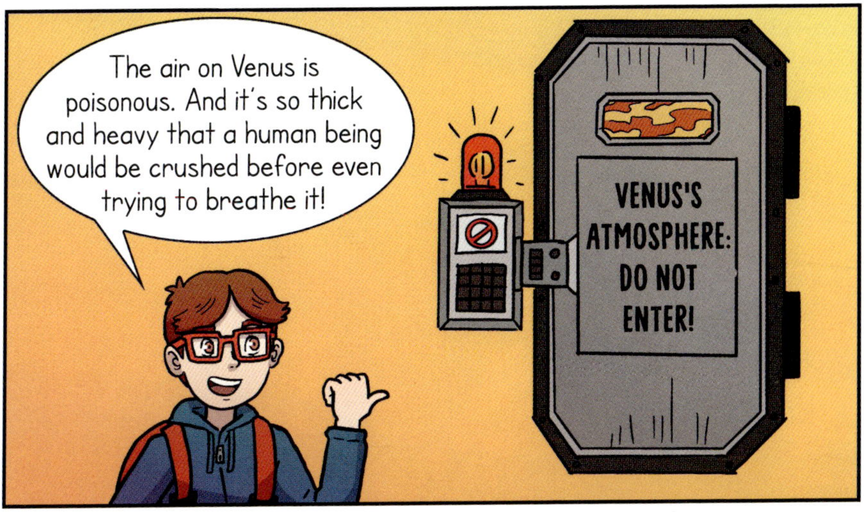
The air on Venus is poisonous. And it's so thick and heavy that a human being would be crushed before even trying to breathe it!
VENUS'S ATMOSPHERE: DO NOT ENTER!

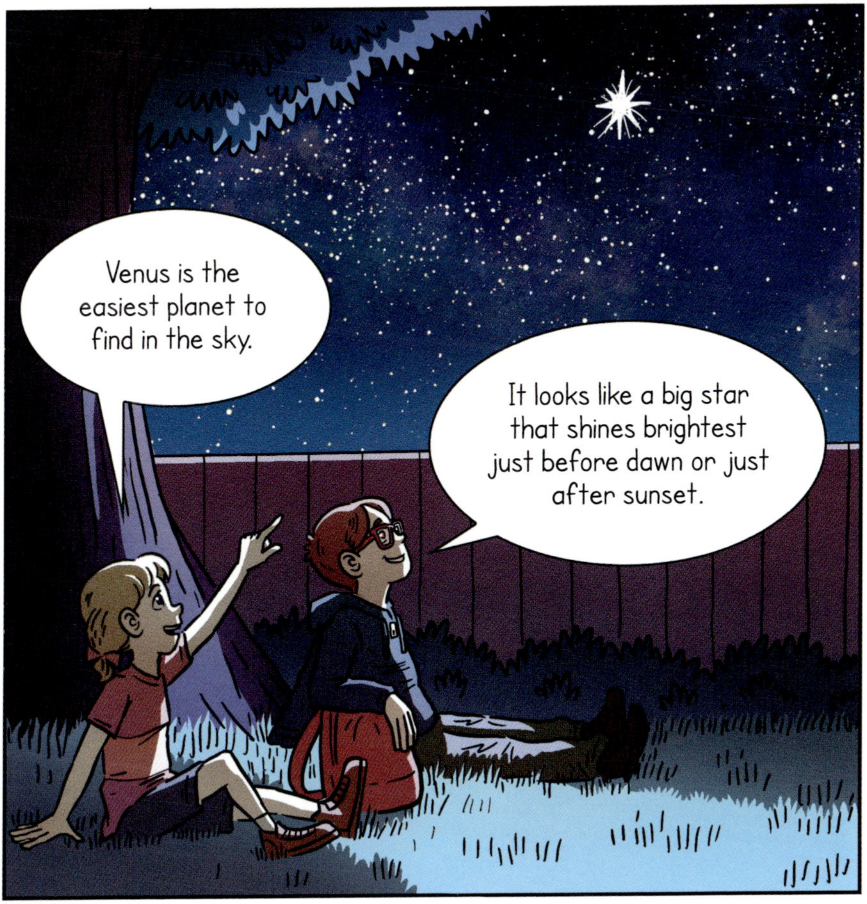
Venus is the easiest planet to find in the sky.
It looks like a big star that shines brightest just before dawn or just after sunset.

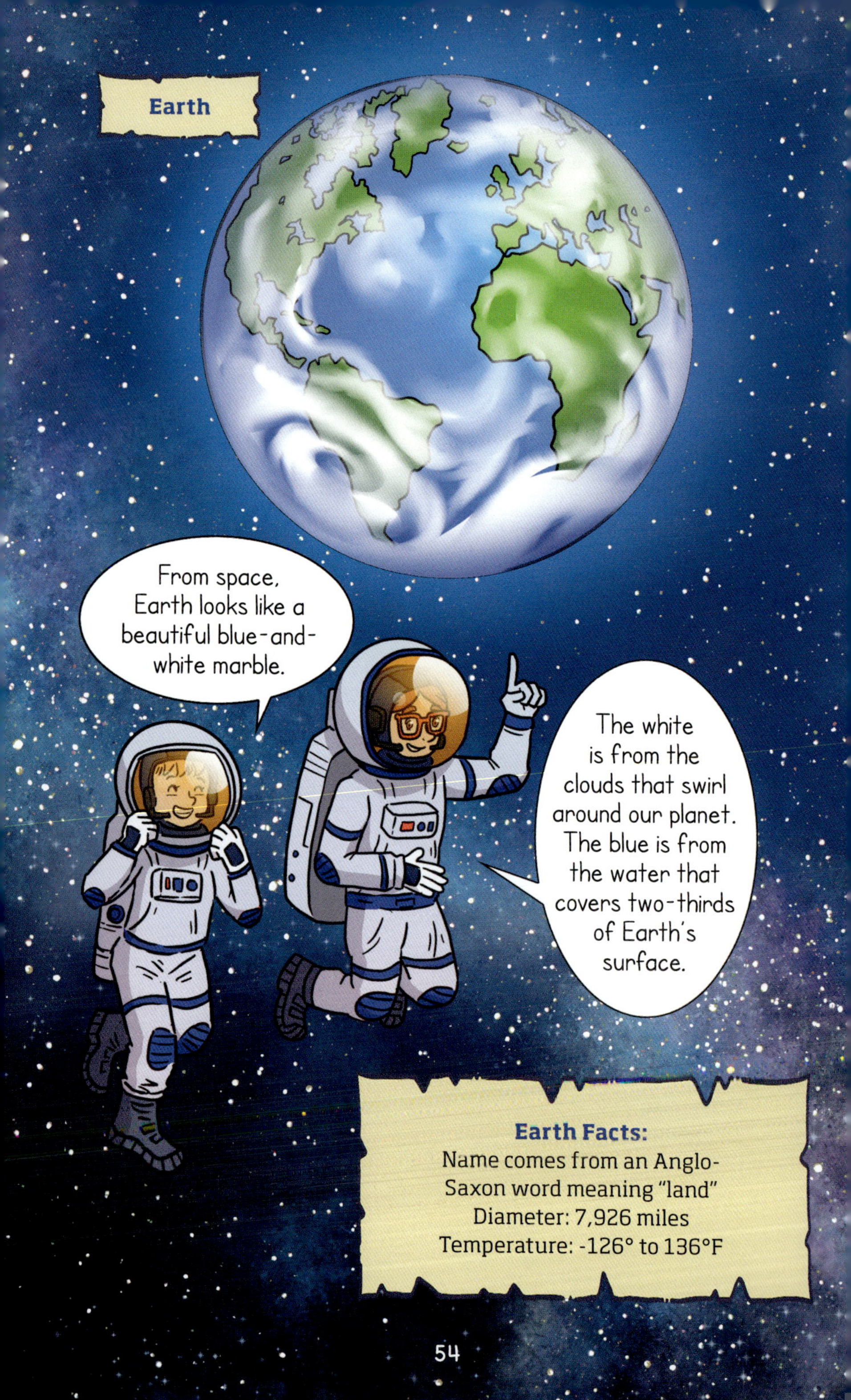
Earth
From space, Earth looks like a beautiful blue-and-white marble.
The white is from the clouds that swirl around our planet. The blue is from the water that covers two-thirds of Earth's surface.
Earth Facts:
Name comes from an Anglo-Saxon word meaning "land"
Diameter: 7,926 miles
Temperature: -126° to 136°F

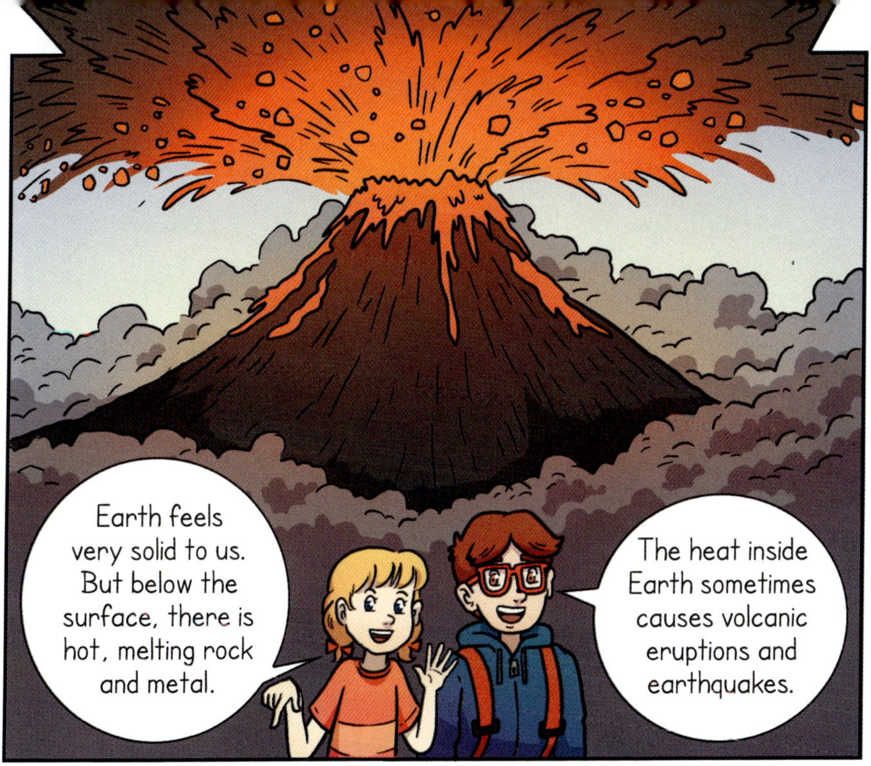
Earth feels very solid to us. But below the surface, there is hot, melting rock and metal.
The heat inside Earth sometimes causes volcanic eruptions and earthquakes.

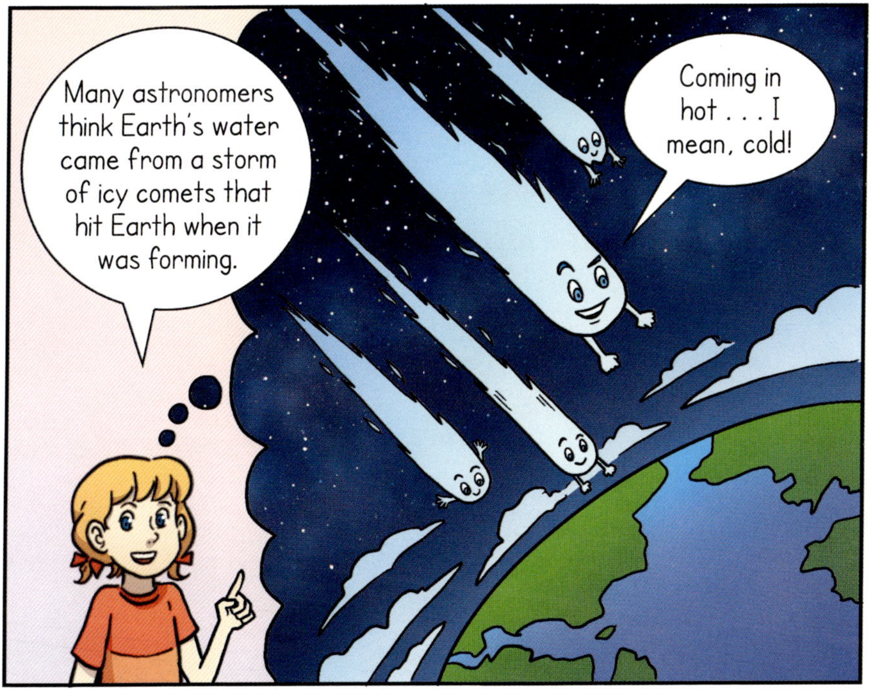
Many astronomers think Earth's water came from a storm of icy comets that hit Earth when it was forming.
Coming in hot . . . I mean, cold!

The Moon

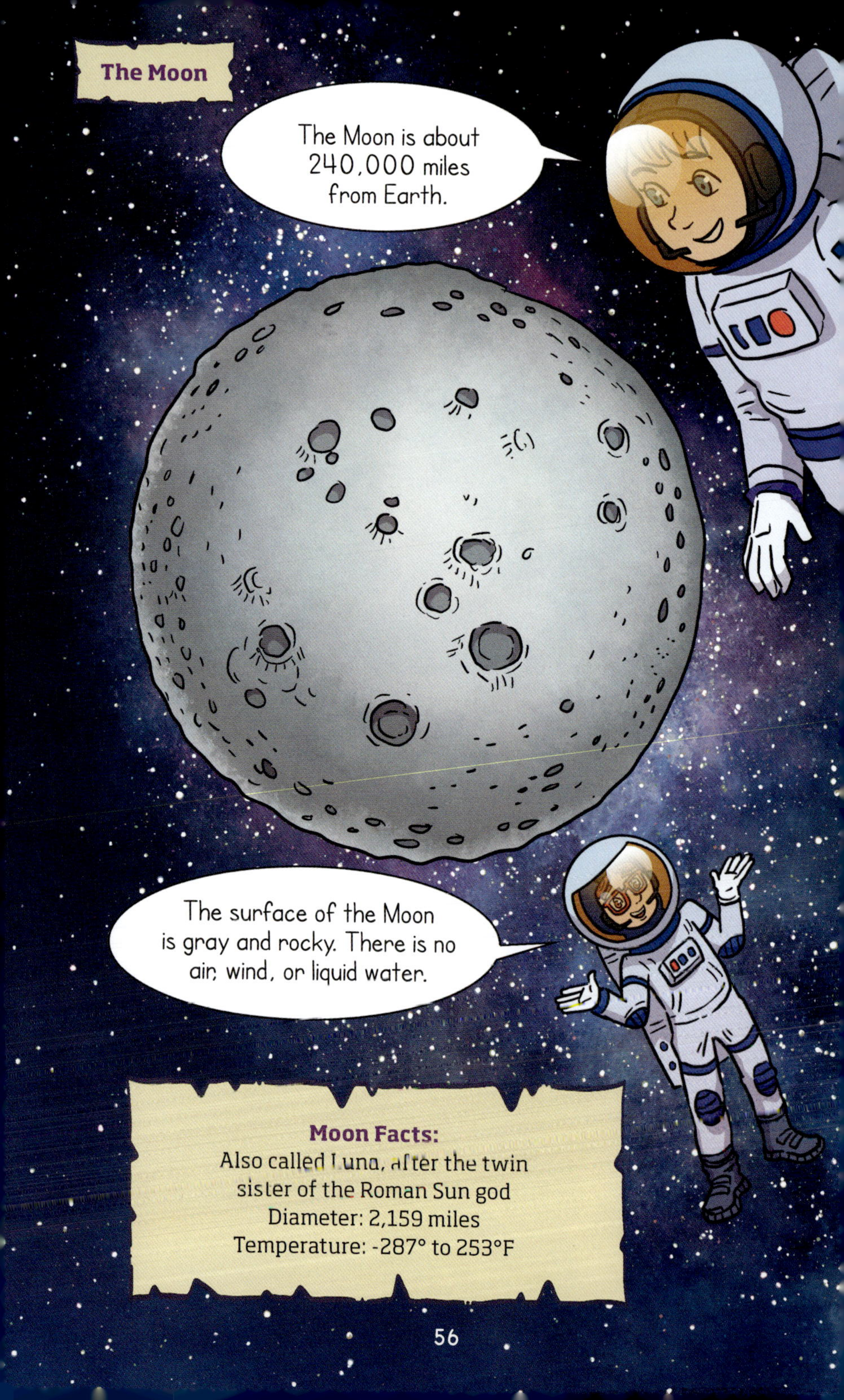
The Moon is about 240,000 miles from Earth.
The surface of the Moon is gray and rocky. There is no air, wind, or liquid water.

Moon Facts:
Also called Luna, after the twin sister of the Roman Sun god
Diameter: 2,159 miles
Temperature: -287° to 253°F

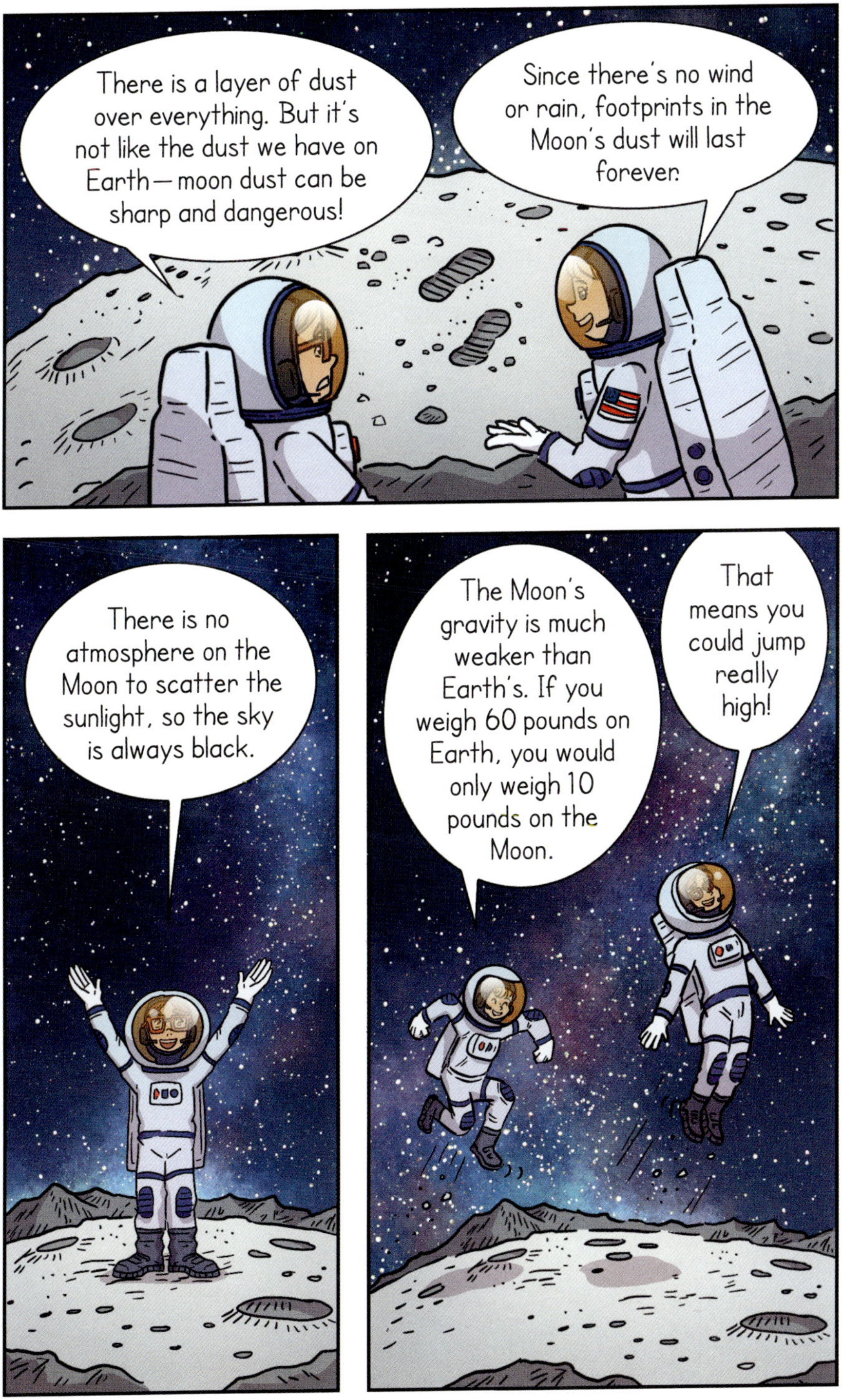
There is a layer of dust over everything. But it's not like the dust we have on Earth—moon dust can be sharp and dangerous!
Since there's no wind or rain, footprints in the Moon's dust will last forever.
There is no atmosphere on the Moon to scatter the sunlight, so the sky is always black.
The Moon's gravity is much weaker than Earth's. If you weigh 60 pounds on Earth, you would only weigh 10 pounds on the Moon.
That means you could jump really high!

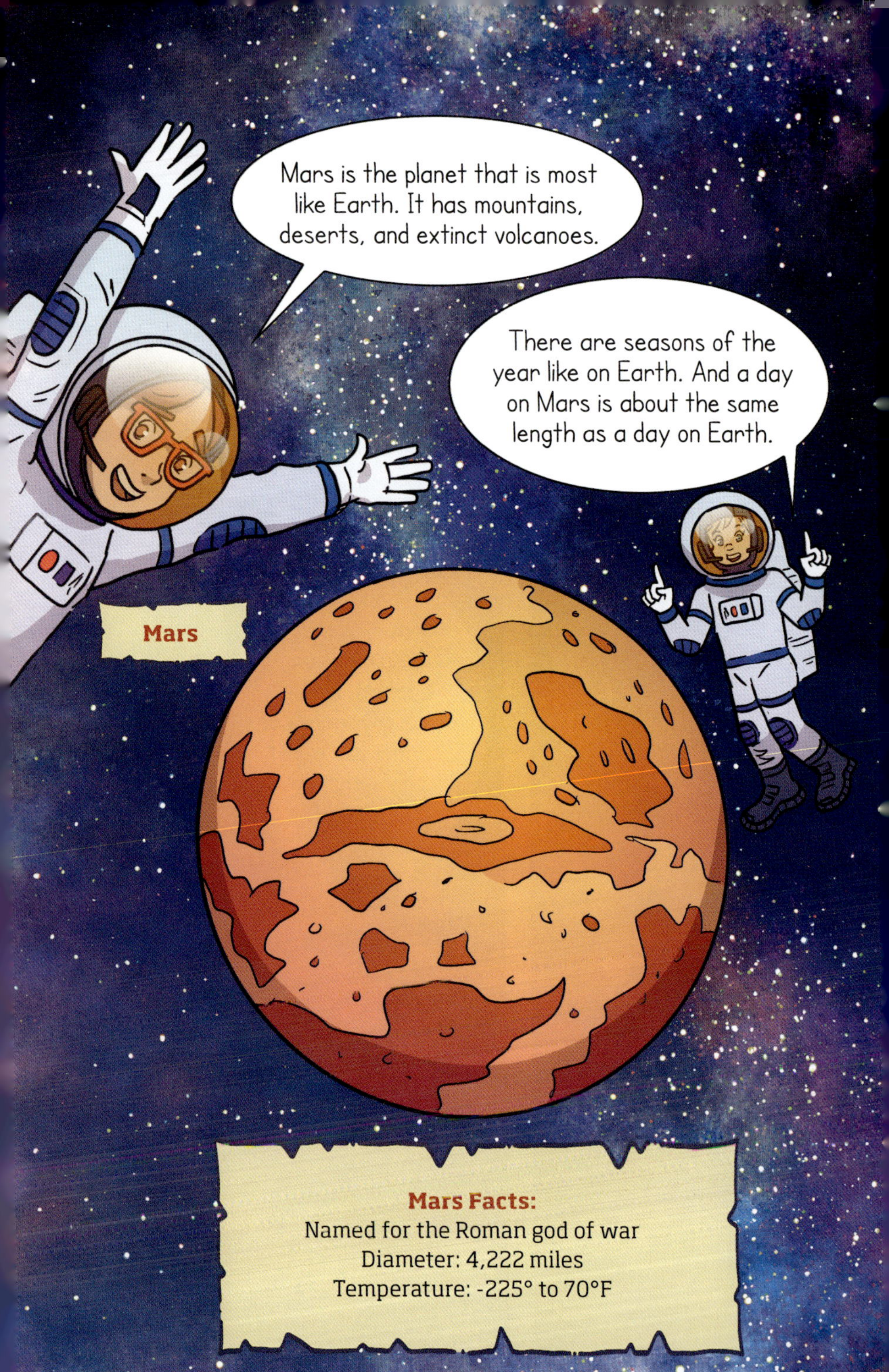
Mars is the planet that is most like Earth. It has mountains, deserts, and extinct volcanoes.
There are seasons of the year like on Earth. And a day on Mars is about the same length as a day on Earth.
Mars
Mars Facts:
Named for the Roman god of war
Diameter: 4,222 miles
Temperature: -225° to 70°F

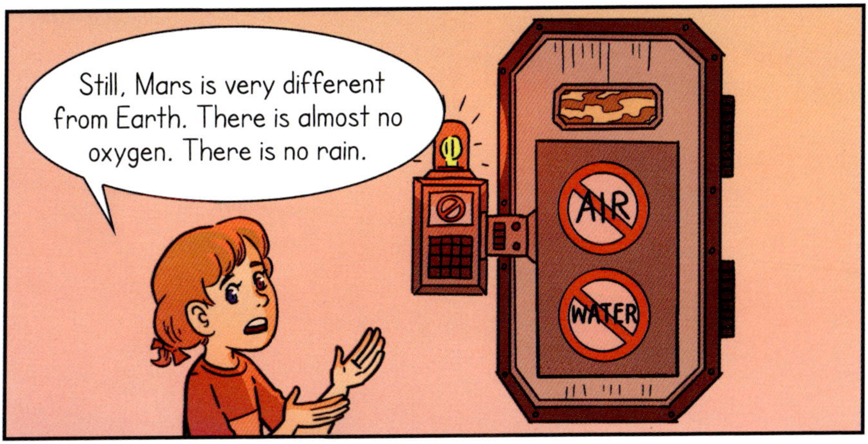
Still, Mars is very different from Earth. There is almost no oxygen. There is no rain.
AIR
WATER

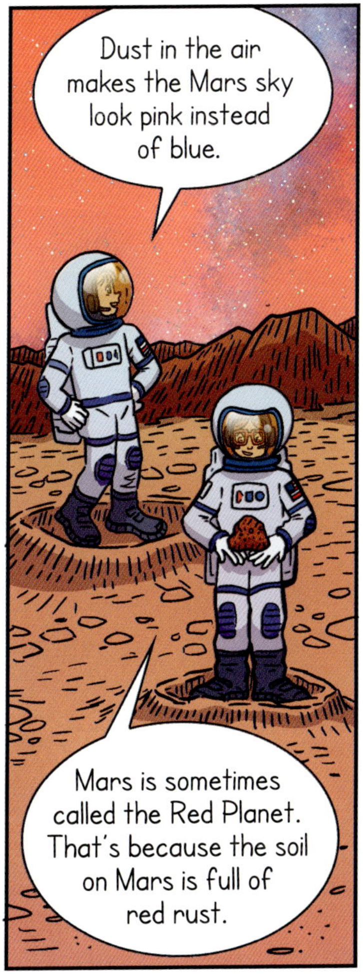
Dust in the air makes the Mars sky look pink instead of blue.
Mars is sometimes called the Red Planet. That's because the soil on Mars is full of red rust.

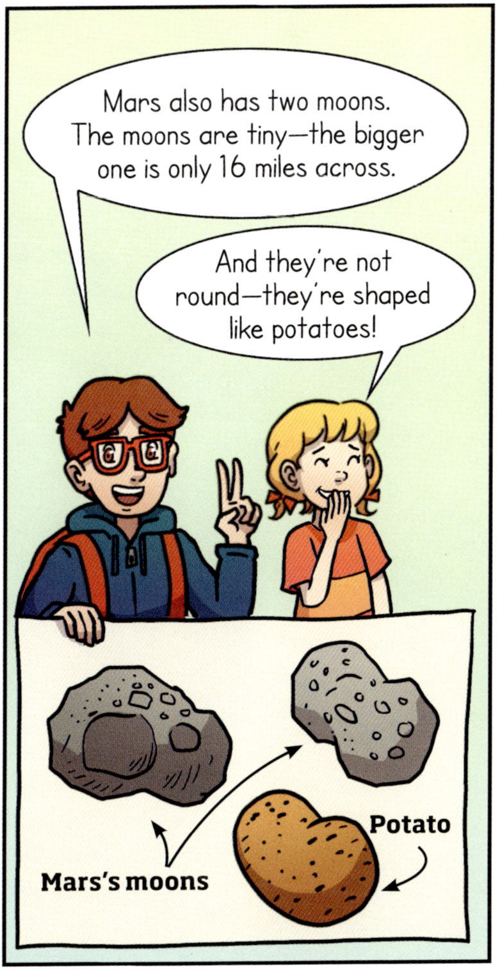
Mars also has two moons. The moons are tiny—the bigger one is only 16 miles across.
And they're not round—they're shaped like potatoes!
Potato
Mars's moons

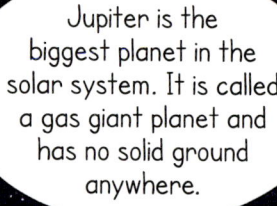

Jupiter is the biggest planet in the solar system. It is called a gas giant planet and has no solid ground anywhere.

Jupiter has 92 moons—that we know about!

Jupiter

Jupiter Facts:
Named for the leader of all the Roman gods
Diameter: 88,846 miles
Temperature: averages -234°F

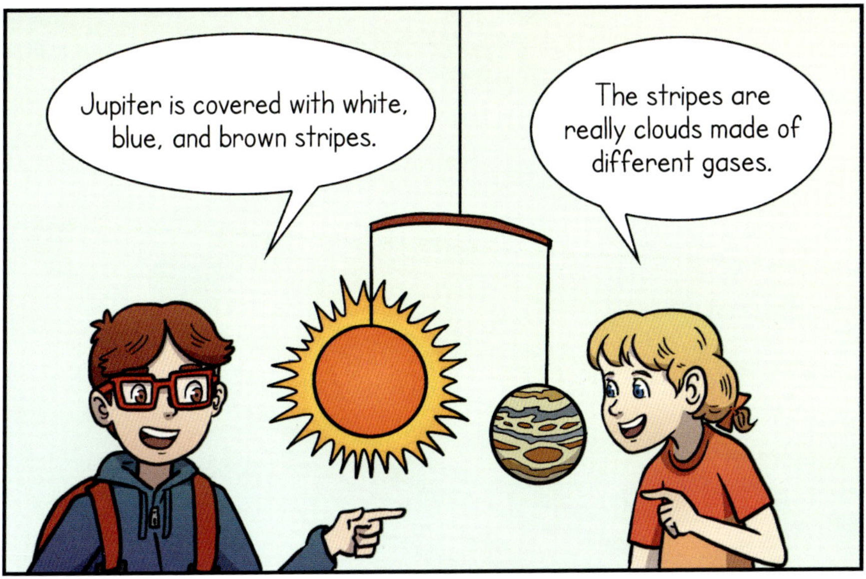
Jupiter is covered with white, blue, and brown stripes.
The stripes are really clouds made of different gases.

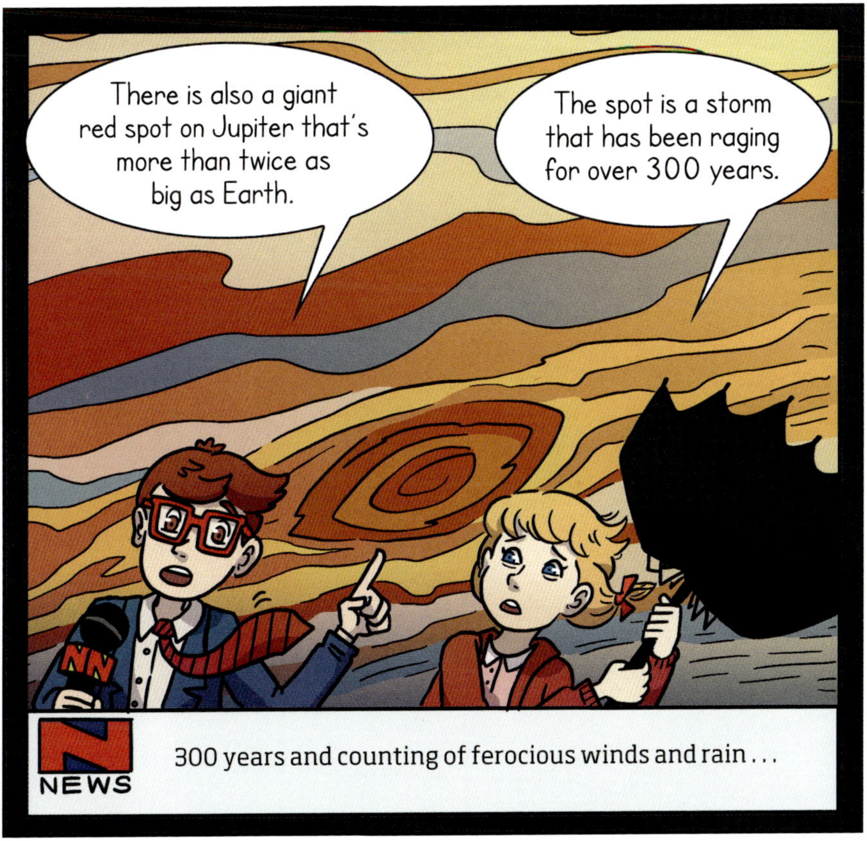
There is also a giant red spot on Jupiter that's more than twice as big as Earth.
The spot is a storm that has been raging for over 300 years.
NN
NEWS
300 years and counting of ferocious winds and rain . . .

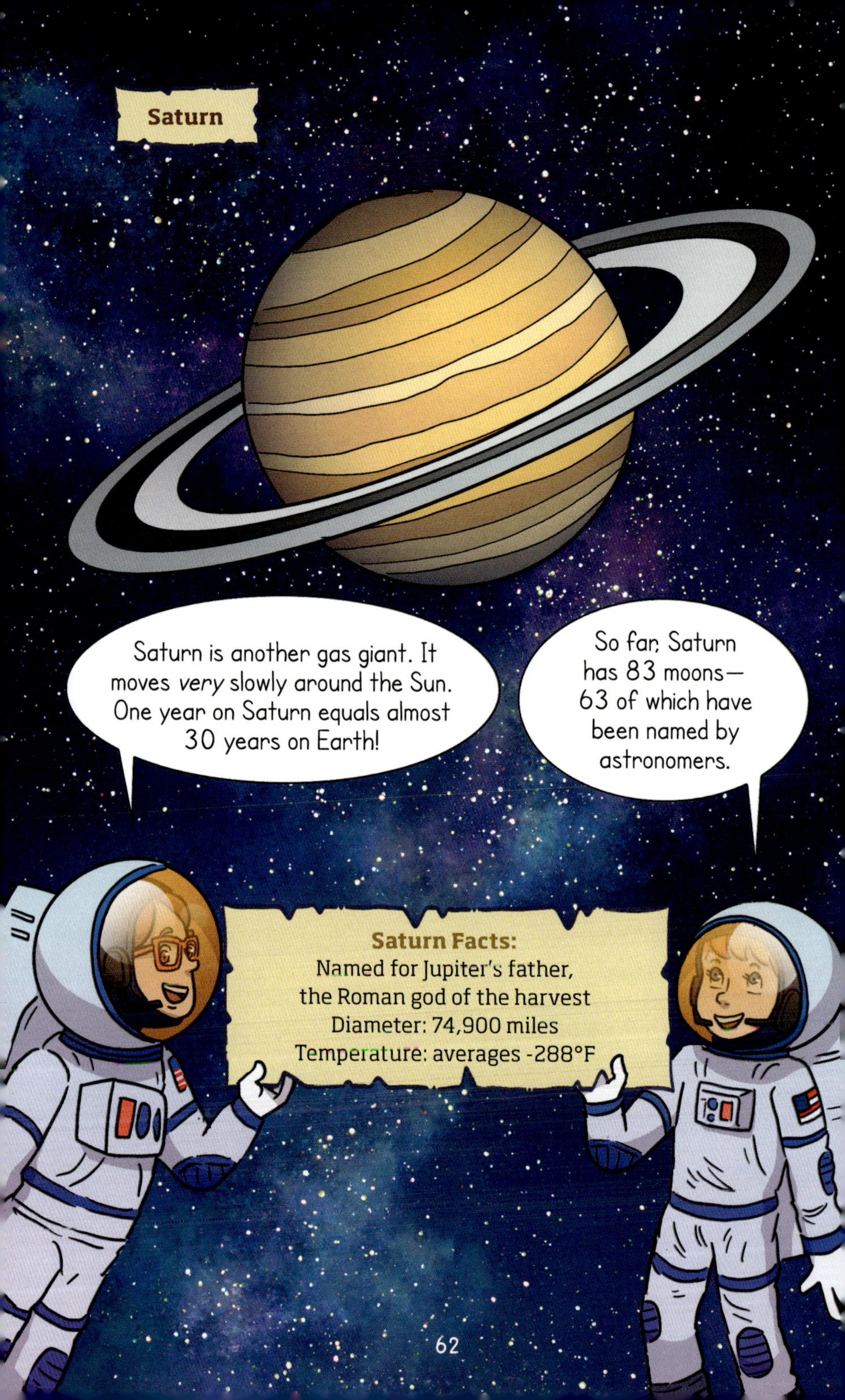
Saturn
Saturn is another gas giant. It moves *very* slowly around the Sun. One year on Saturn equals almost 30 years on Earth!
So far, Saturn has 83 moons—63 of which have been named by astronomers.
Saturn Facts:
Named for Jupiter's father, the Roman god of the harvest
Diameter: 74,900 miles
Temperature: averages -288°F

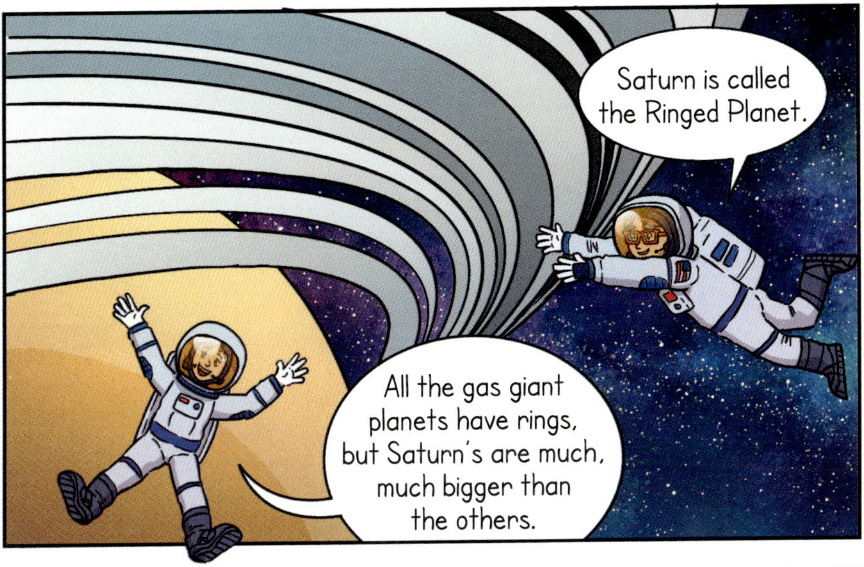
Saturn is called the Ringed Planet.
All the gas giant planets have rings, but Saturn's are much, much bigger than the others.

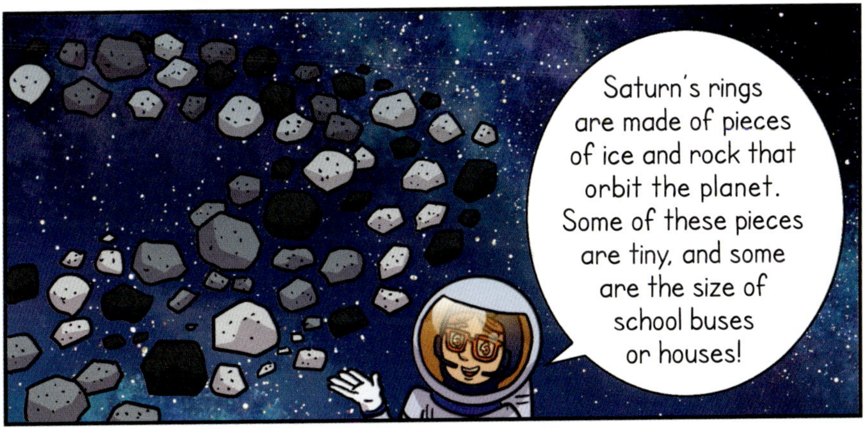
Saturn's rings are made of pieces of ice and rock that orbit the planet. Some of these pieces are tiny, and some are the size of school buses or houses!

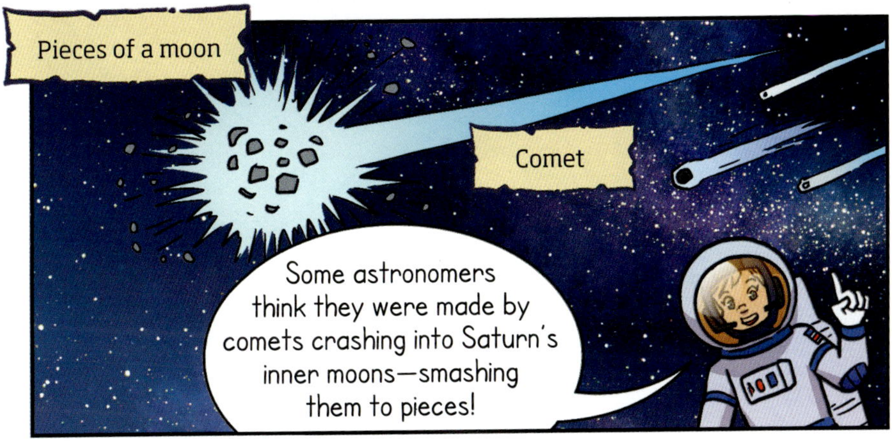
Pieces of a moon
Comet
Some astronomers think they were made by comets crashing into Saturn's inner moons—smashing them to pieces!

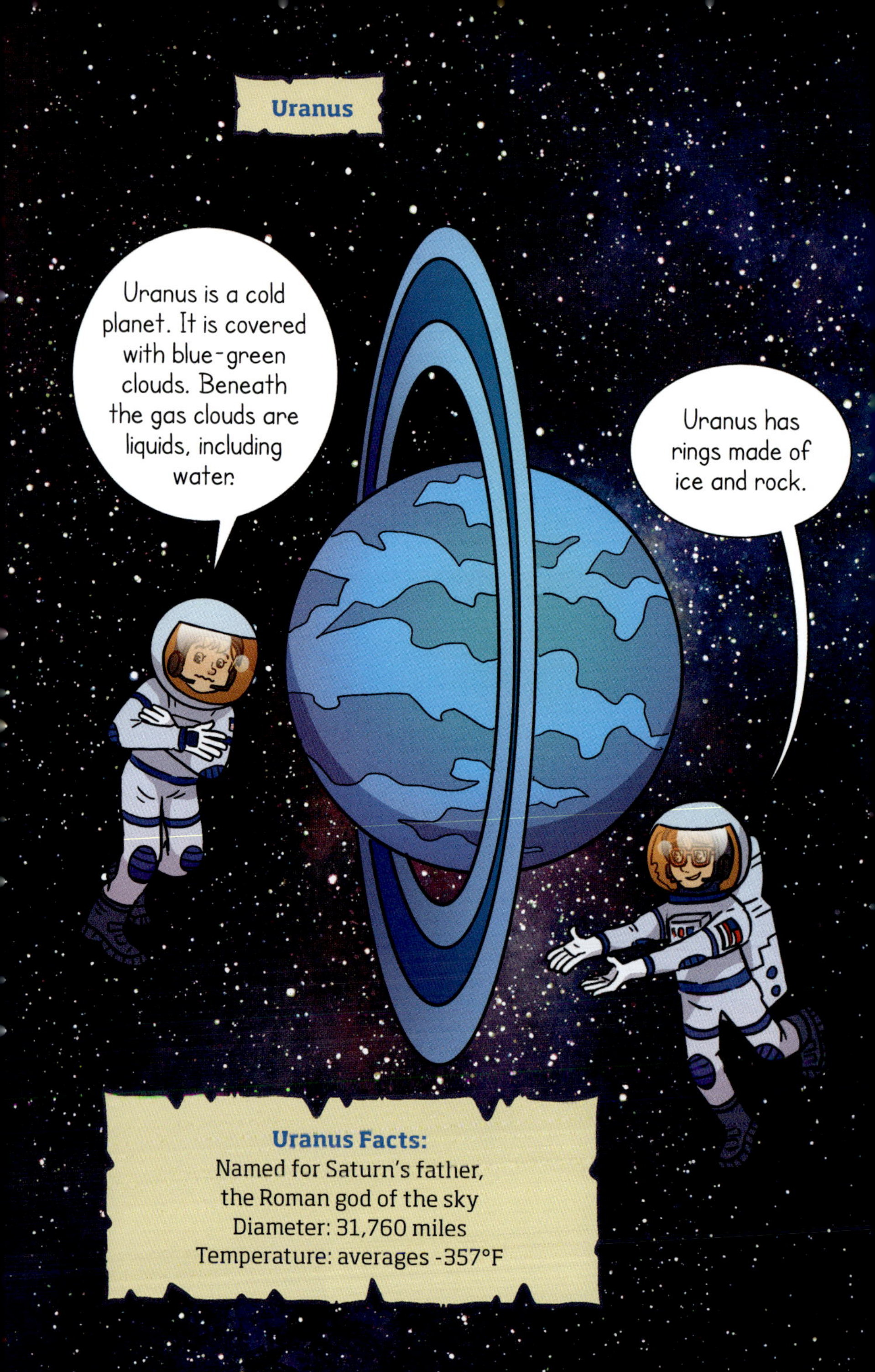
Uranus
Uranus is a cold planet. It is covered with blue-green clouds. Beneath the gas clouds are liquids, including water.
Uranus has rings made of ice and rock.
Uranus Facts:
Named for Saturn's father, the Roman god of the sky
Diameter: 31,760 miles
Temperature: averages -357°F

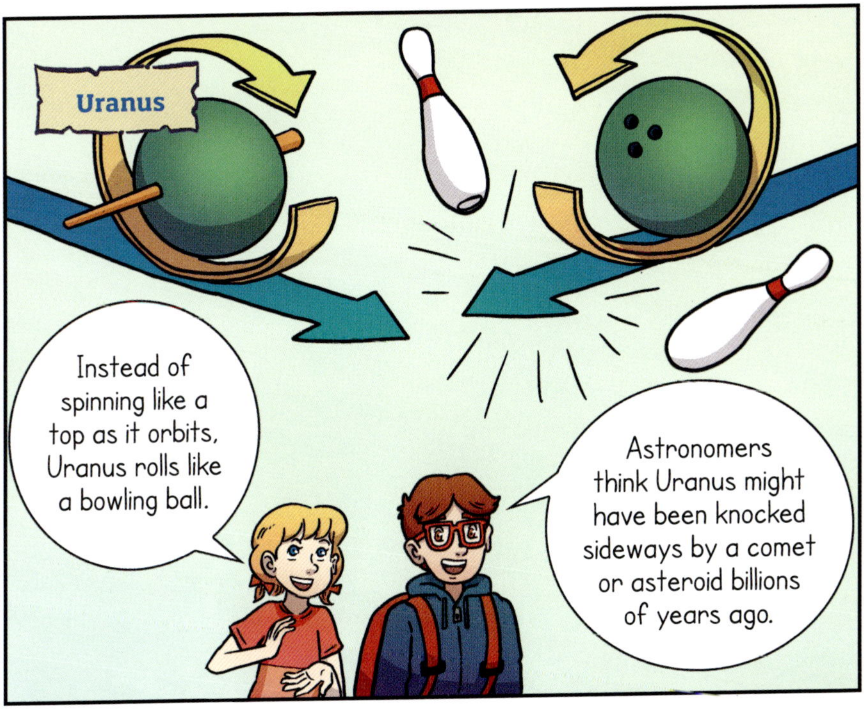
Uranus
Instead of spinning like a top as it orbits, Uranus rolls like a bowling ball.
Astronomers think Uranus might have been knocked sideways by a comet or asteroid billions of years ago.

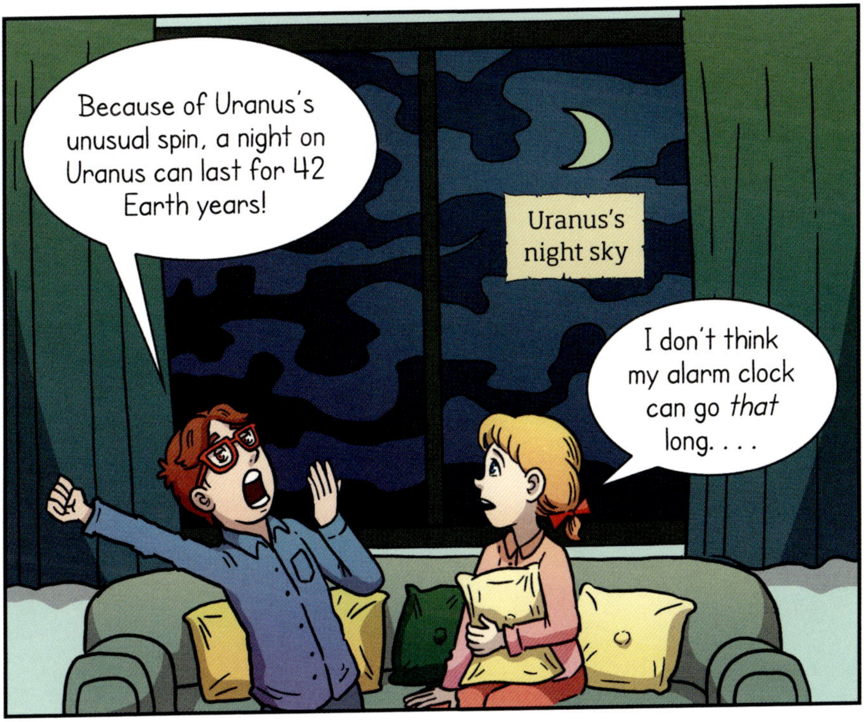
Because of Uranus's unusual spin, a night on Uranus can last for 42 Earth years!
Uranus's night sky
I don't think my alarm clock can go *that* long. . . .

Neptune

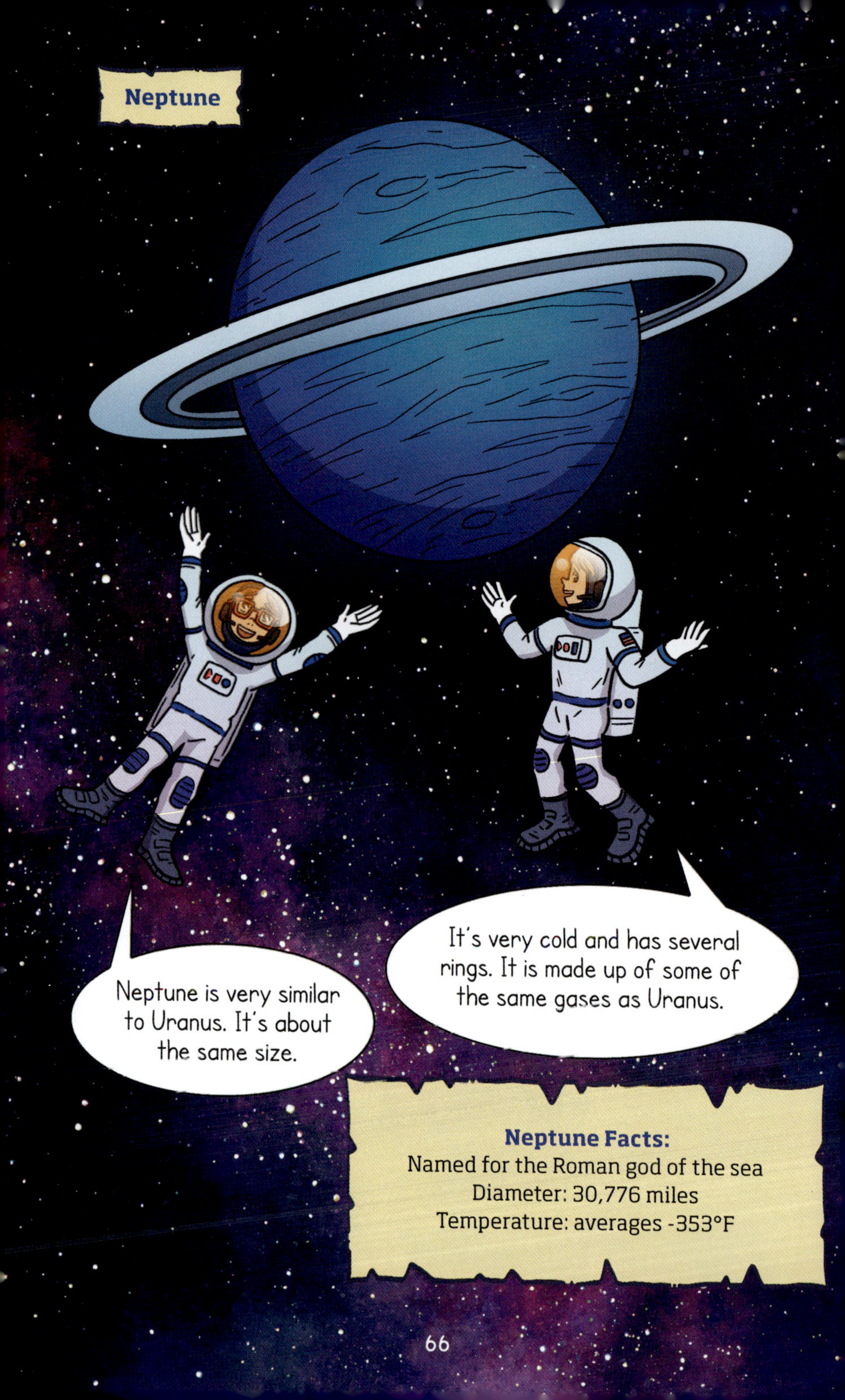
Neptune is very similar to Uranus. It's about the same size.
It's very cold and has several rings. It is made up of some of the same gases as Uranus.

Neptune Facts:
Named for the Roman god of the sea
Diameter: 30,776 miles
Temperature: averages -353°F

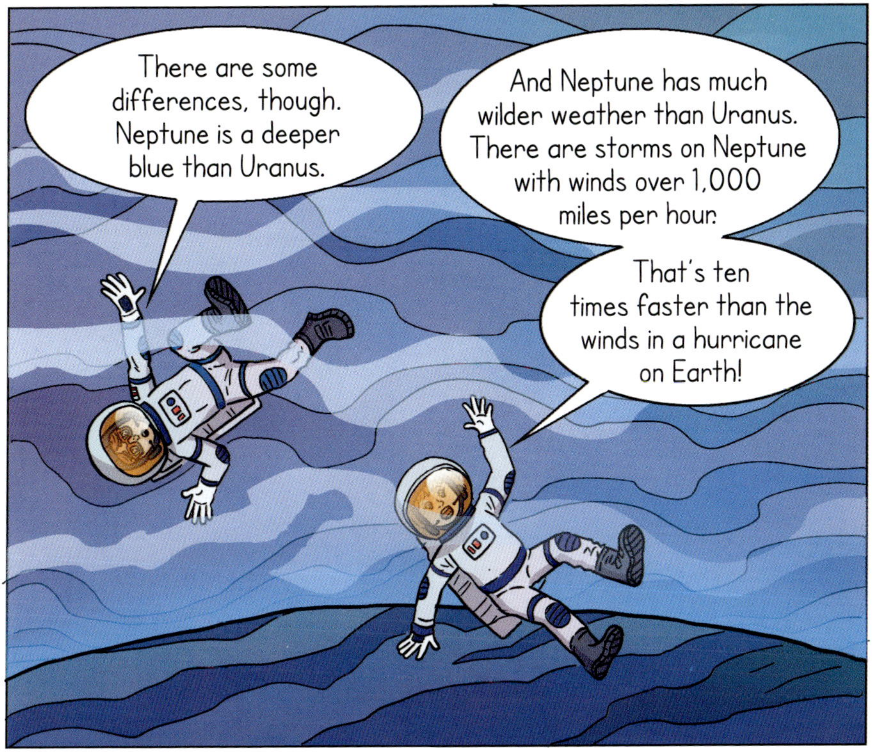
There are some differences, though. Neptune is a deeper blue than Uranus.
And Neptune has much wilder weather than Uranus. There are storms on Neptune with winds over 1,000 miles per hour.
That's ten times faster than the winds in a hurricane on Earth!

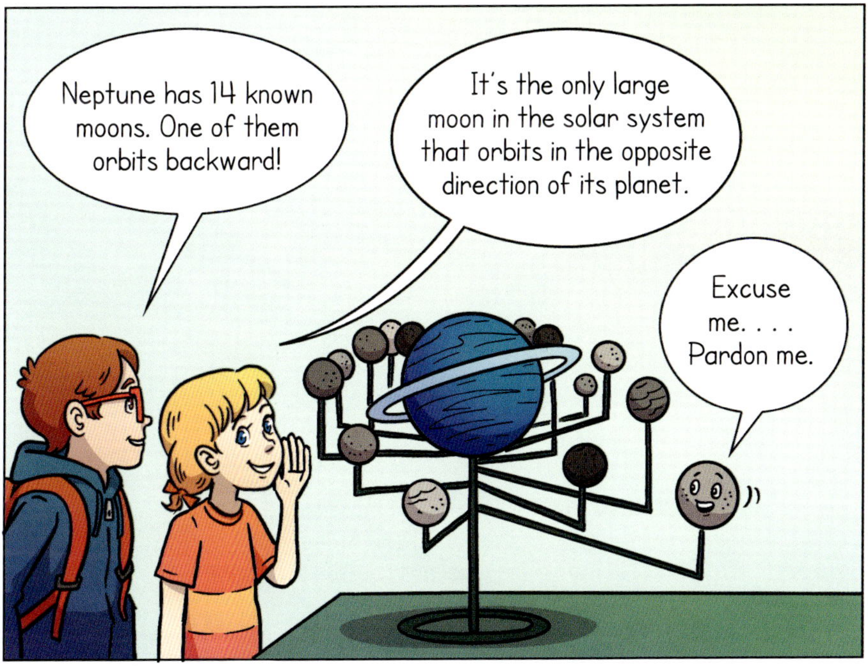
Neptune has 14 known moons. One of them orbits backward!
It's the only large moon in the solar system that orbits in the opposite direction of its planet.
Excuse me. . . . Pardon me.

Pluto is made up of a rocky core surrounded by ice and frozen gases. For many years, Pluto was known as the ninth planet in our solar system.

But as astronomers learned more about the outer solar system, they realized that Pluto was only one of many objects like it out there.

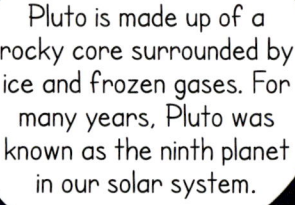

Pluto

Pluto Facts:
Named for the Roman god of the underworld
Diameter: 1,430 miles
Temperature: averages -387° to -369°F

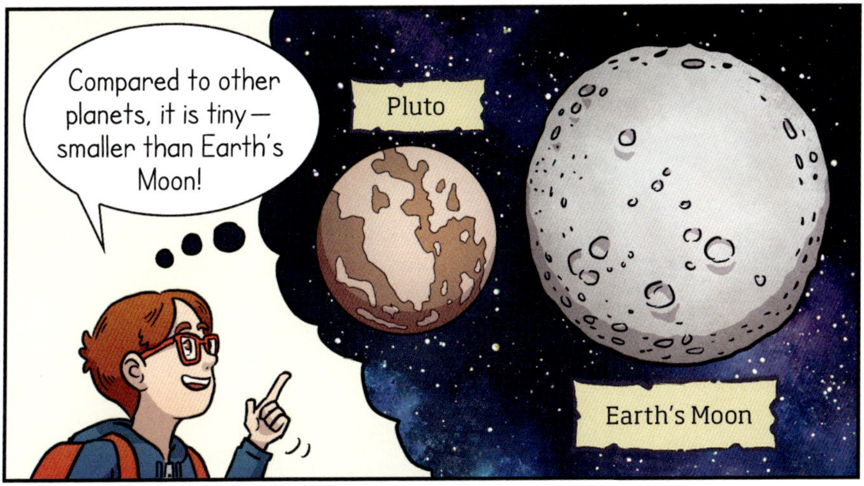
Compared to other planets, it is tiny—smaller than Earth's Moon!
Pluto
Earth's Moon

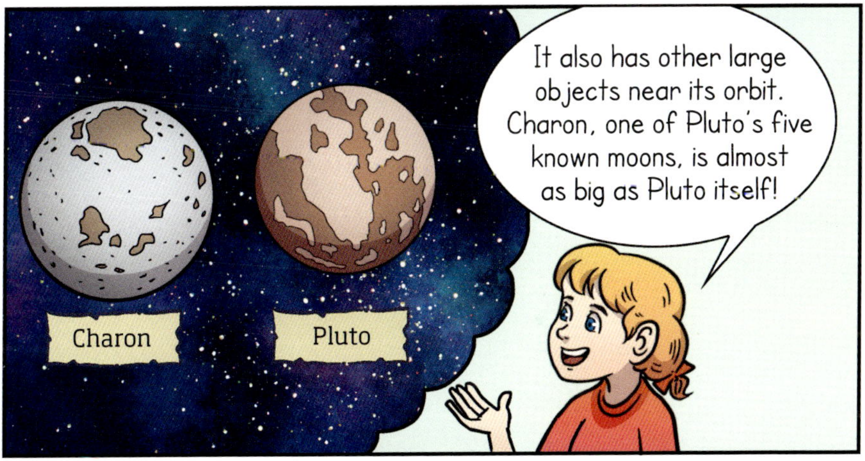
It also has other large objects near its orbit. Charon, one of Pluto's five known moons, is almost as big as Pluto itself!
Charon
Pluto

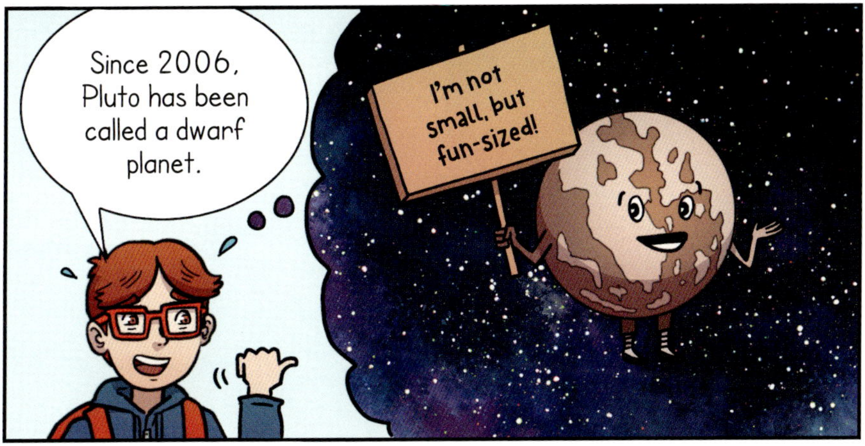
Since 2006, Pluto has been called a dwarf planet.
I'm not small, but fun-sized!

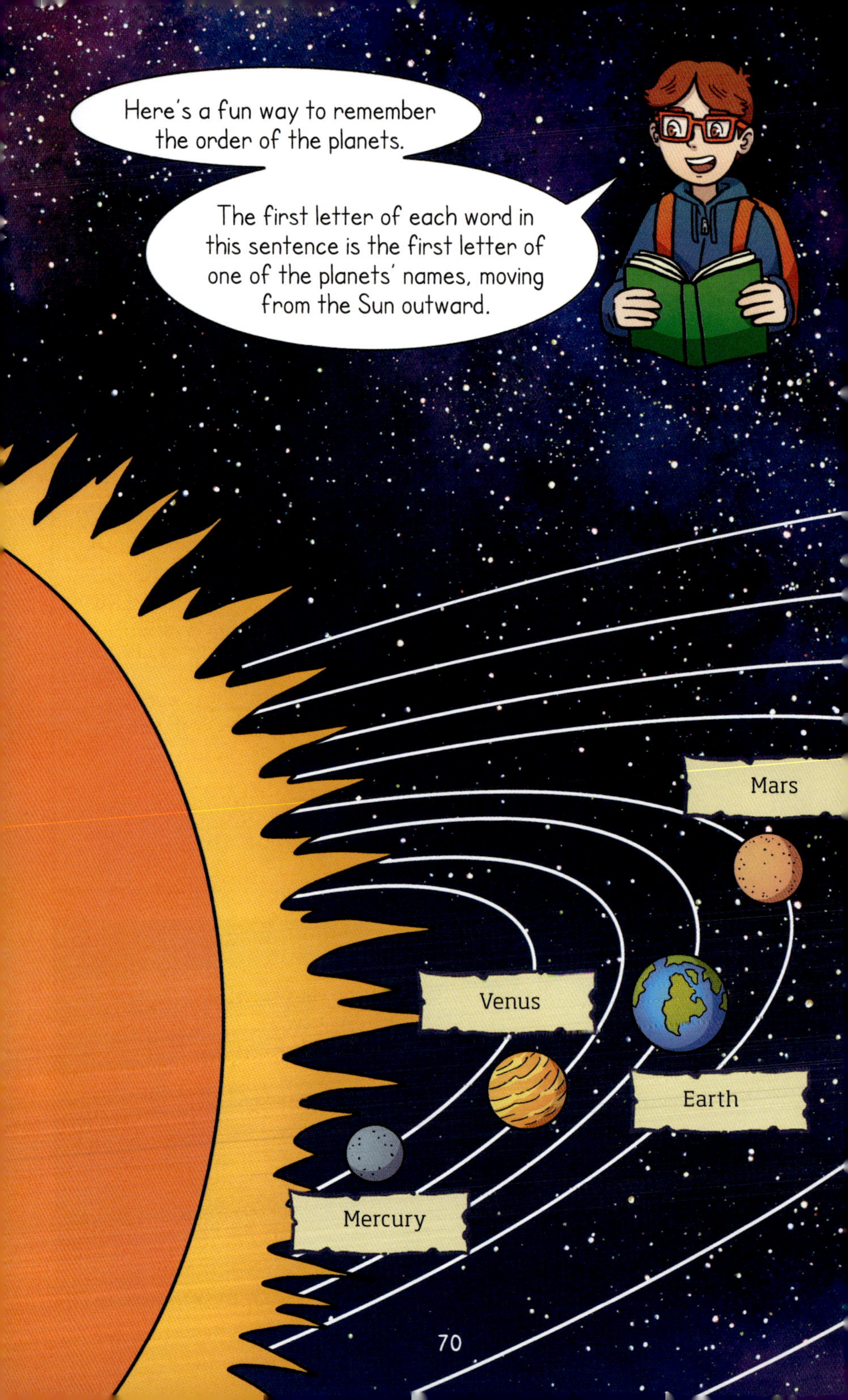
Here's a fun way to remember the order of the planets.
The first letter of each word in this sentence is the first letter of one of the planets' names, moving from the Sun outward.
Mars
Venus
Earth
Mercury

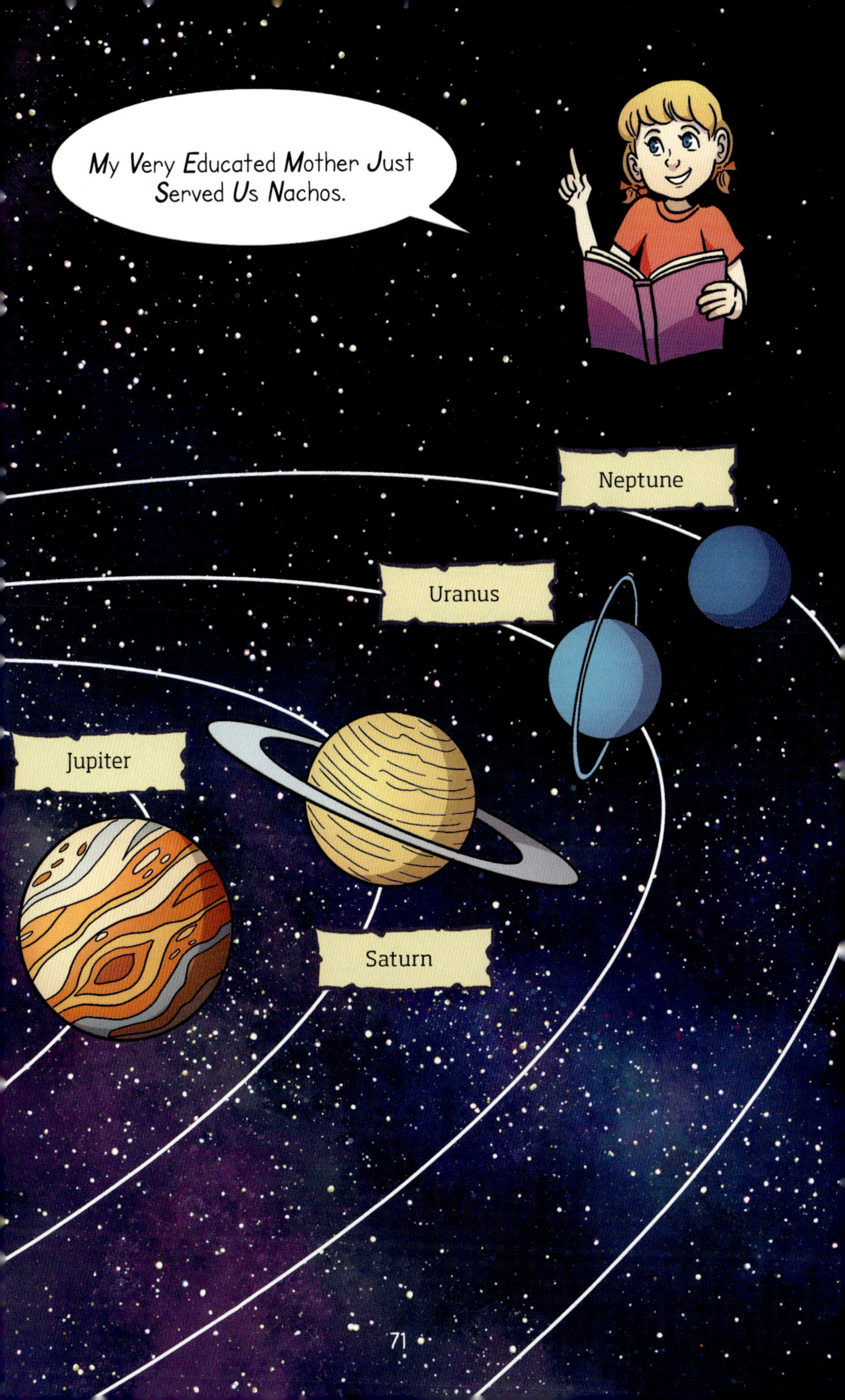
My Very Educated Mother Just Served Us Nachos.
Neptune
Uranus
Jupiter
Saturn

CHAPTER FIVE
Space Travel

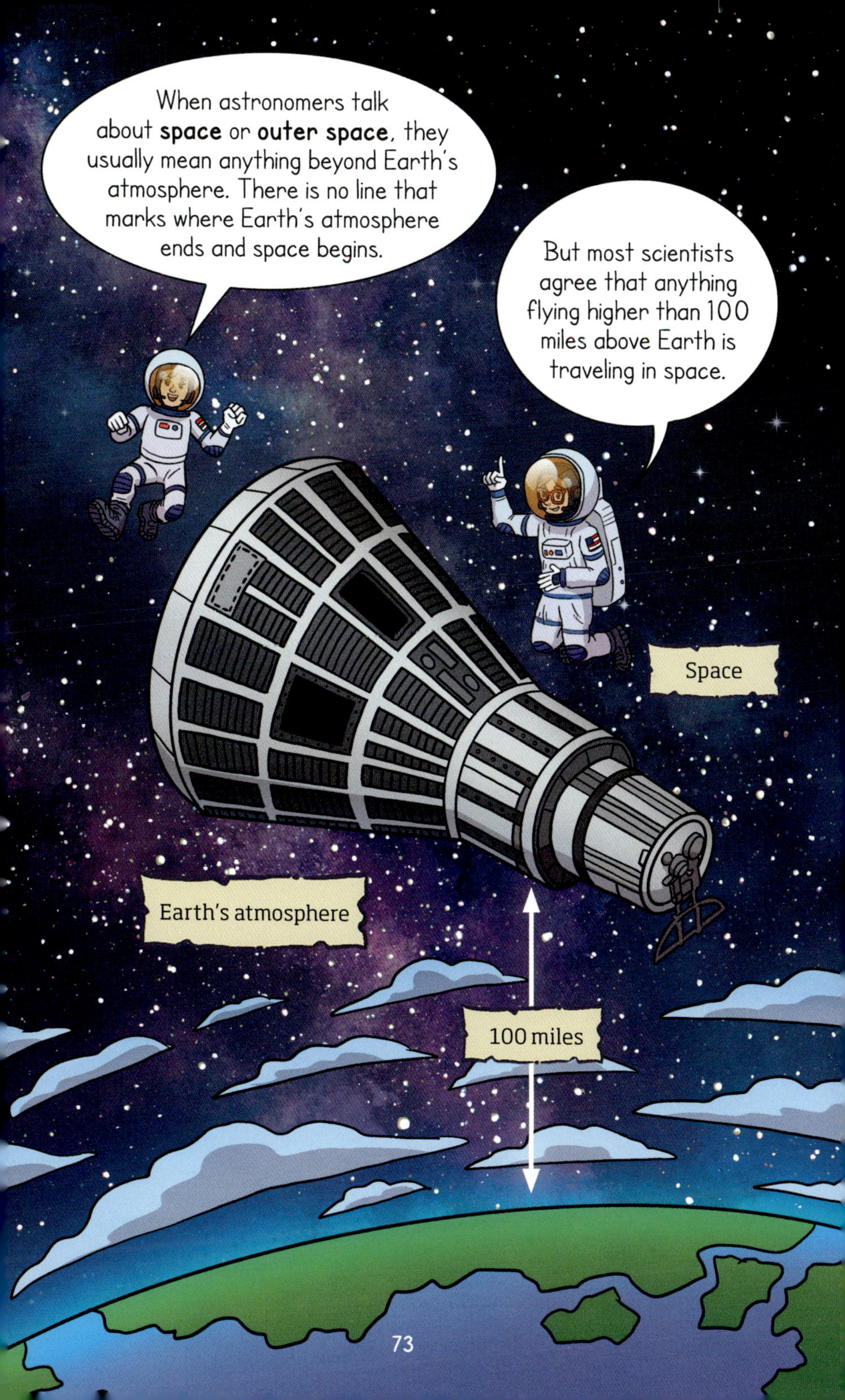
When astronomers talk about **space** or **outer space**, they usually mean anything beyond Earth's atmosphere. There is no line that marks where Earth's atmosphere ends and space begins.
But most scientists agree that anything flying higher than 100 miles above Earth is traveling in space.
Space
Earth's atmosphere
100 miles

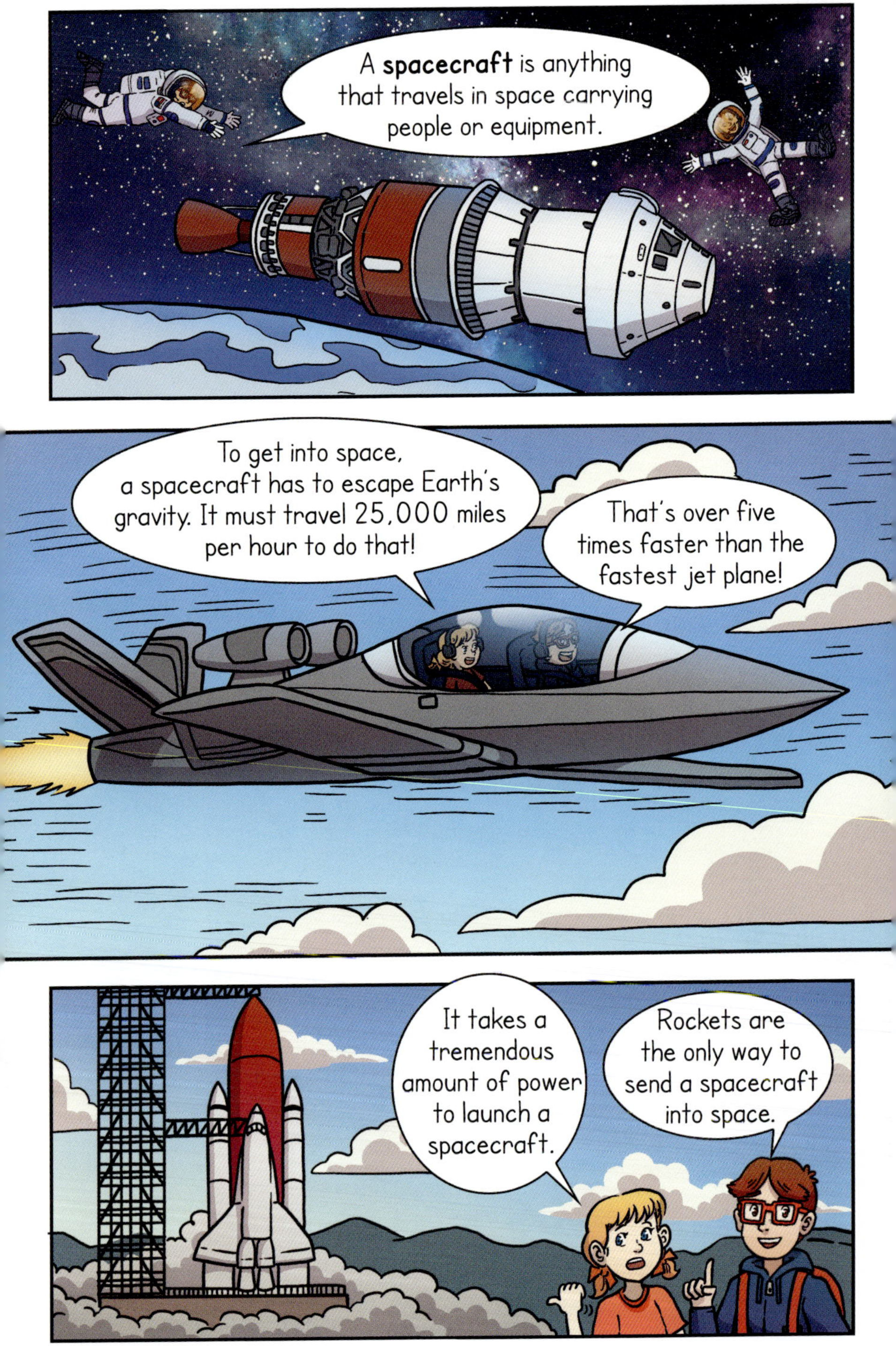
A **spacecraft** is anything that travels in space carrying people or equipment.
To get into space, a spacecraft has to escape Earth's gravity. It must travel 25,000 miles per hour to do that!
That's over five times faster than the fastest jet plane!
It takes a tremendous amount of power to launch a spacecraft.
Rockets are the only way to send a spacecraft into space.

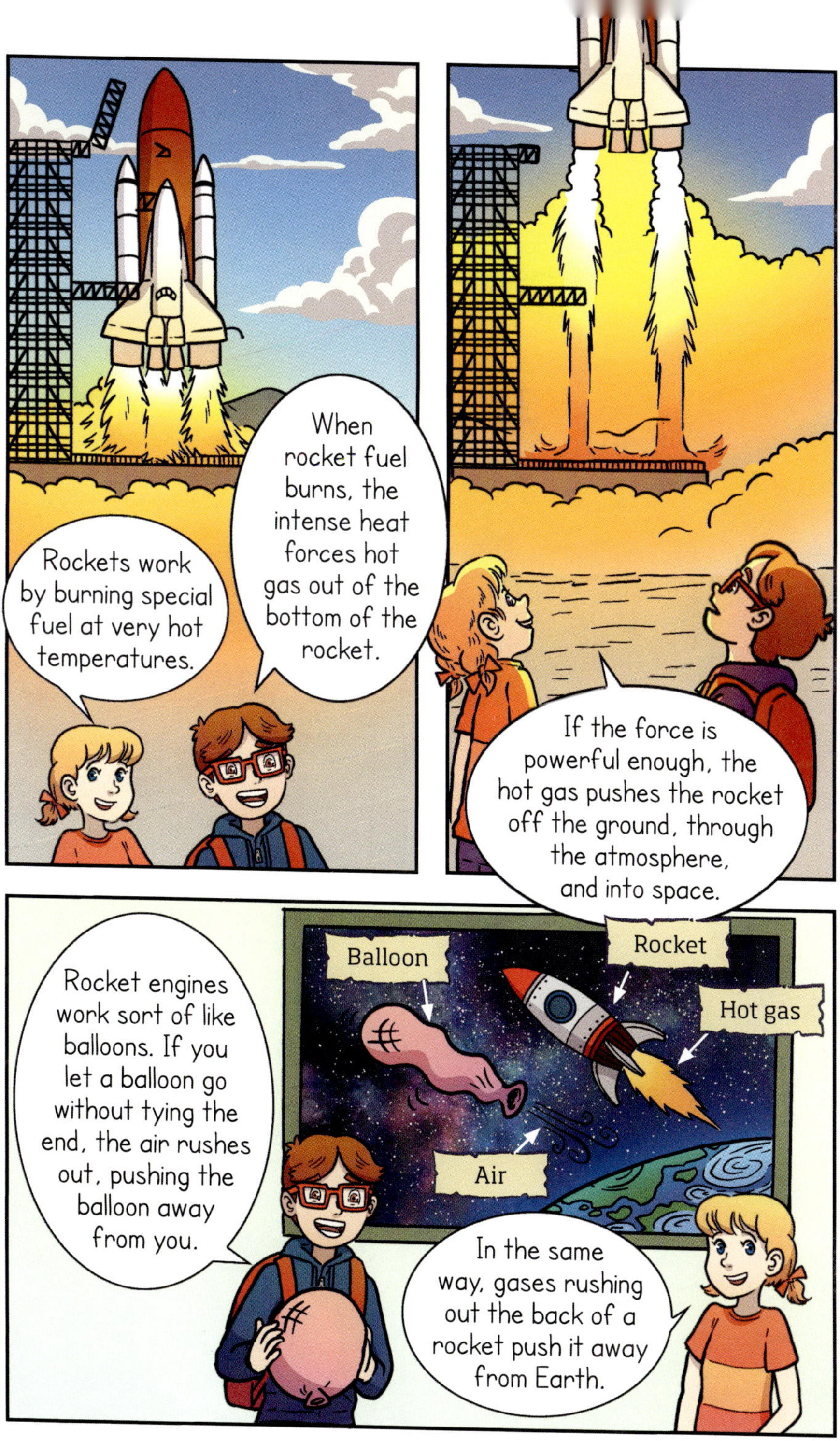

Rockets work by burning special fuel at very hot temperatures.
When rocket fuel burns, the intense heat forces hot gas out of the bottom of the rocket.
If the force is powerful enough, the hot gas pushes the rocket off the ground, through the atmosphere, and into space.
Rocket engines work sort of like balloons. If you let a balloon go without tying the end, the air rushes out, pushing the balloon away from you.
Balloon
Rocket
Hot gas
Air
In the same way, gases rushing out the back of a rocket push it away from Earth.

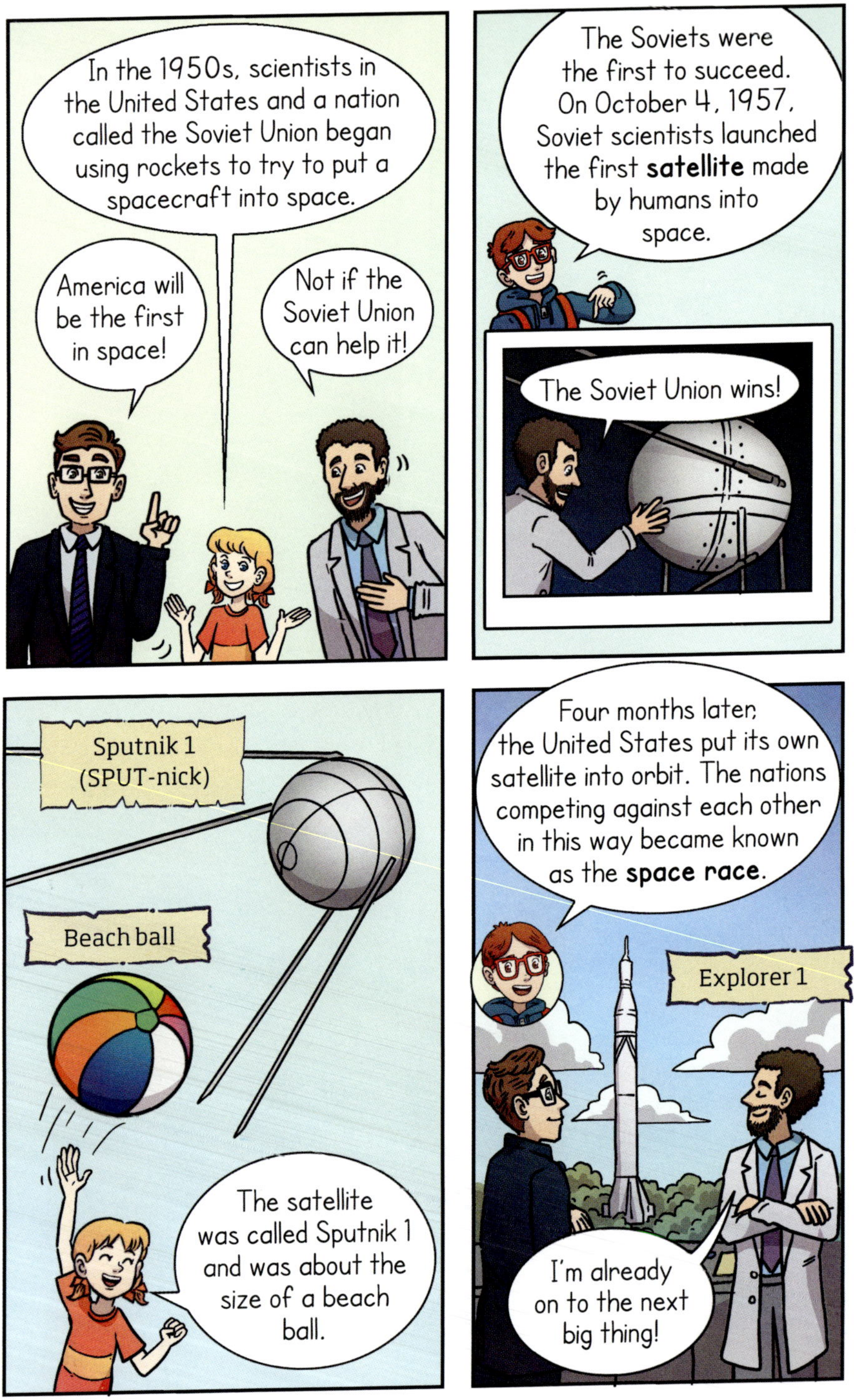
In the 1950s, scientists in the United States and a nation called the Soviet Union began using rockets to try to put a spacecraft into space.
America will be the first in space!
Not if the Soviet Union can help it!
The Soviets were the first to succeed. On October 4, 1957, Soviet scientists launched the first **satellite** made by humans into space.
The Soviet Union wins!
Sputnik 1 (SPUT-nick)
Beach ball
The satellite was called Sputnik 1 and was about the size of a beach ball.
Four months later, the United States put its own satellite into orbit. The nations competing against each other in this way became known as the **space race**.
Explorer 1
I'm already on to the next big thing!

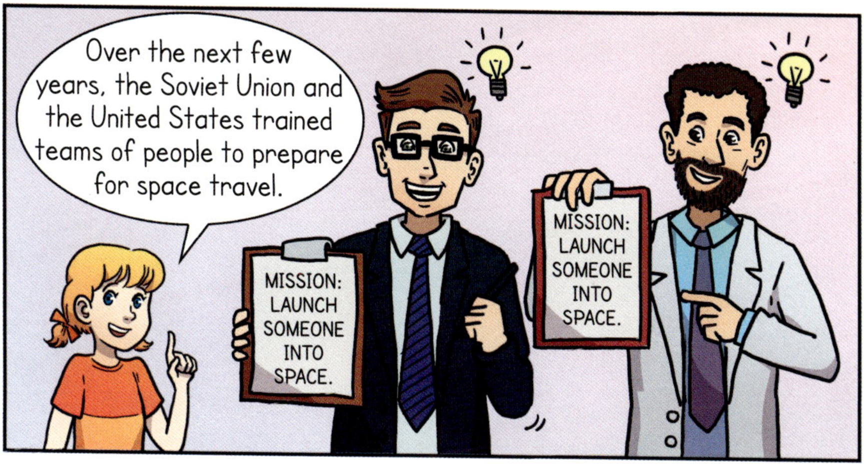
Over the next few years, the Soviet Union and the United States trained teams of people to prepare for space travel.
MISSION: LAUNCH SOMEONE INTO SPACE.
MISSION: LAUNCH SOMEONE INTO SPACE.

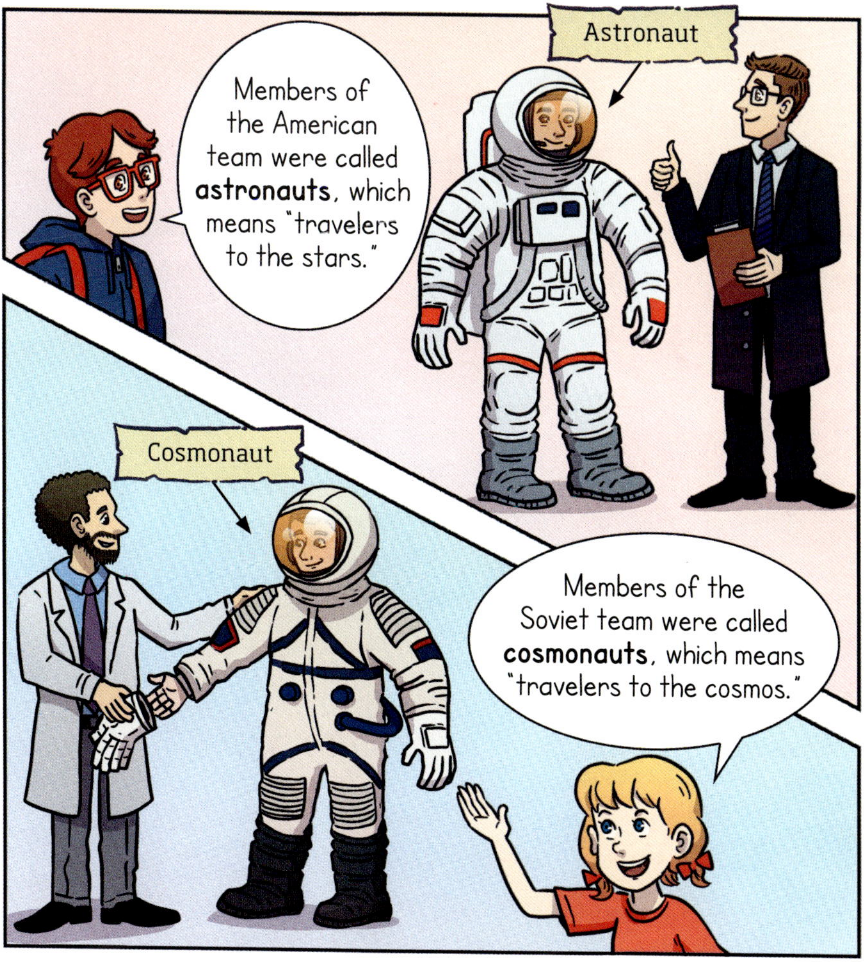
Members of the American team were called **astronauts**, which means "travelers to the stars."
Astronaut
Cosmonaut
Members of the Soviet team were called **cosmonauts**, which means "travelers to the cosmos."

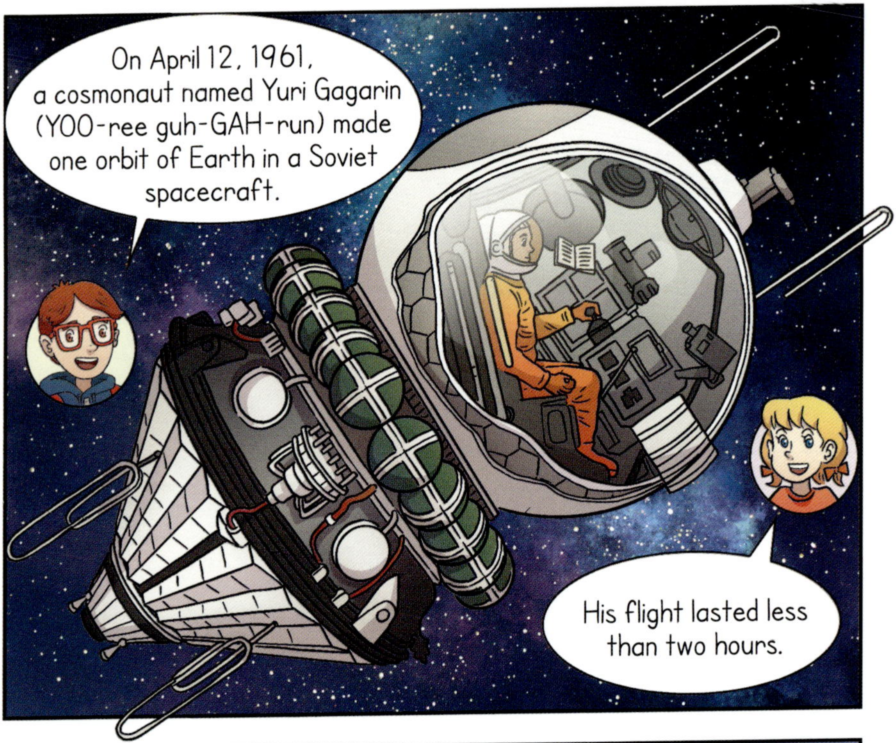
On April 12, 1961, a cosmonaut named Yuri Gagarin (YOO-ree guh-GAH-run) made one orbit of Earth in a Soviet spacecraft.
His flight lasted less than two hours.

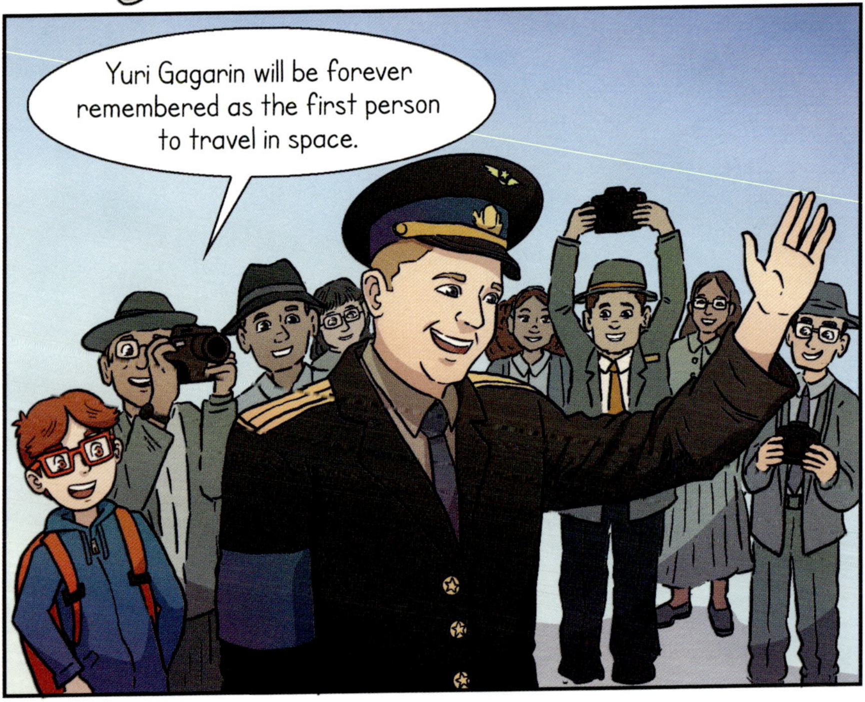
Yuri Gagarin will be forever remembered as the first person to travel in space.

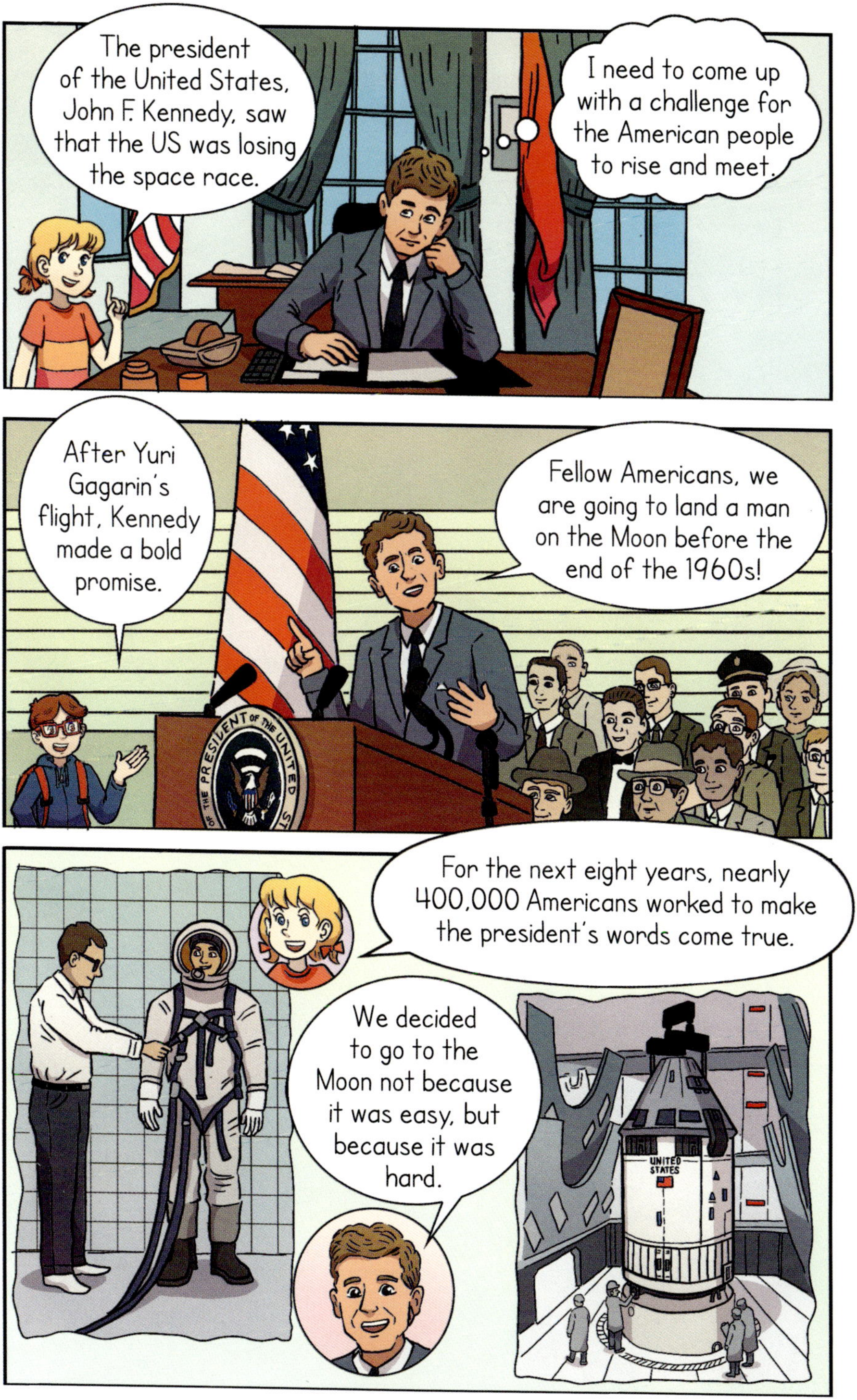
The president of the United States, John F. Kennedy, saw that the US was losing the space race.
I need to come up with a challenge for the American people to rise and meet.
After Yuri Gagarin's flight, Kennedy made a bold promise.
Fellow Americans, we are going to land a man on the Moon before the end of the 1960s!
For the next eight years, nearly 400,000 Americans worked to make the president's words come true.
We decided to go to the Moon not because it was easy, but because it was hard.
UNITED STATES

Space Travelers

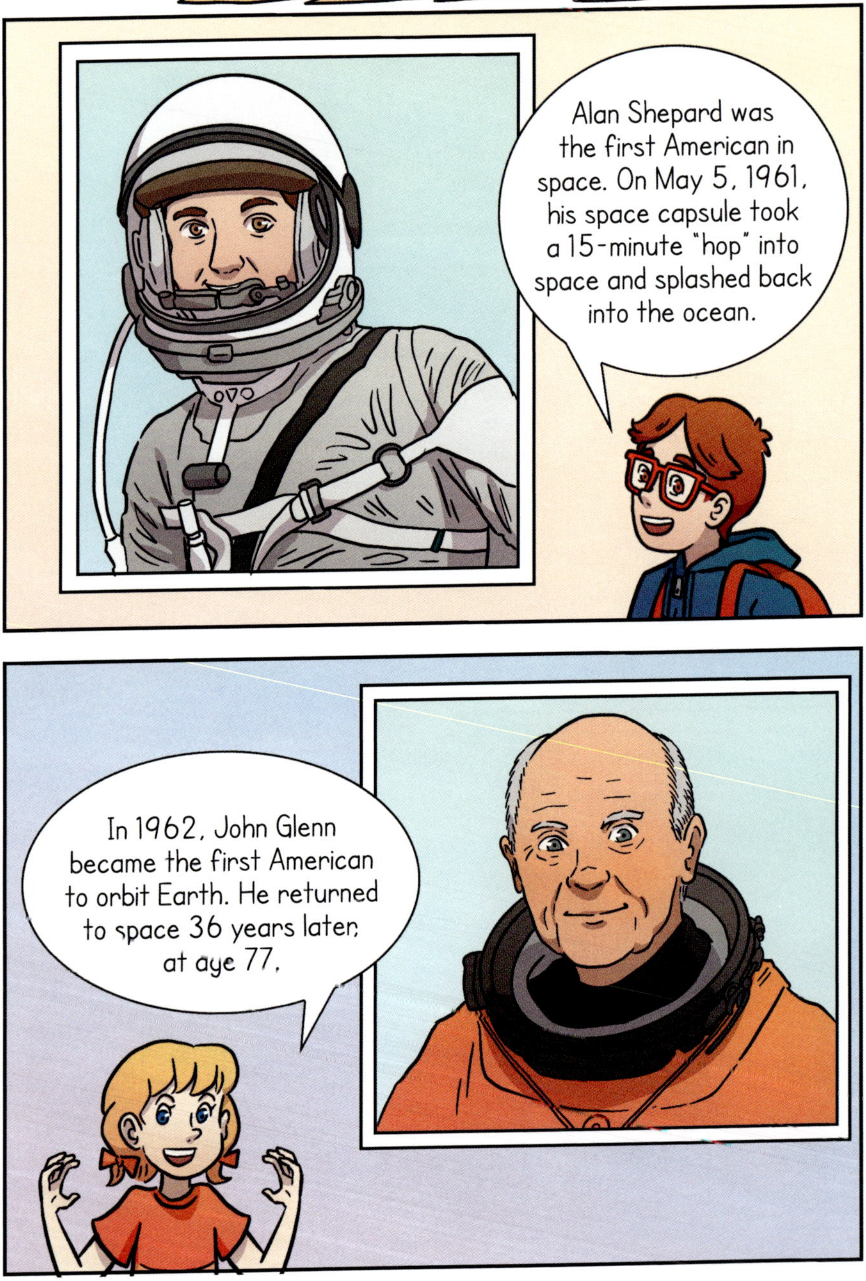
Alan Shepard was the first American in space. On May 5, 1961, his space capsule took a 15-minute "hop" into space and splashed back into the ocean.
In 1962, John Glenn became the first American to orbit Earth. He returned to space 36 years later, at age 77.

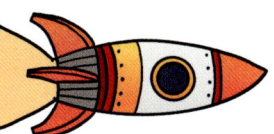

Hall of Fame

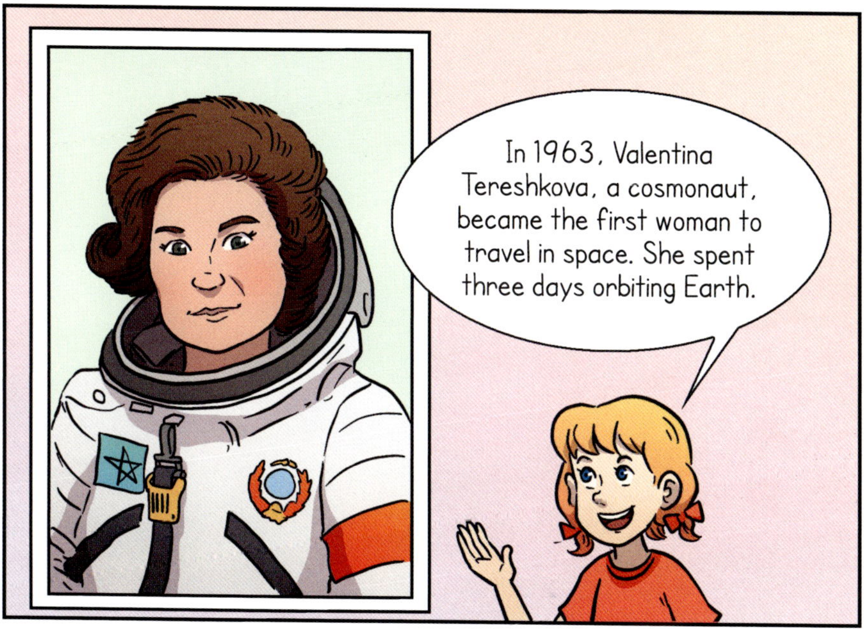
In 1963, Valentina Tereshkova, a cosmonaut, became the first woman to travel in space. She spent three days orbiting Earth.

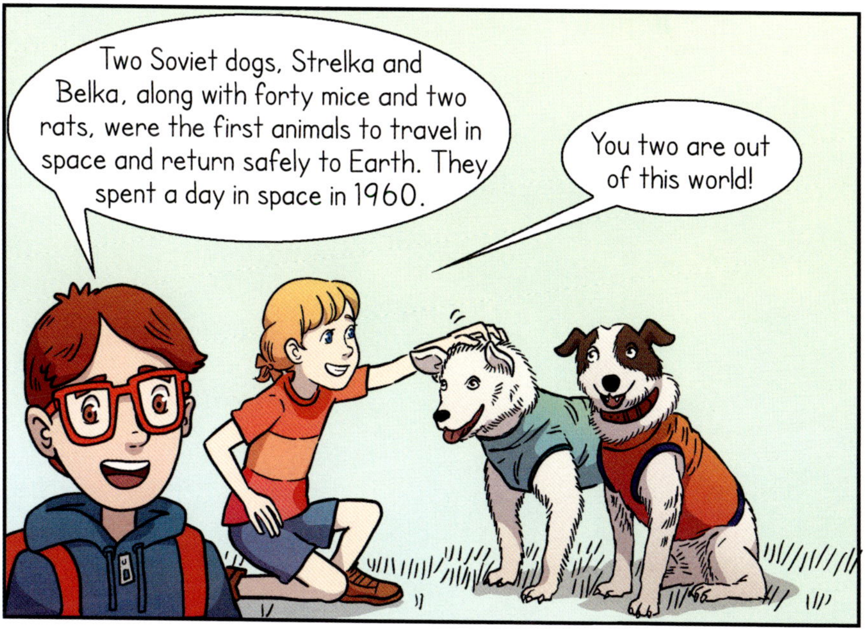
Two Soviet dogs, Strelka and Belka, along with forty mice and two rats, were the first animals to travel in space and return safely to Earth. They spent a day in space in 1960.
You two are out of this world!

CHAPTER SIX
From Earth to the Moon

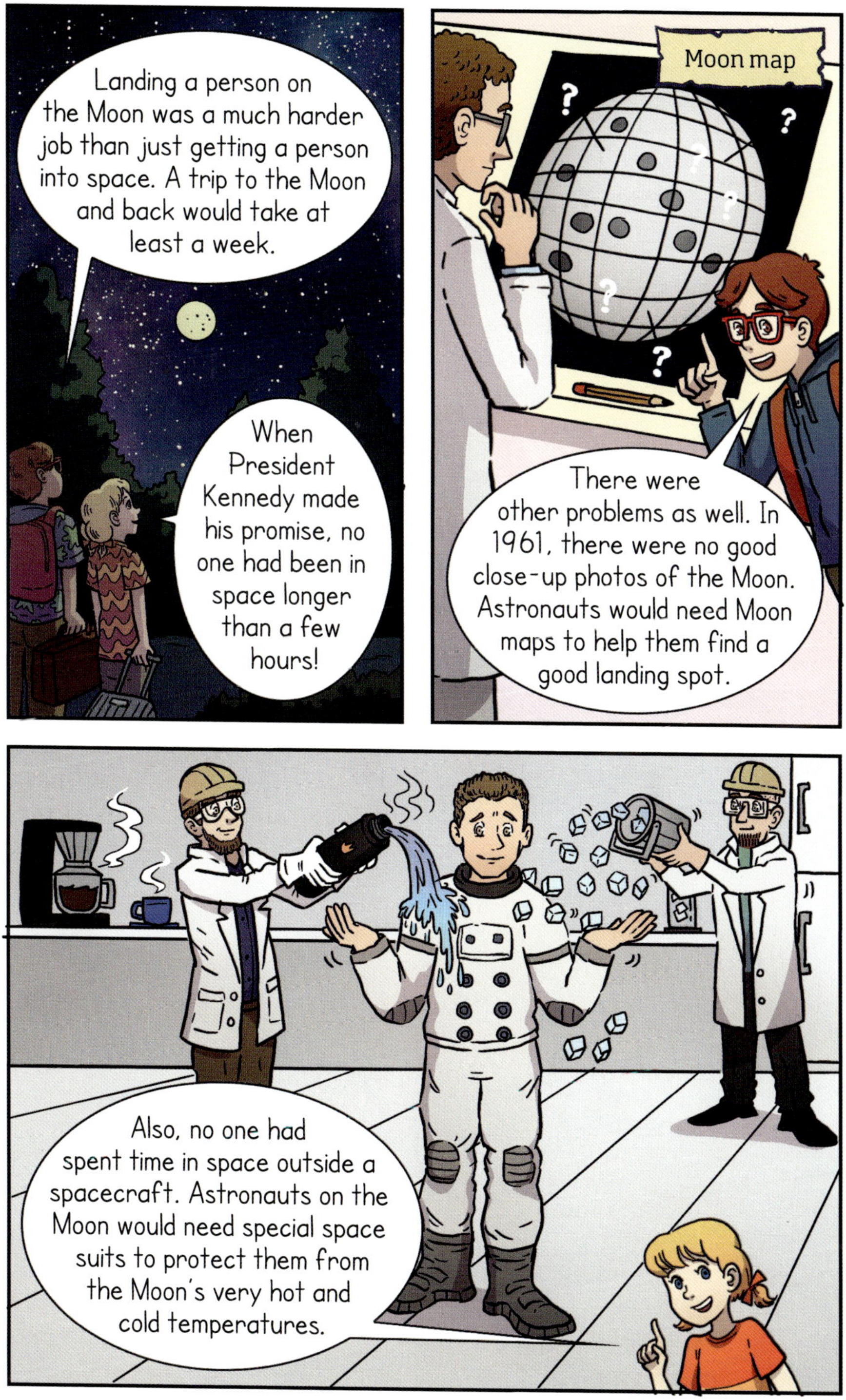
Landing a person on the Moon was a much harder job than just getting a person into space. A trip to the Moon and back would take at least a week.
When President Kennedy made his promise, no one had been in space longer than a few hours!
Moon map
There were other problems as well. In 1961, there were no good close-up photos of the Moon. Astronauts would need Moon maps to help them find a good landing spot.
Also, no one had spent time in space outside a spacecraft. Astronauts on the Moon would need special space suits to protect them from the Moon's very hot and cold temperatures.

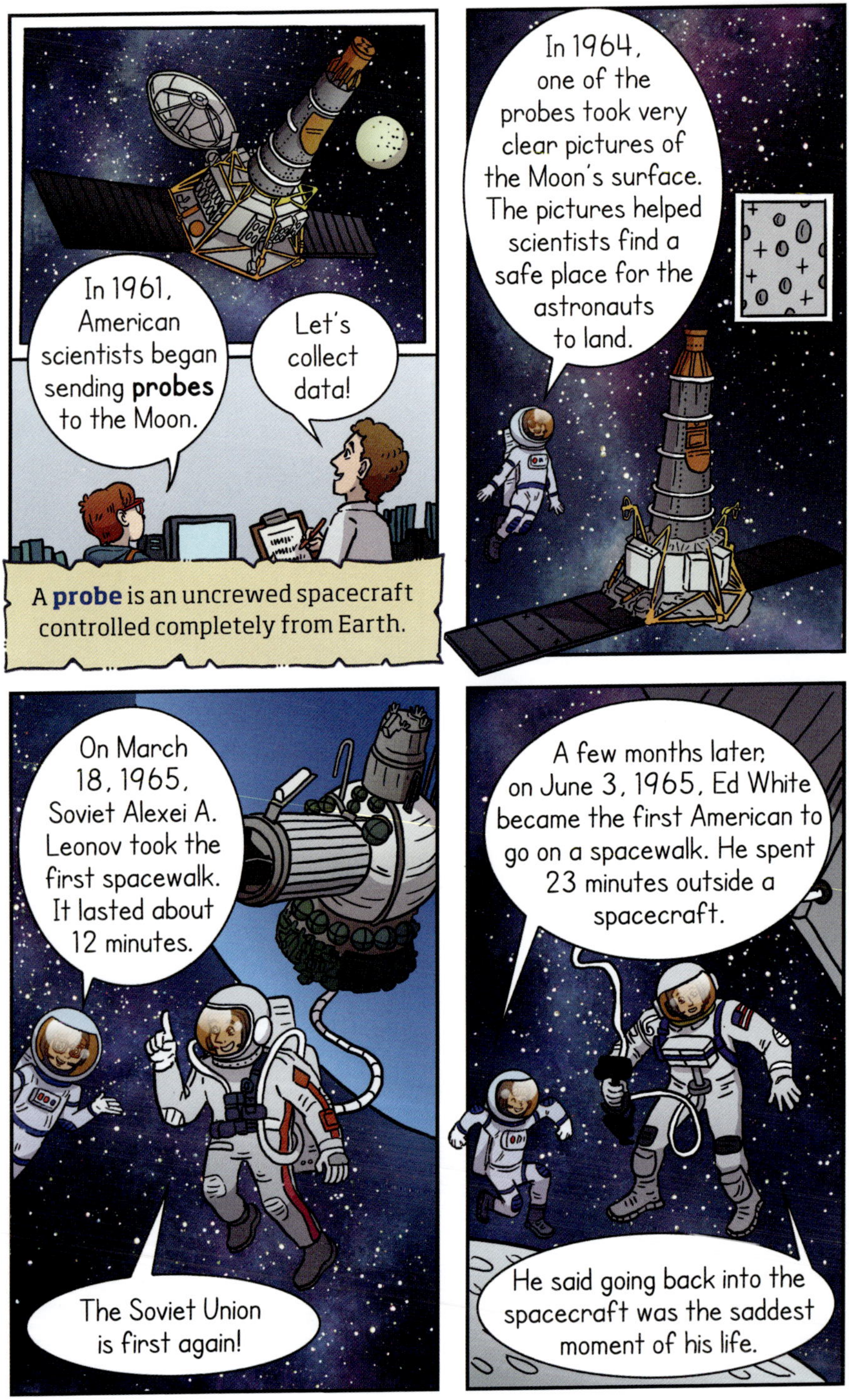
In 1961, American scientists began sending **probes** to the Moon.
Let's collect data!
A **probe** is an uncrewed spacecraft controlled completely from Earth.
In 1964, one of the probes took very clear pictures of the Moon's surface. The pictures helped scientists find a safe place for the astronauts to land.
On March 18, 1965, Soviet Alexei A. Leonov took the first spacewalk. It lasted about 12 minutes.
The Soviet Union is first again!
A few months later, on June 3, 1965, Ed White became the first American to go on a spacewalk. He spent 23 minutes outside a spacecraft.
He said going back into the spacecraft was the saddest moment of his life.

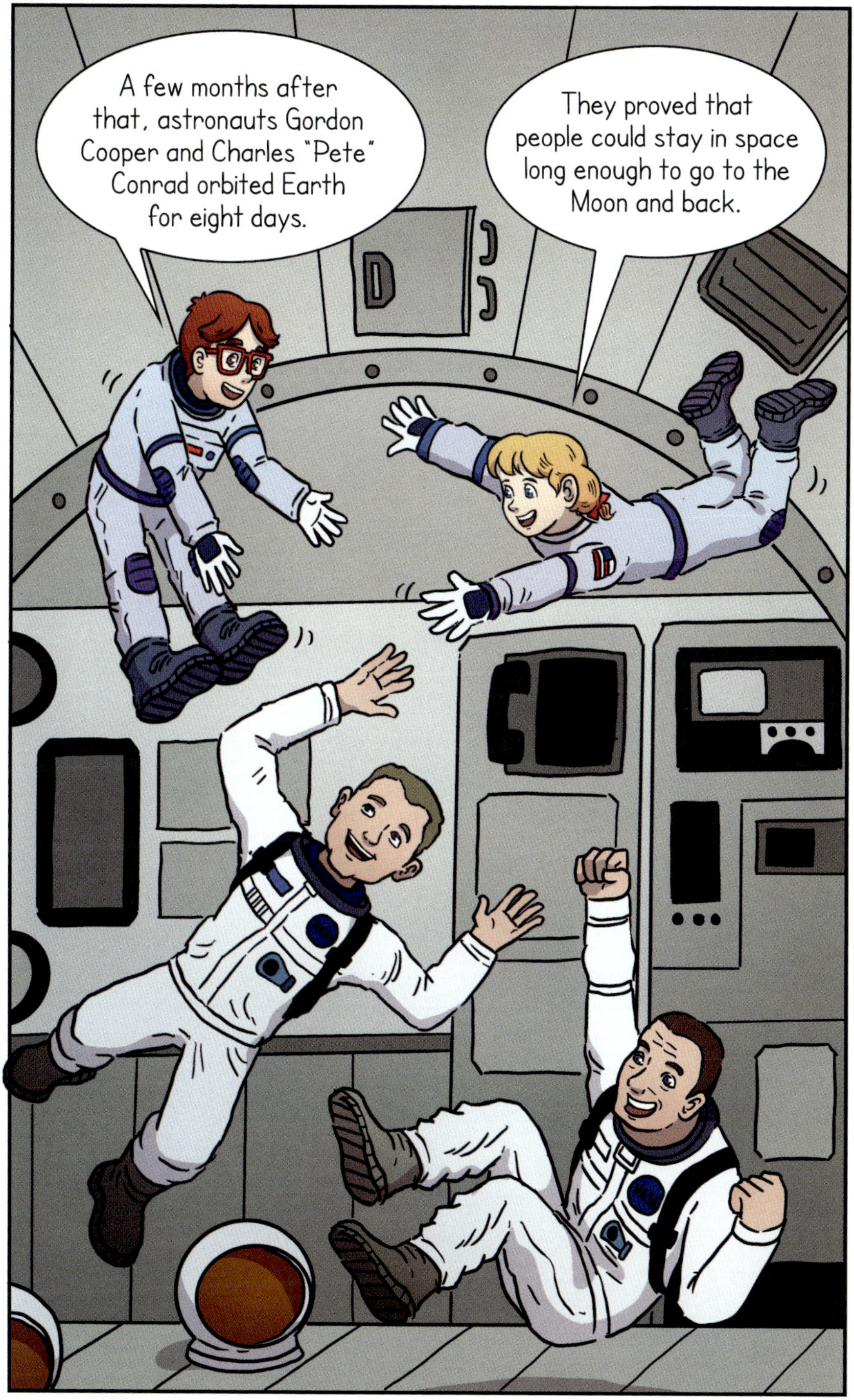
A few months after that, astronauts Gordon Cooper and Charles "Pete" Conrad orbited Earth for eight days.
They proved that people could stay in space long enough to go to the Moon and back.

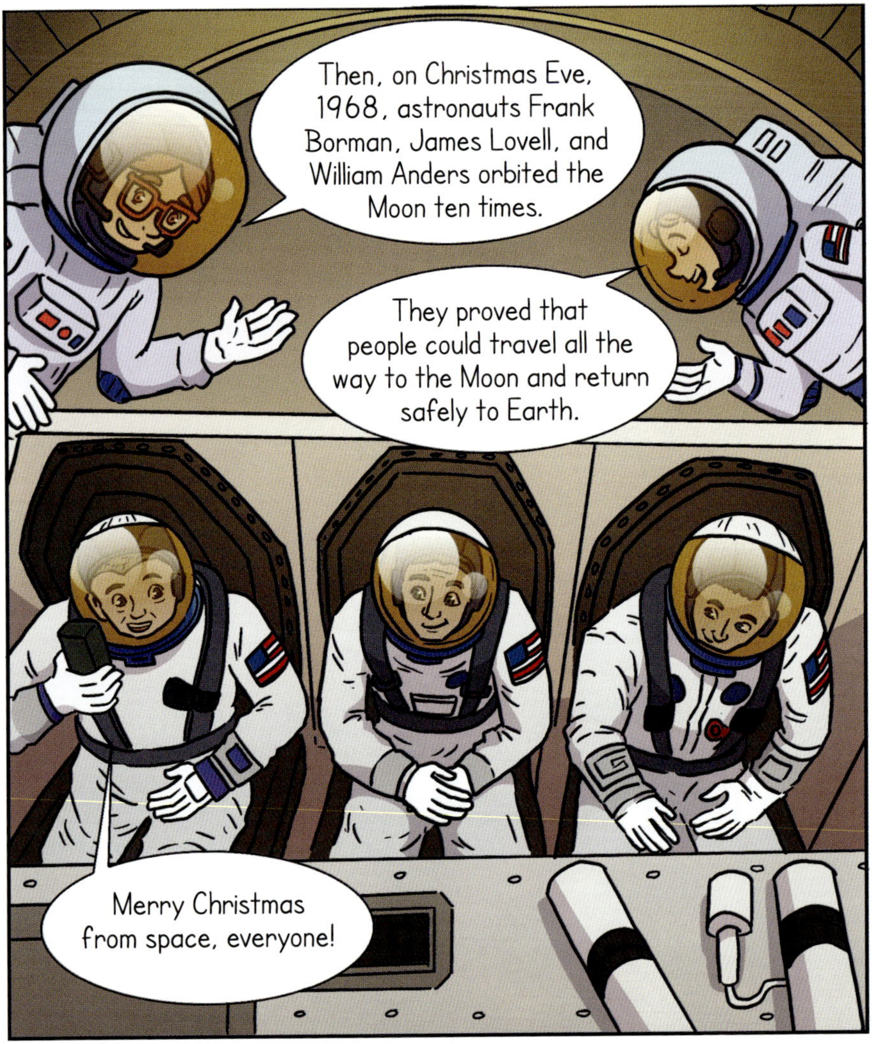
Then, on Christmas Eve, 1968, astronauts Frank Borman, James Lovell, and William Anders orbited the Moon ten times.
They proved that people could travel all the way to the Moon and return safely to Earth.
Merry Christmas from space, everyone!

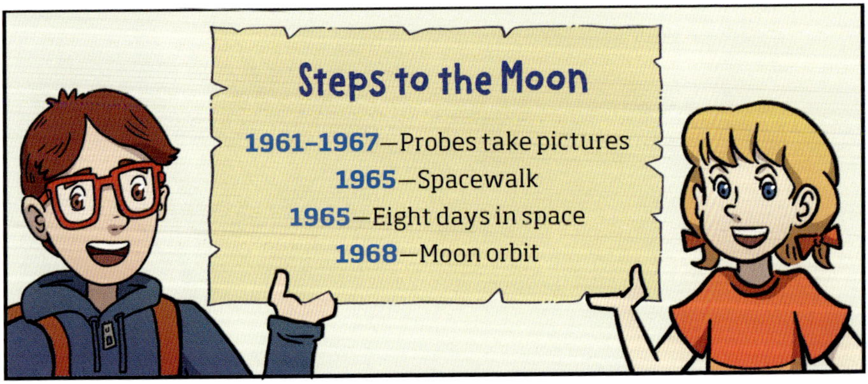
Steps to the Moon
1961–1967—Probes take pictures
1965—Spacewalk
1965—Eight days in space
1968—Moon orbit

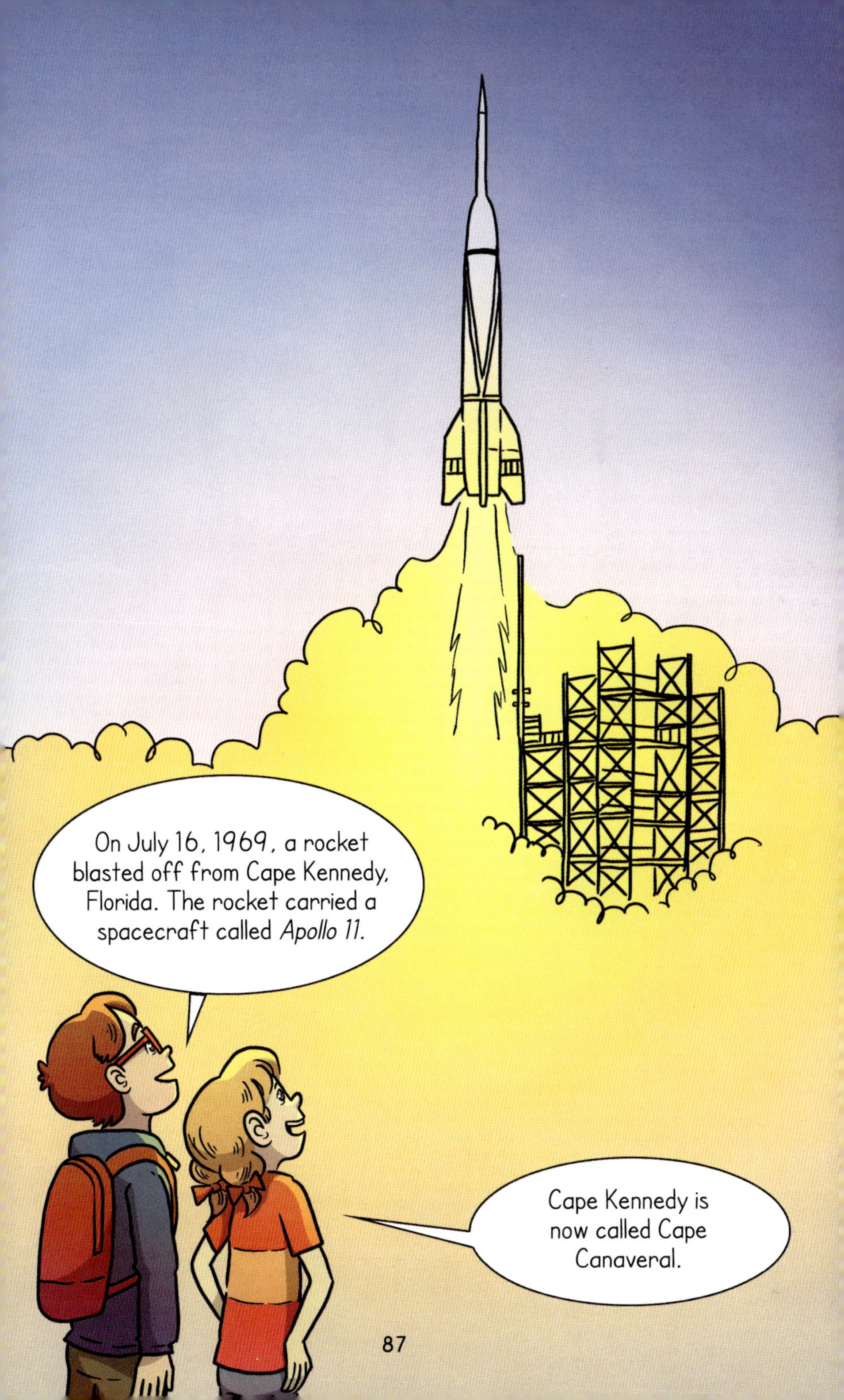
On July 16, 1969, a rocket blasted off from Cape Kennedy, Florida. The rocket carried a spacecraft called *Apollo 11*.
Cape Kennedy is now called Cape Canaveral.

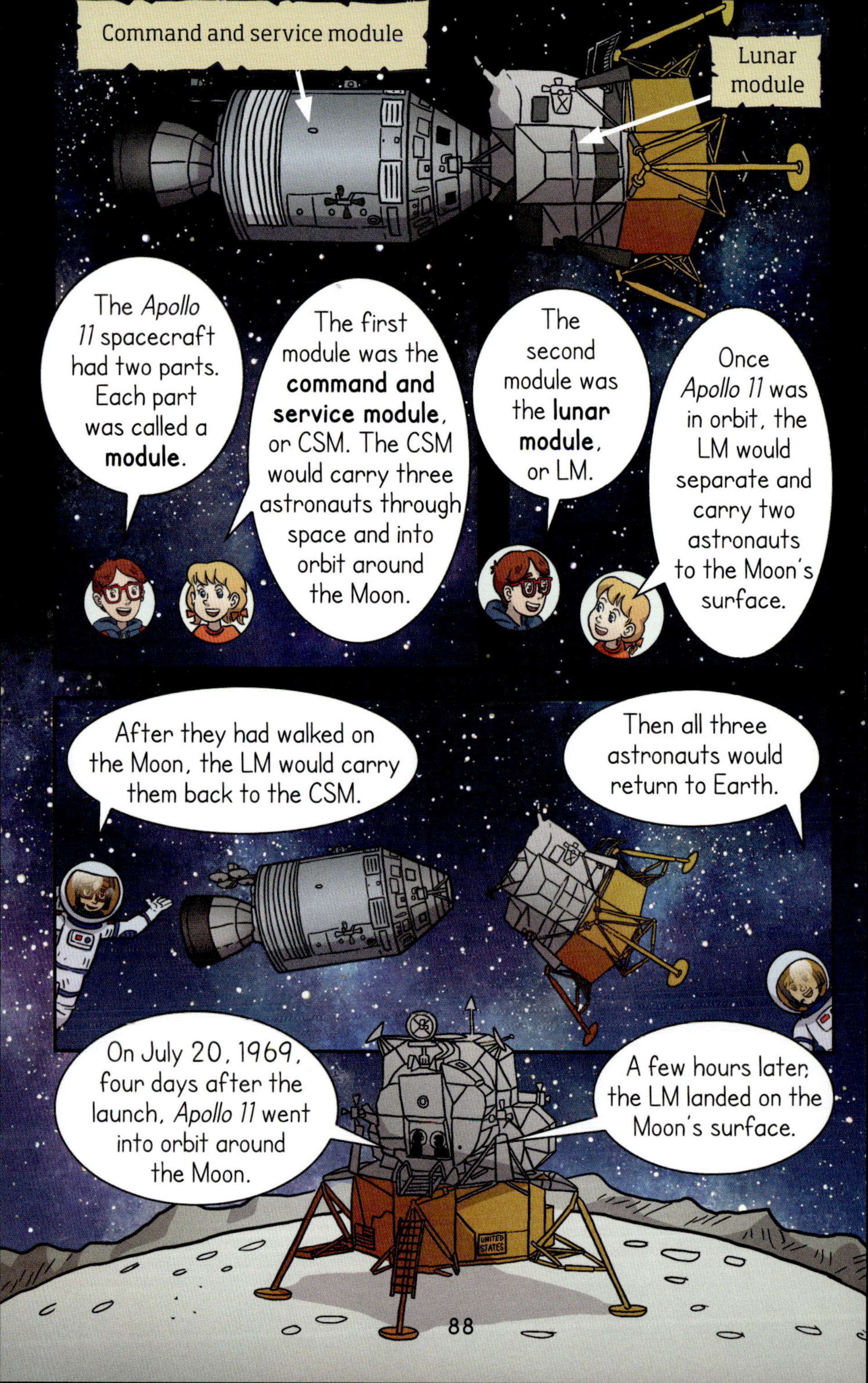
Command and service module
Lunar module
The *Apollo 11* spacecraft had two parts. Each part was called a **module**.
The first module was the **command and service module**, or CSM. The CSM would carry three astronauts through space and into orbit around the Moon.
The second module was the **lunar module**, or LM.
Once *Apollo 11* was in orbit, the LM would separate and carry two astronauts to the Moon's surface.
After they had walked on the Moon, the LM would carry them back to the CSM.
Then all three astronauts would return to Earth.
On July 20, 1969, four days after the launch, *Apollo 11* went into orbit around the Moon.
A few hours later, the LM landed on the Moon's surface.
UNITED STATES

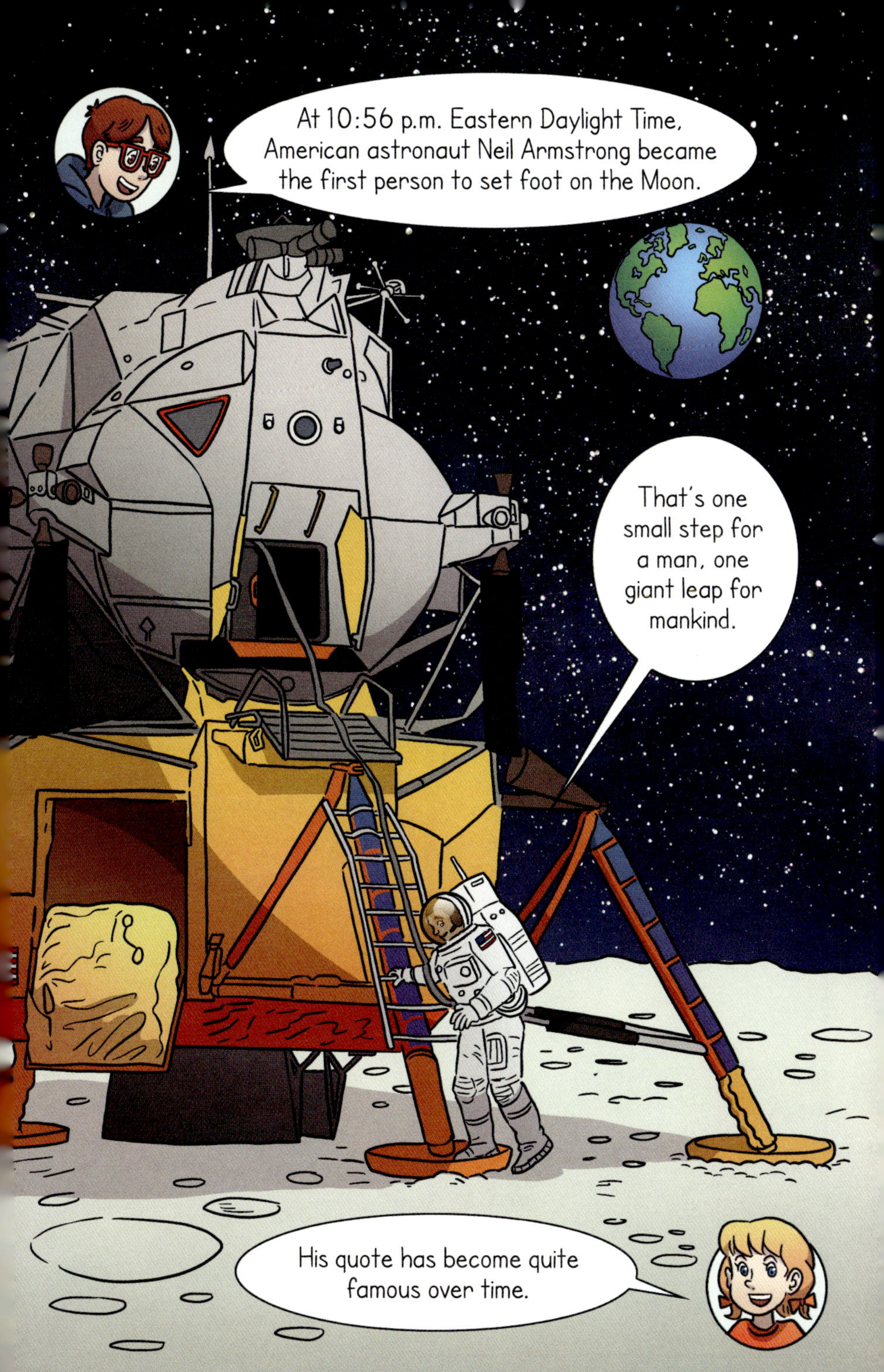
At 10:56 p.m. Eastern Daylight Time, American astronaut Neil Armstrong became the first person to set foot on the Moon.
That's one small step for a man, one giant leap for mankind.
His quote has become quite famous over time.

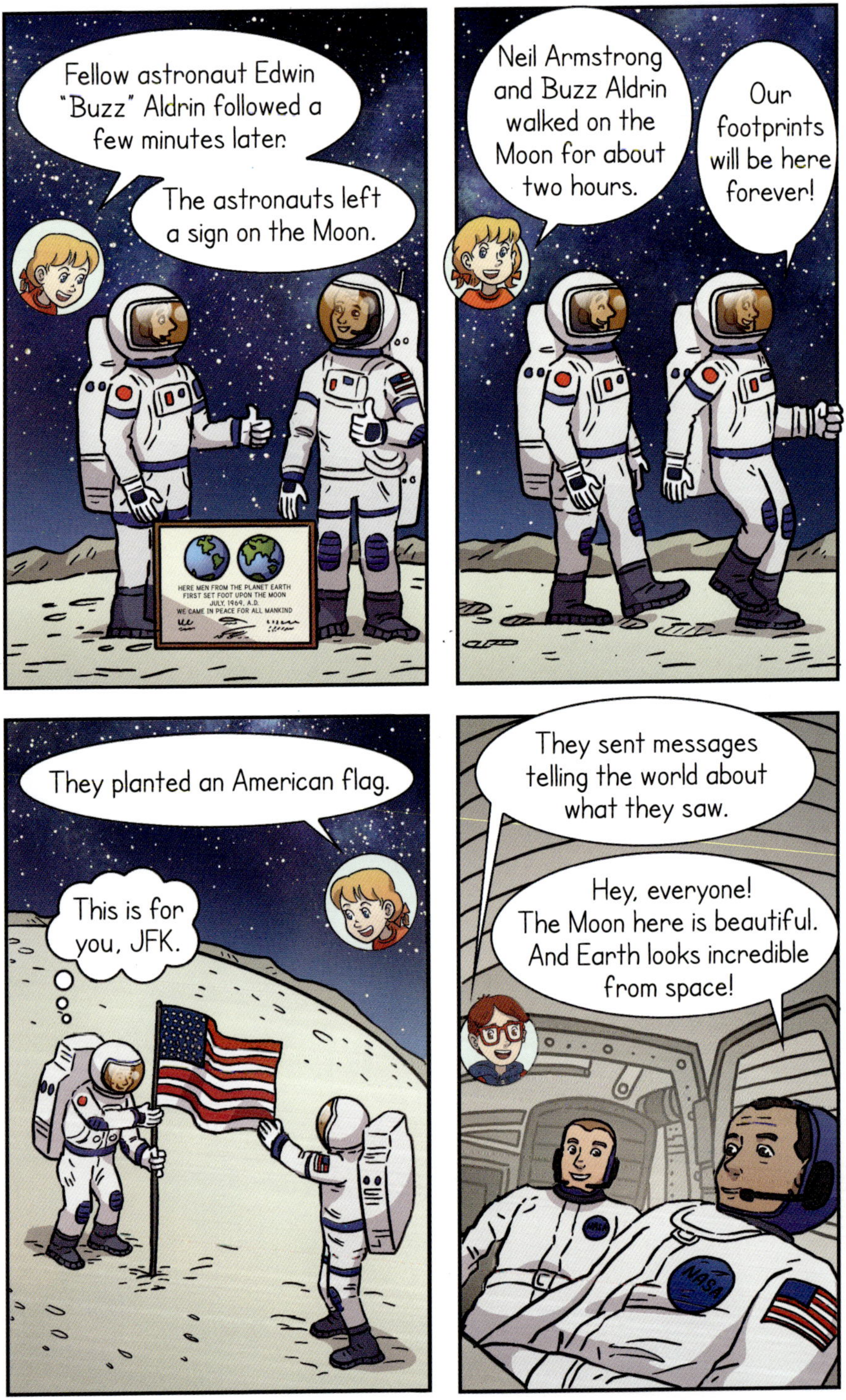
Fellow astronaut Edwin "Buzz" Aldrin followed a few minutes later.
The astronauts left a sign on the Moon.
HERE MEN FROM THE PLANET EARTH FIRST SET FOOT UPON THE MOON JULY, 1969, A.D. WE CAME IN PEACE FOR ALL MANKIND
Neil Armstrong and Buzz Aldrin walked on the Moon for about two hours.
Our footprints will be here forever!
They planted an American flag.
This is for you, JFK.
They sent messages telling the world about what they saw.
Hey, everyone! The Moon here is beautiful. And Earth looks incredible from space!
NASA

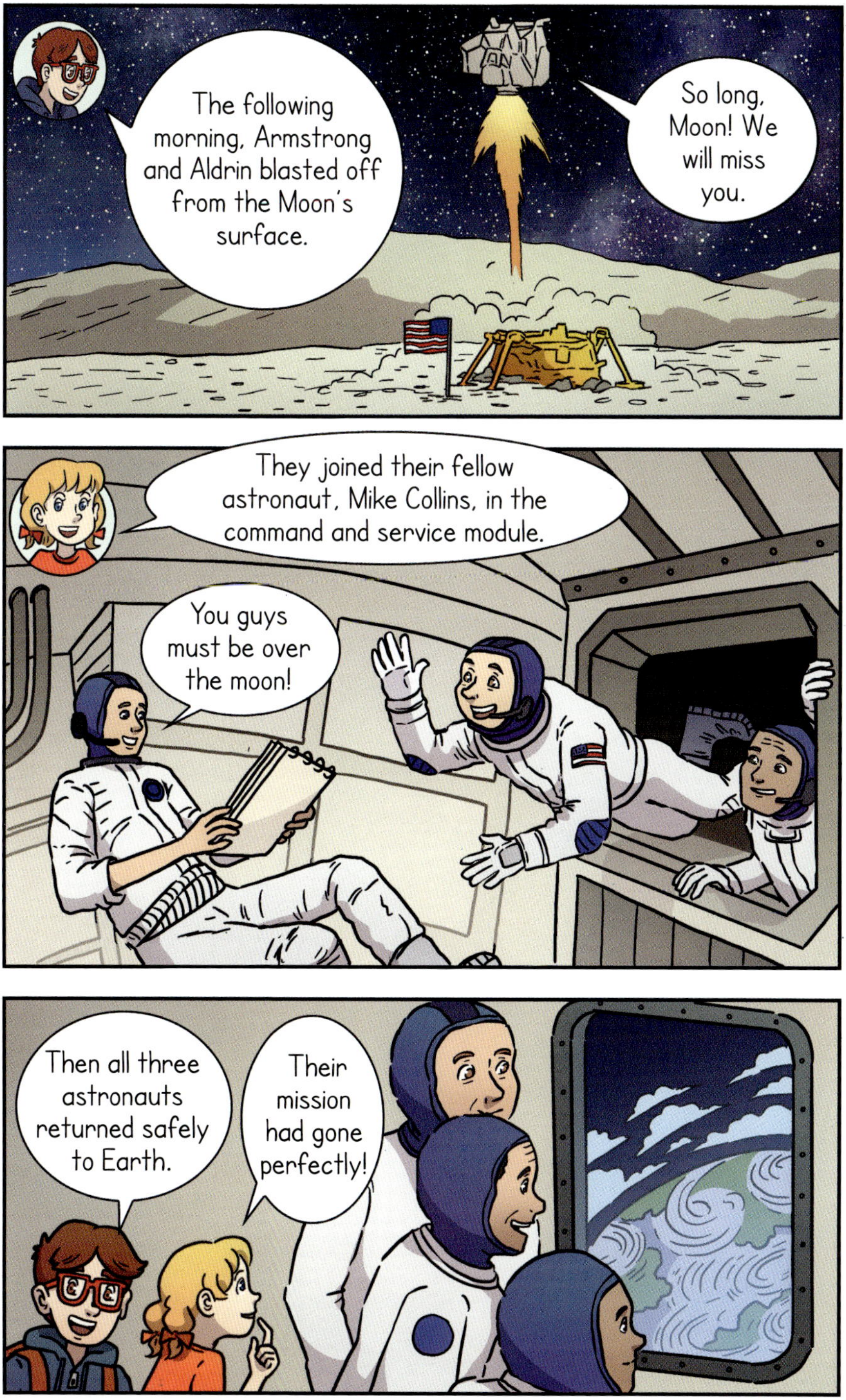
The following morning, Armstrong and Aldrin blasted off from the Moon's surface.
So long, Moon! We will miss you.
They joined their fellow astronaut, Mike Collins, in the command and service module.
You guys must be over the moon!
Then all three astronauts returned safely to Earth.
Their mission had gone perfectly!

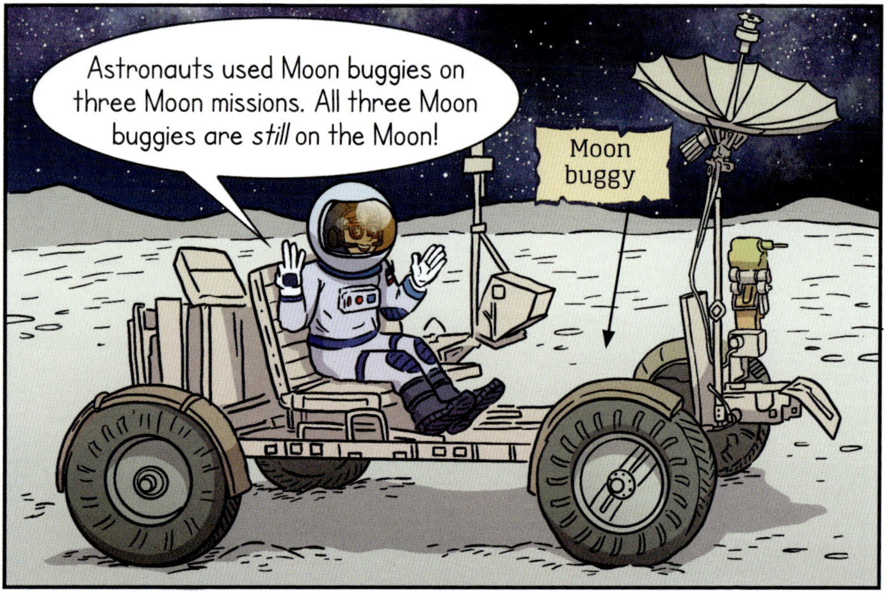
Astronauts used Moon buggies on three Moon missions. All three Moon buggies are *still* on the Moon!
Moon buggy

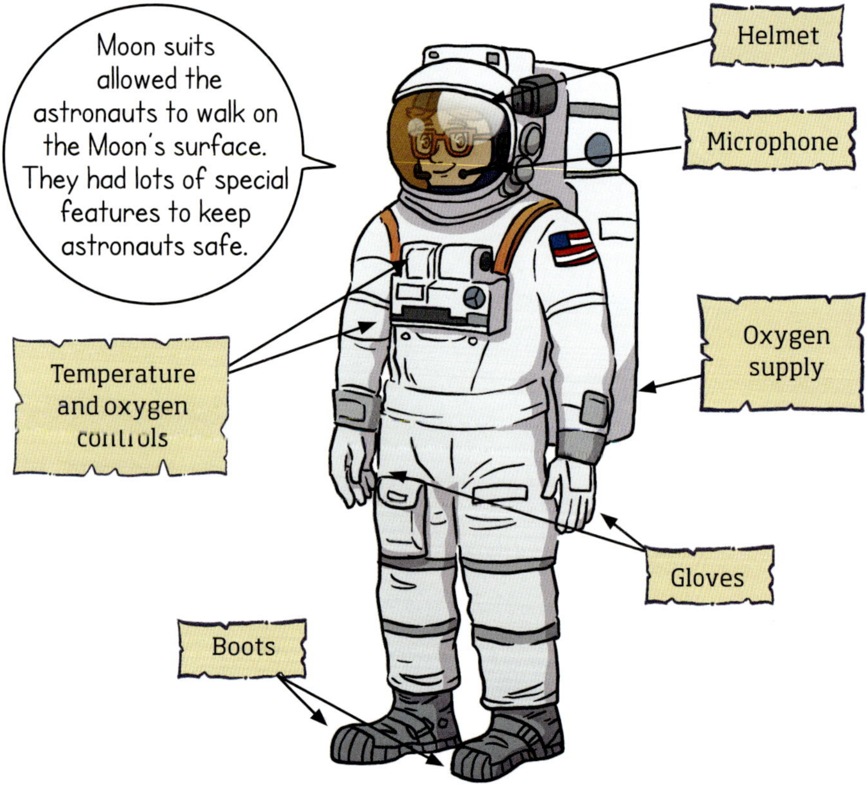
Moon suits allowed the astronauts to walk on the Moon's surface. They had lots of special features to keep astronauts safe.
Helmet
Microphone
Oxygen supply
Temperature and oxygen controls
Gloves
Boots

CHAPTER SEVEN
Space Travel Today

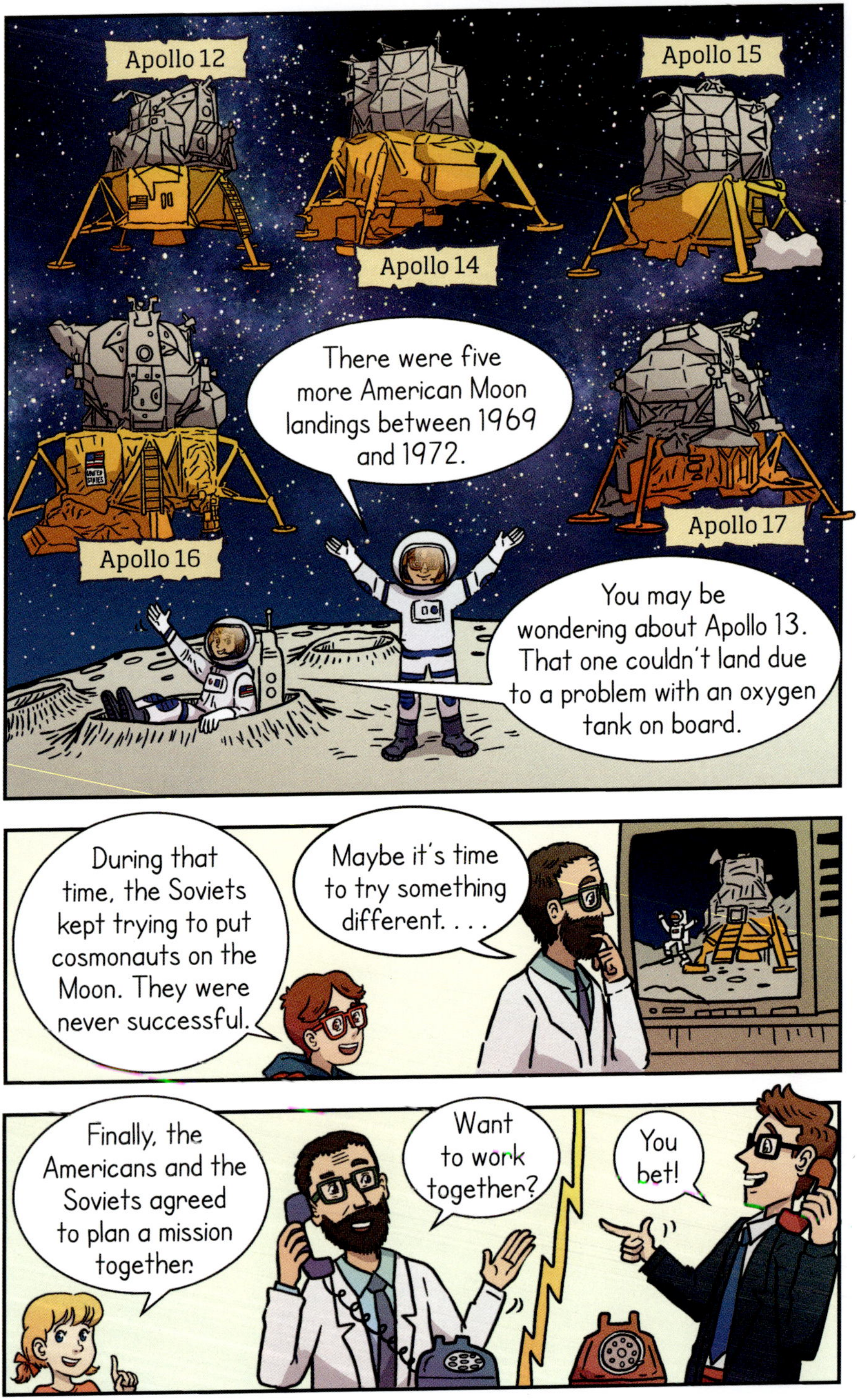
Apollo 12
Apollo 14
Apollo 15
Apollo 16
Apollo 17
There were five more American Moon landings between 1969 and 1972.
You may be wondering about Apollo 13. That one couldn't land due to a problem with an oxygen tank on board.
During that time, the Soviets kept trying to put cosmonauts on the Moon. They were never successful.
Maybe it's time to try something different. . . .
Finally, the Americans and the Soviets agreed to plan a mission together.
Want to work together?
You bet!

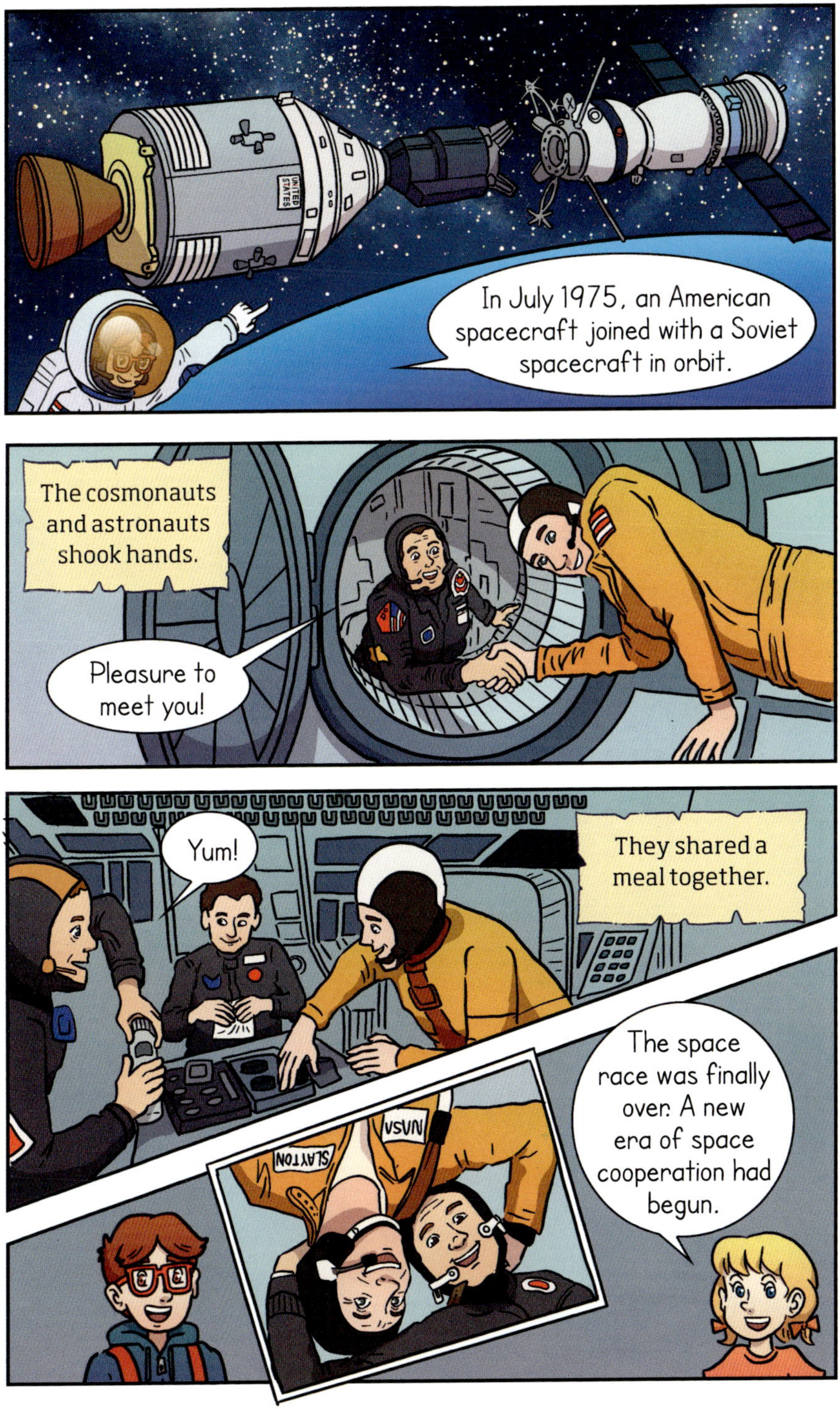
In July 1975, an American spacecraft joined with a Soviet spacecraft in orbit.
The cosmonauts and astronauts shook hands.
Pleasure to meet you!
Yum!
They shared a meal together.
The space race was finally over. A new era of space cooperation had begun.

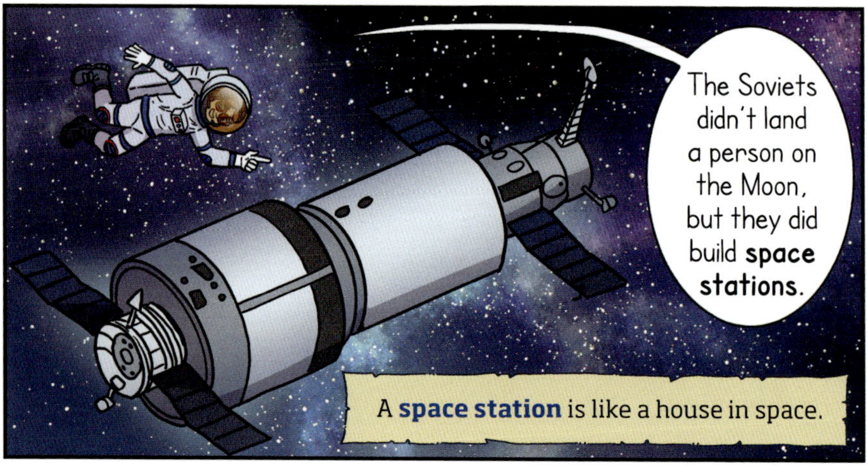
The Soviets didn't land a person on the Moon, but they did build **space stations**.
A **space station** is like a house in space.

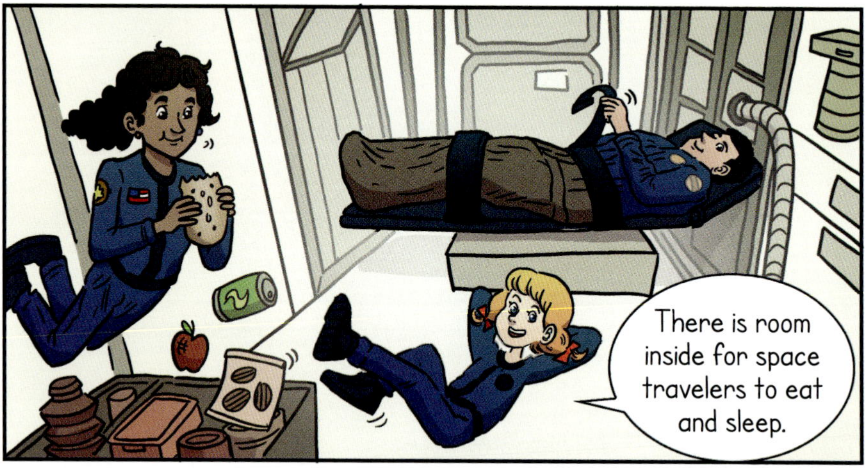
There is room inside for space travelers to eat and sleep.

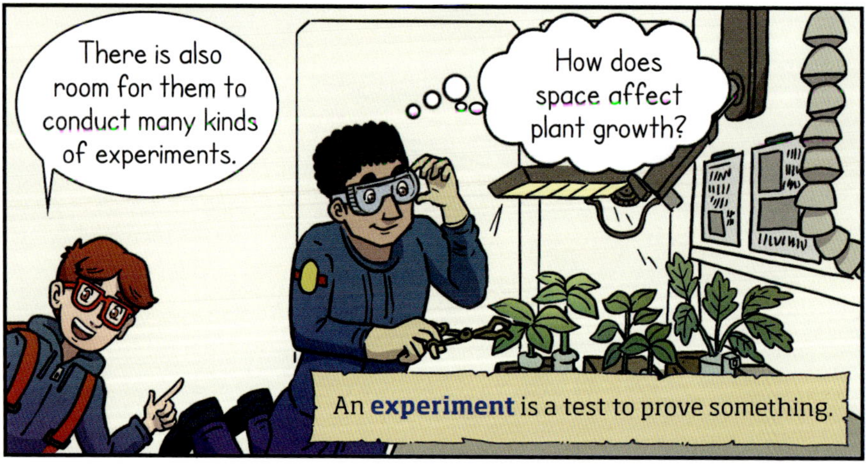
There is also room for them to conduct many kinds of experiments.
How does space affect plant growth?
An **experiment** is a test to prove something.

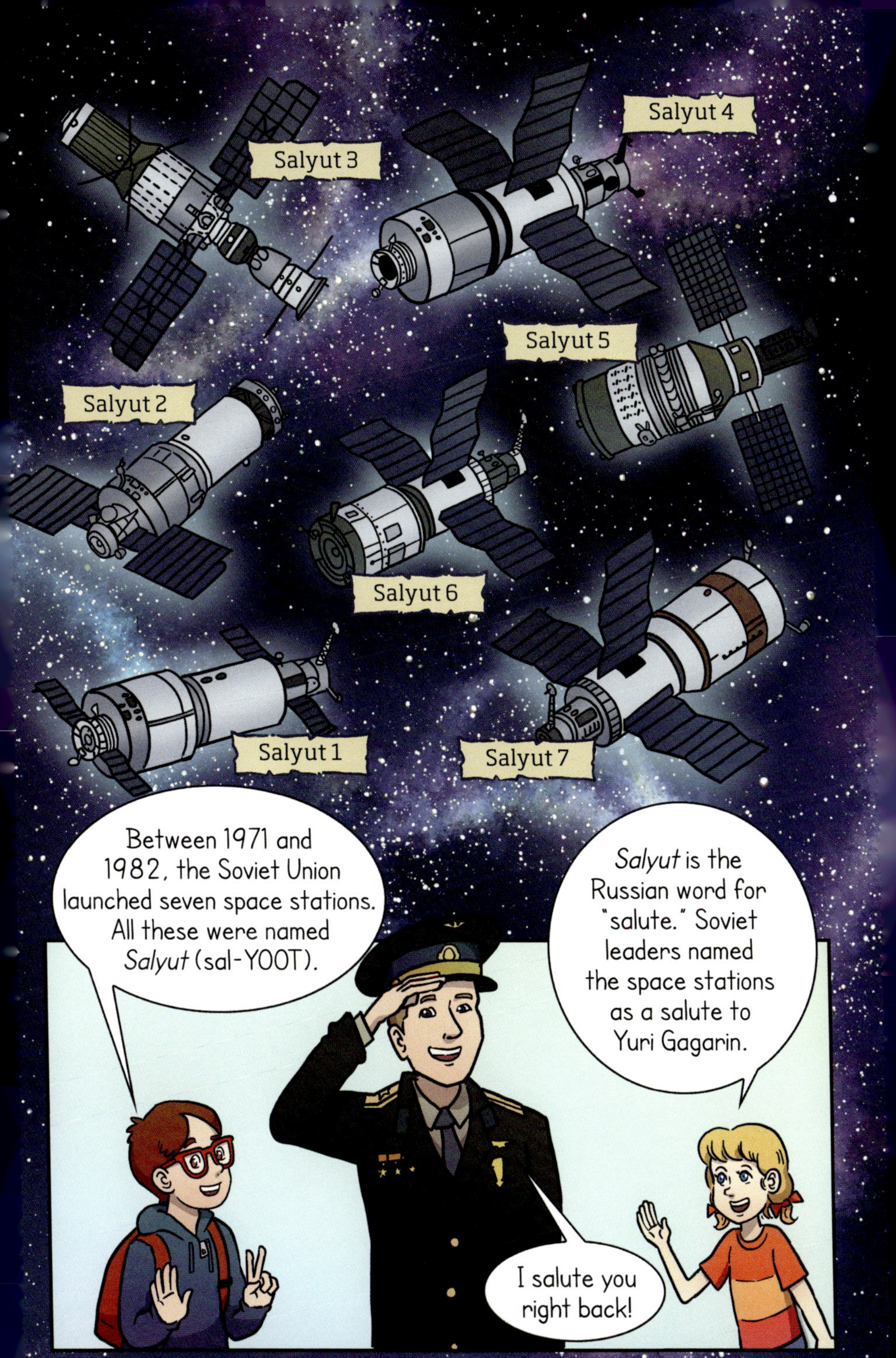
Salyut 3
Salyut 4
Salyut 5
Salyut 2
Salyut 6
Salyut 1
Salyut 7
Between 1971 and 1982, the Soviet Union launched seven space stations. All these were named *Salyut* (sal-YOOT).
Salyut is the Russian word for "salute." Soviet leaders named the space stations as a salute to Yuri Gagarin.
I salute you right back!

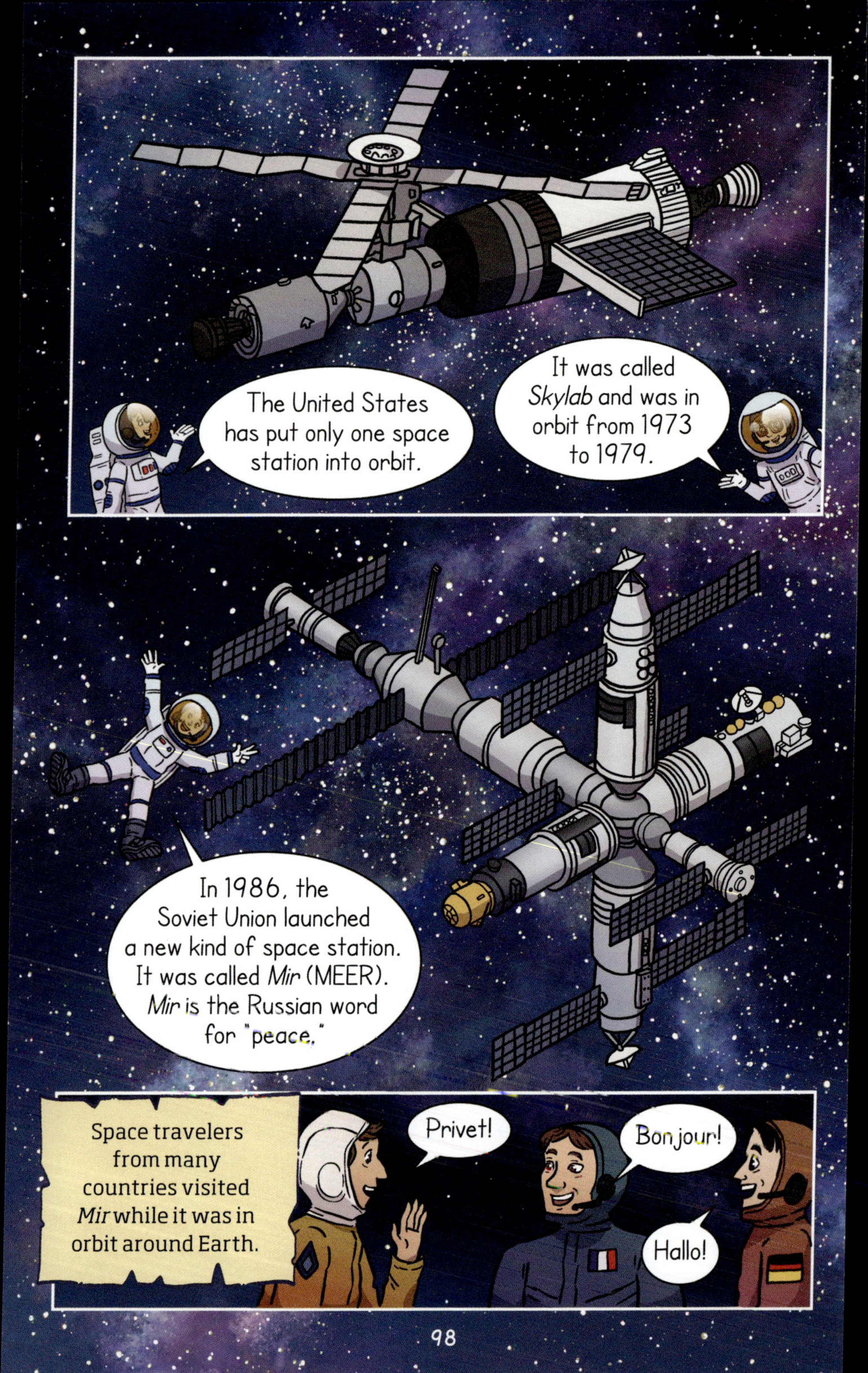
The United States has put only one space station into orbit.
It was called *Skylab* and was in orbit from 1973 to 1979.
In 1986, the Soviet Union launched a new kind of space station. It was called *Mir* (MEER). *Mir* is the Russian word for "peace."
Space travelers from many countries visited *Mir* while it was in orbit around Earth.
Privet!
Bonjour!
Hallo!

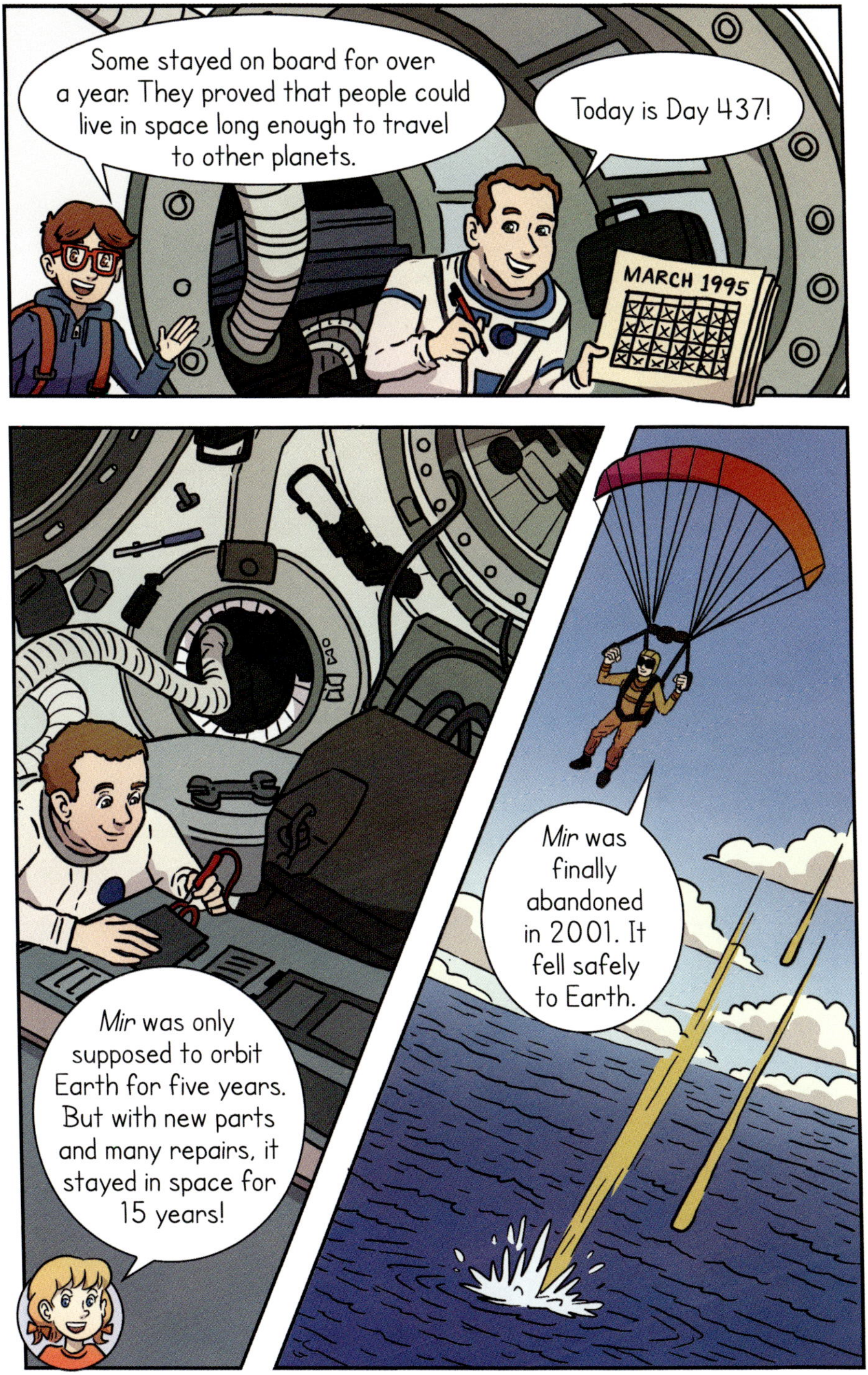
Some stayed on board for over a year. They proved that people could live in space long enough to travel to other planets.
Today is Day 437!
MARCH 1995
Mir was only supposed to orbit Earth for five years. But with new parts and many repairs, it stayed in space for 15 years!
Mir was finally abandoned in 2001. It fell safely to Earth.

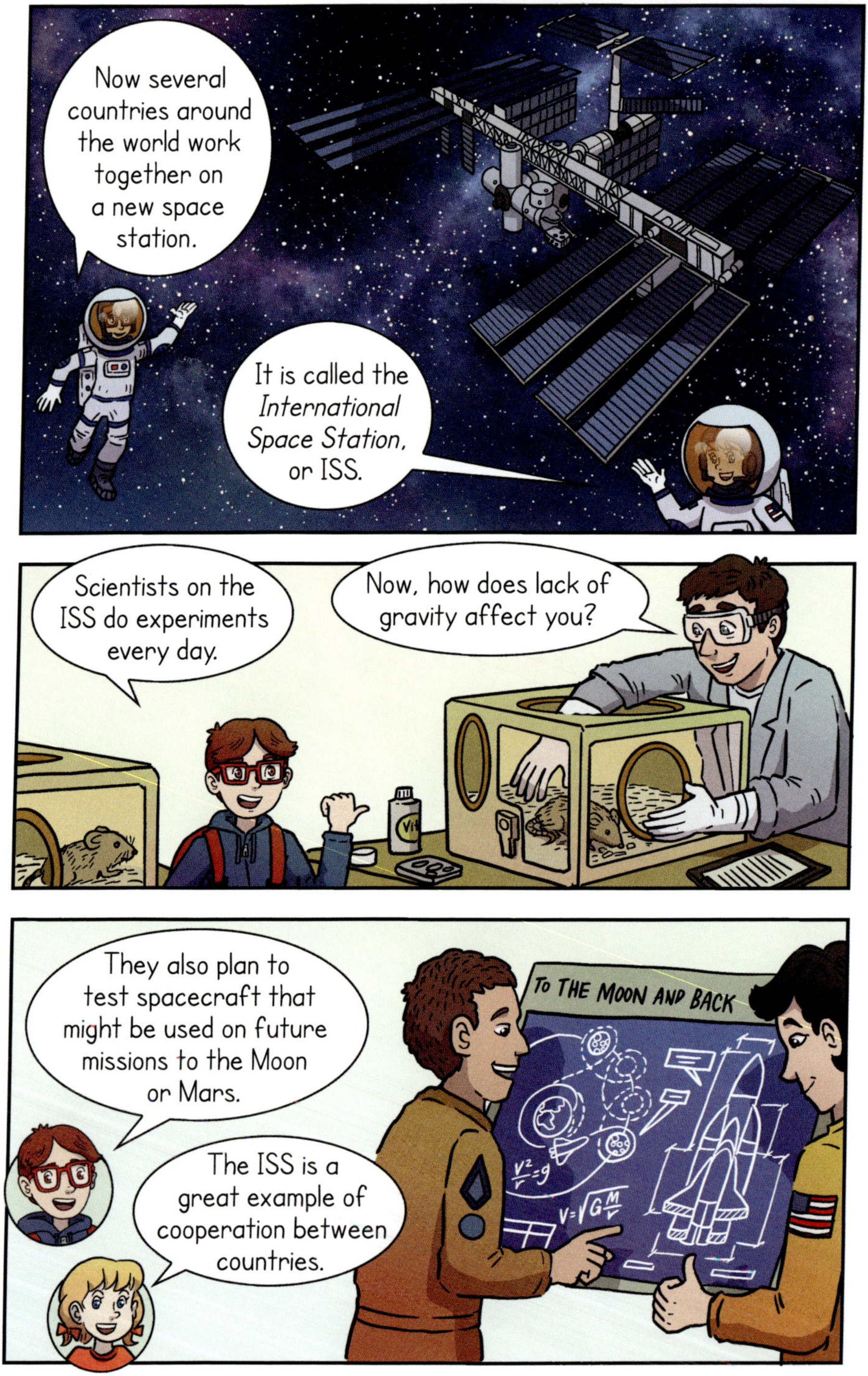
Now several countries around the world work together on a new space station.
It is called the *International Space Station*, or ISS.
Scientists on the ISS do experiments every day.
Now, how does lack of gravity affect you?
They also plan to test spacecraft that might be used on future missions to the Moon or Mars.
TO THE MOON AND BACK
The ISS is a great example of cooperation between countries.

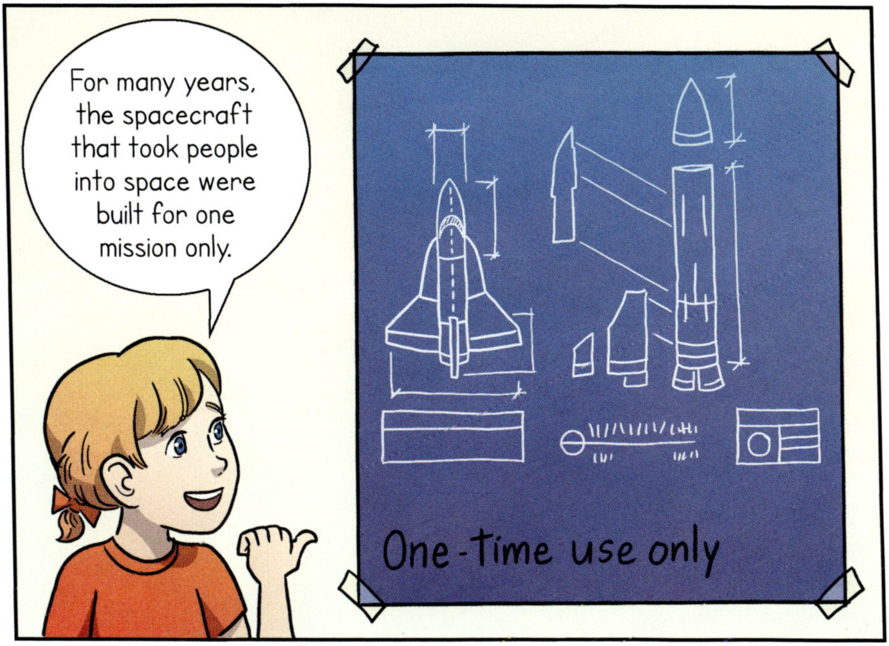
For many years, the spacecraft that took people into space were built for one mission only.
One-time use only

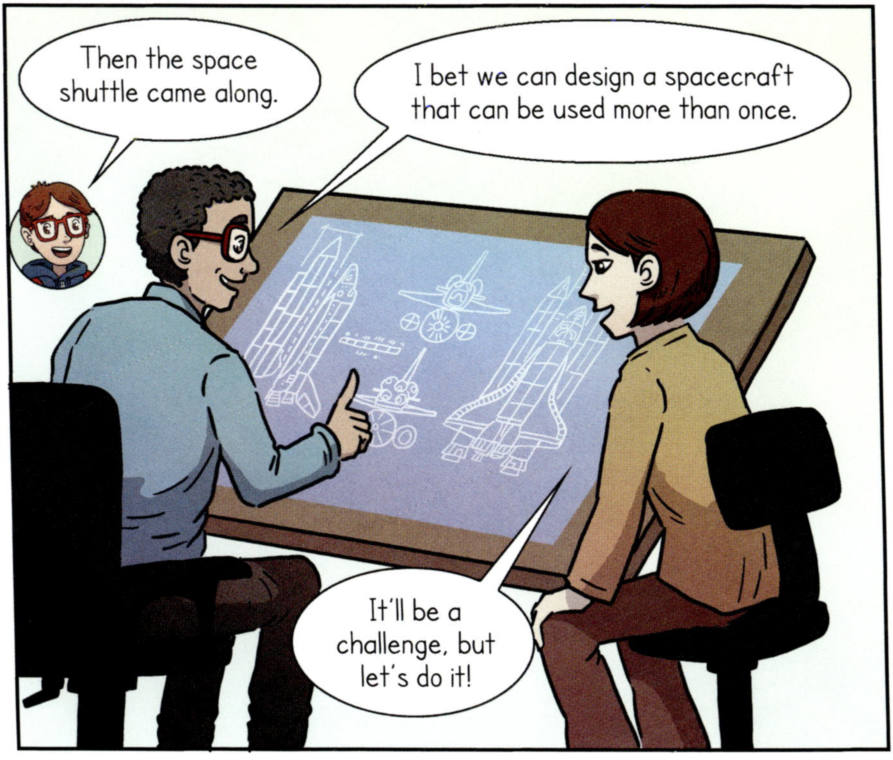
Then the space shuttle came along.
I bet we can design a spacecraft that can be used more than once.
It'll be a challenge, but let's do it!

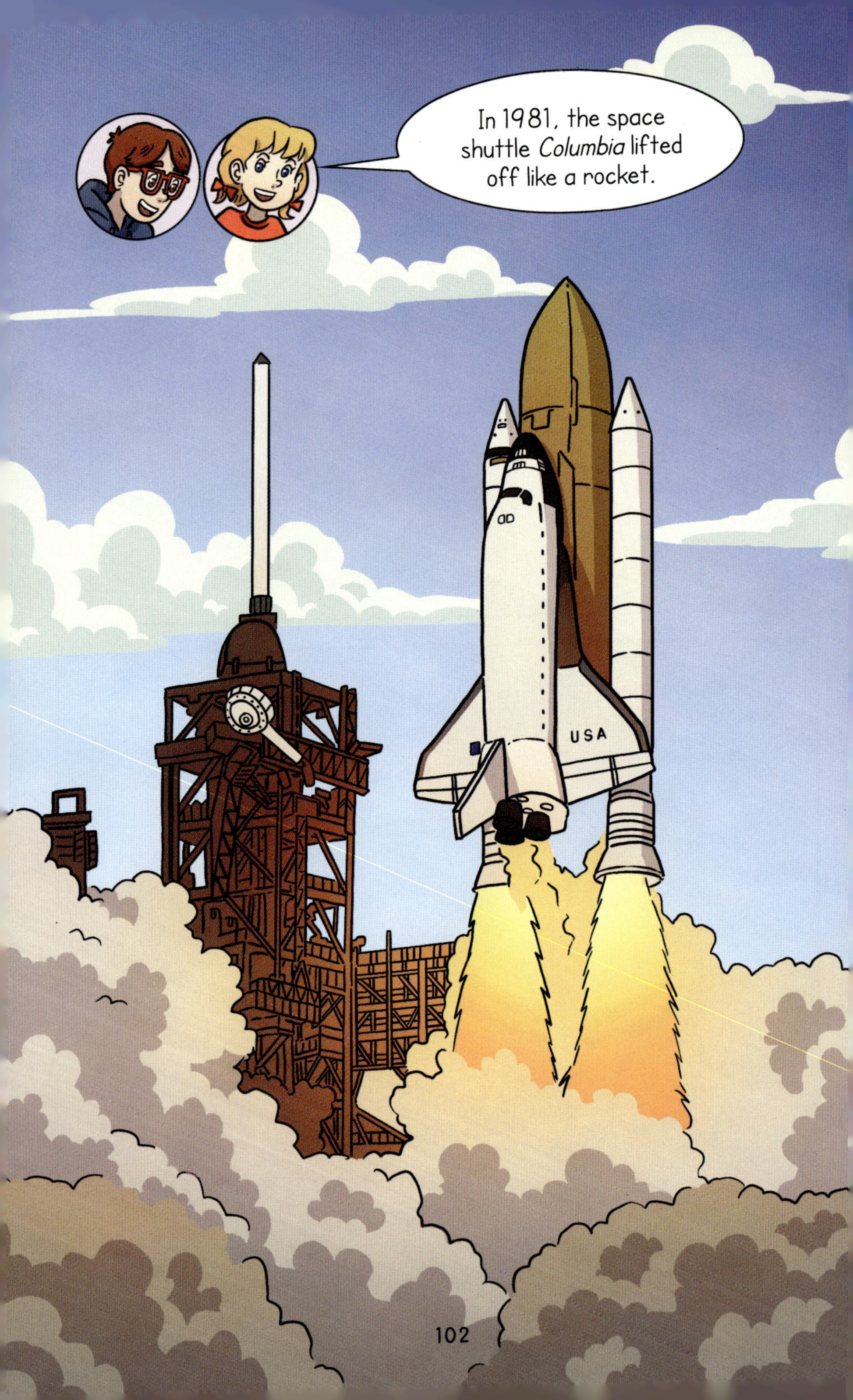
In 1981, the space shuttle *Columbia* lifted off like a rocket.
USA

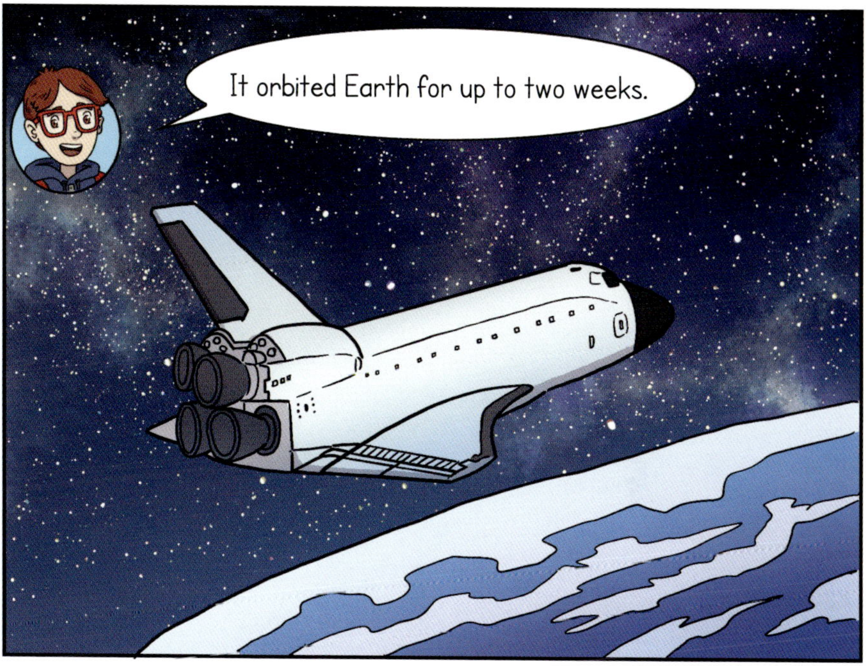
It orbited Earth for up to two weeks.

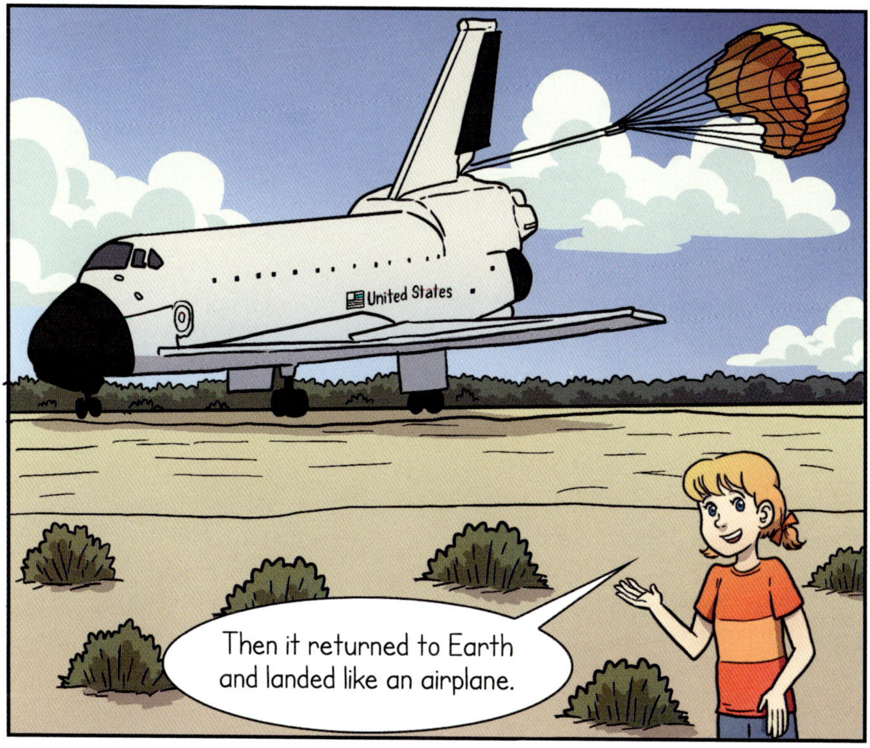
United States
Then it returned to Earth and landed like an airplane.

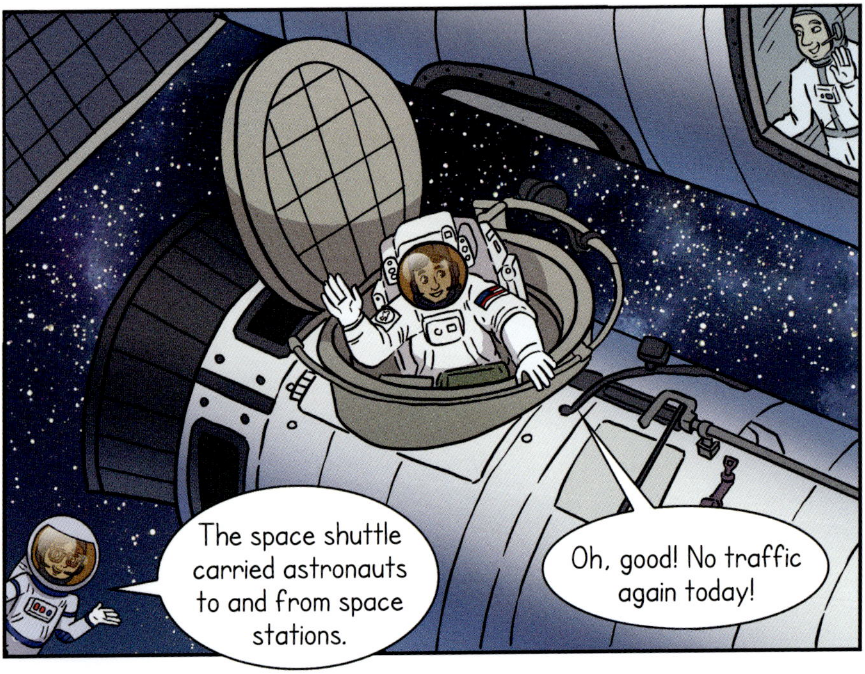

The space shuttle carried astronauts to and from space stations.
Oh, good! No traffic again today!

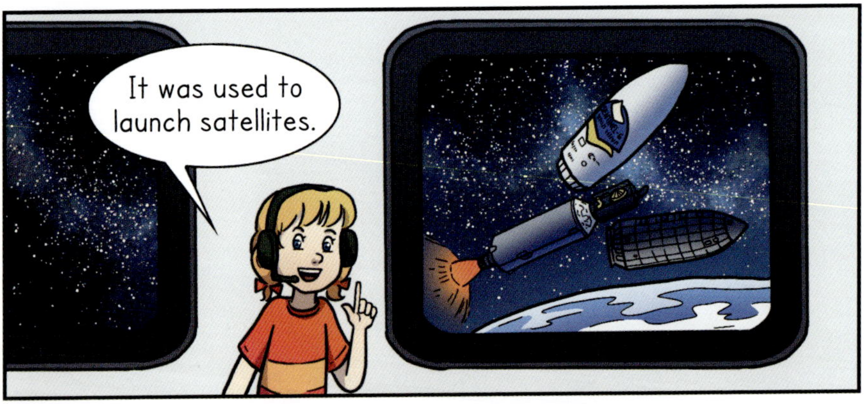

It was used to launch satellites.

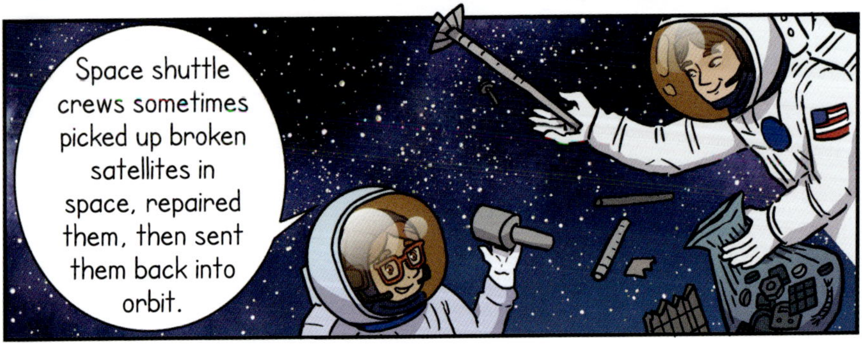

Space shuttle crews sometimes picked up broken satellites in space, repaired them, then sent them back into orbit.

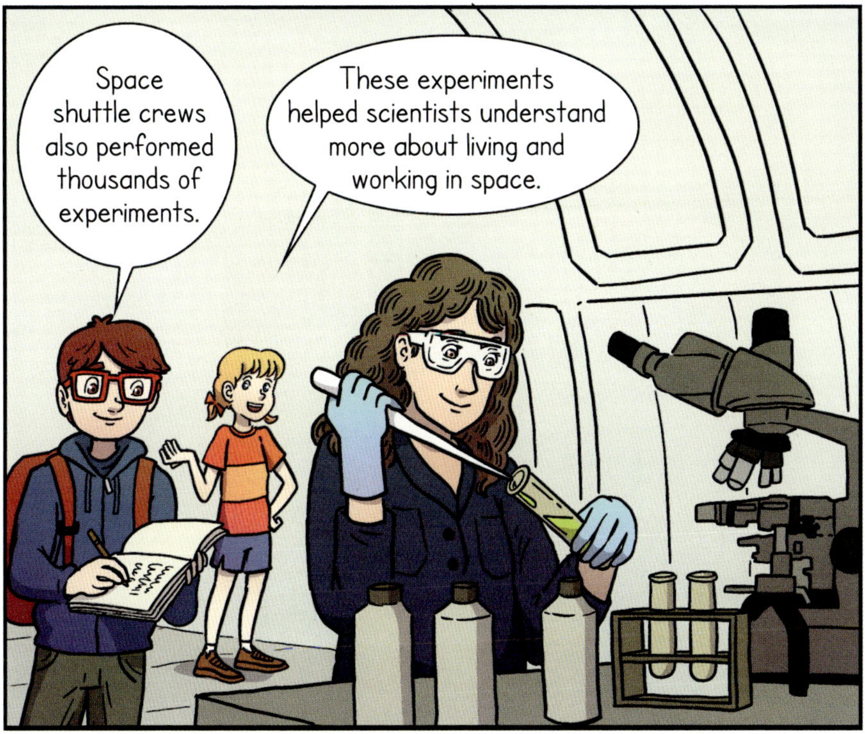
Space shuttle crews also performed thousands of experiments.
These experiments helped scientists understand more about living and working in space.

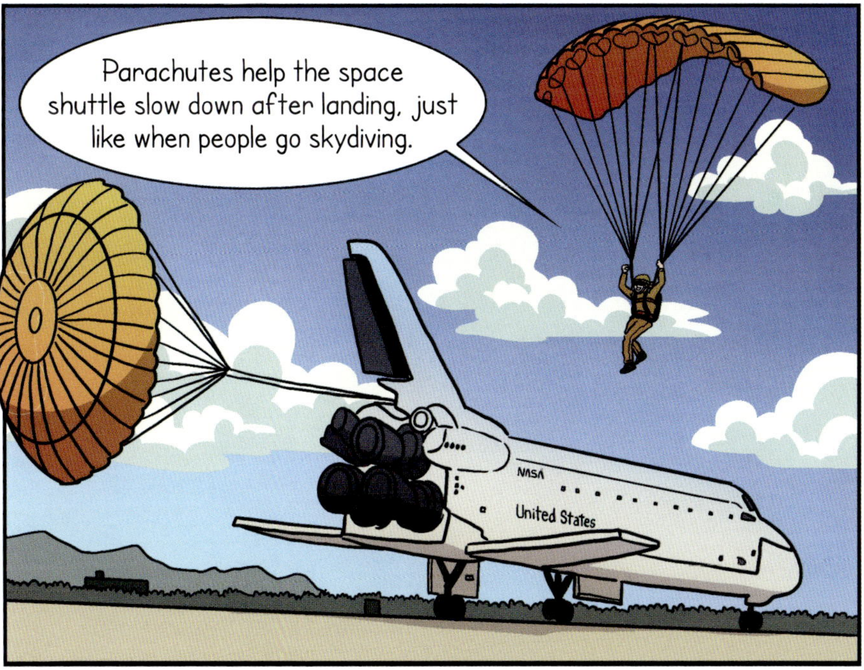
Parachutes help the space shuttle slow down after landing, just like when people go skydiving.
NASA
United States

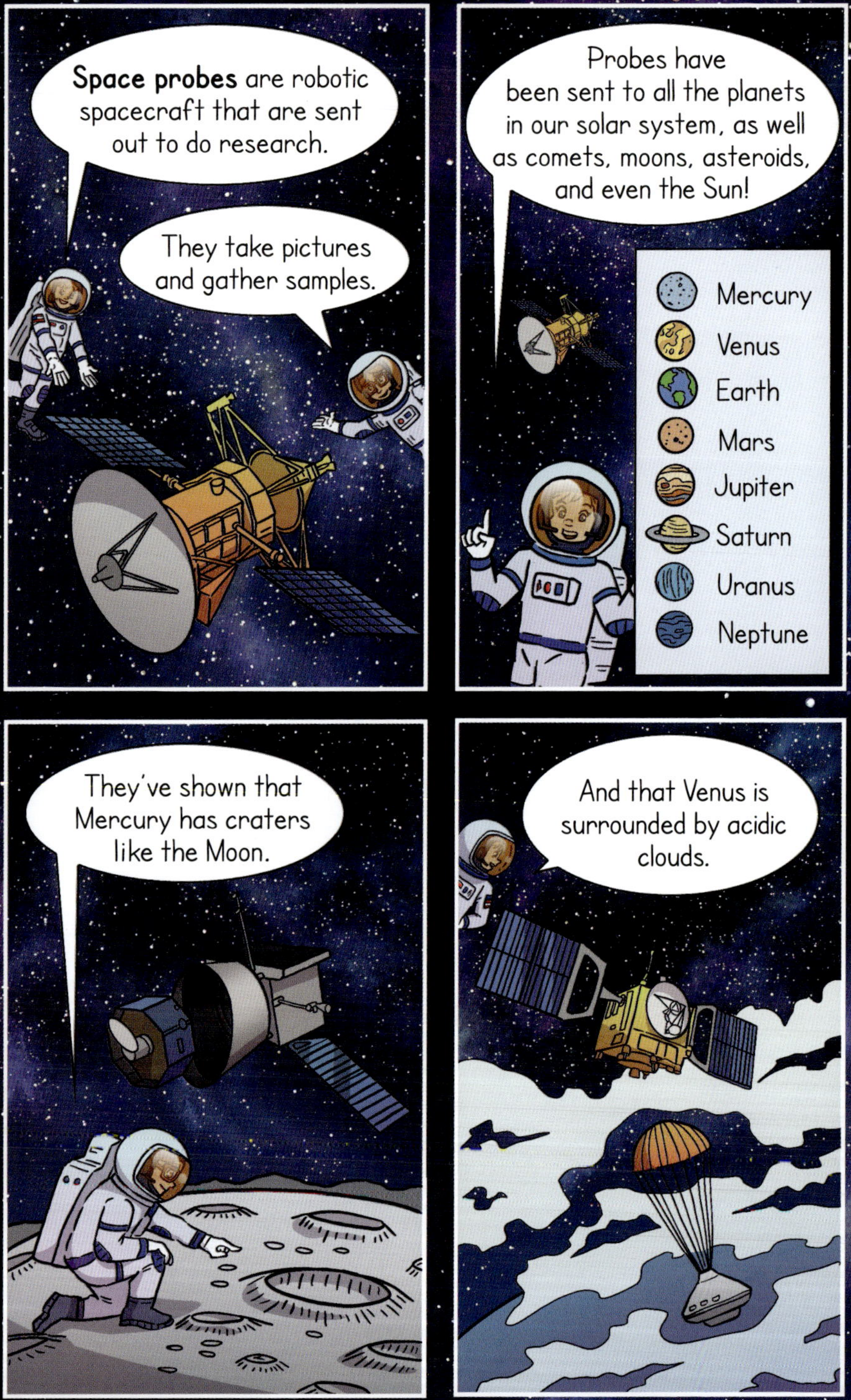
Space probes are robotic spacecraft that are sent out to do research.
They take pictures and gather samples.
Probes have been sent to all the planets in our solar system, as well as comets, moons, asteroids, and even the Sun!
Mercury
Venus
Earth
Mars
Jupiter
Saturn
Uranus
Neptune
They've shown that Mercury has craters like the Moon.
And that Venus is surrounded by acidic clouds.

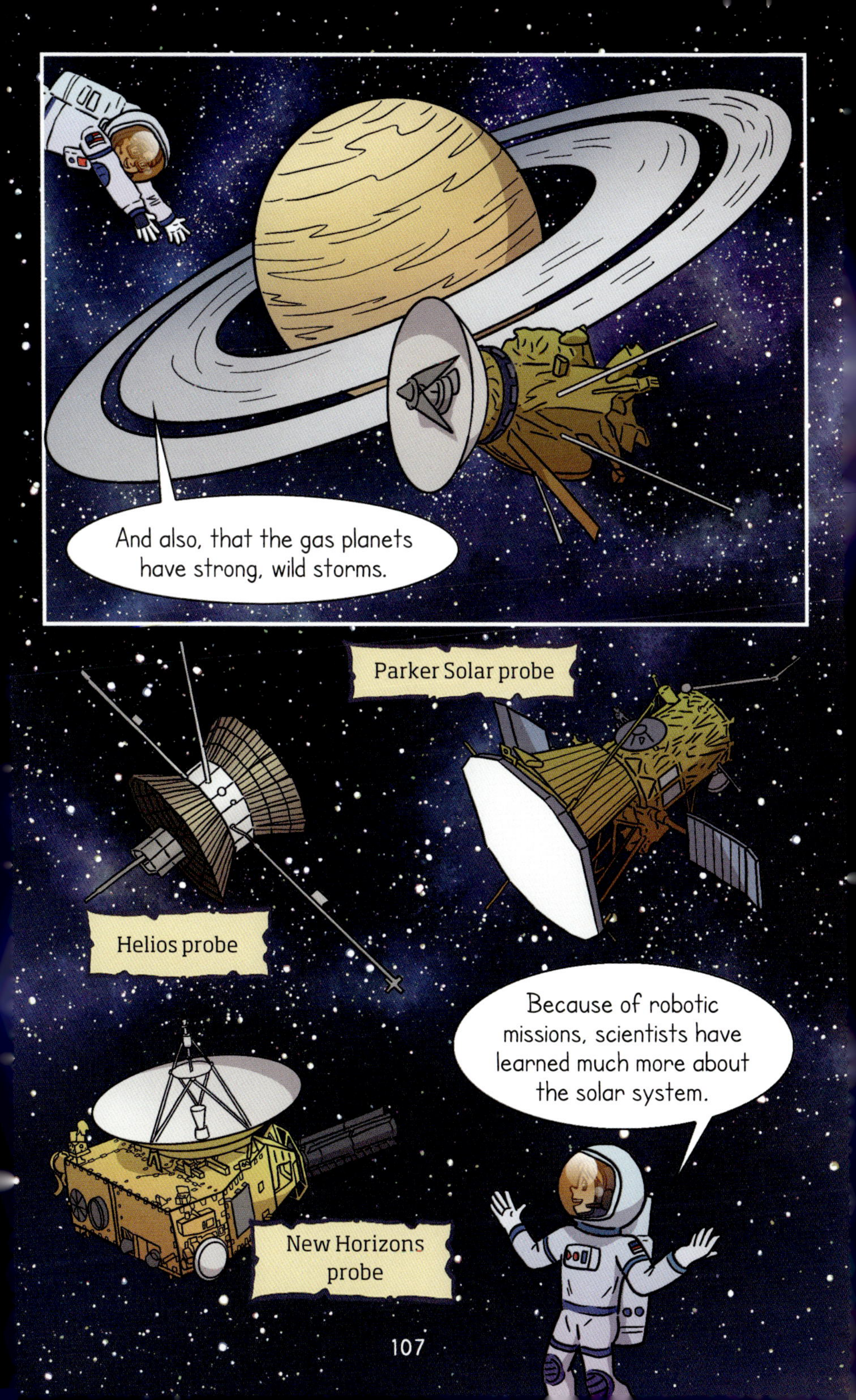
And also, that the gas planets have strong, wild storms.
Parker Solar probe
Helios probe
Because of robotic missions, scientists have learned much more about the solar system.
New Horizons probe

CHAPTER EIGHT

Living and Working in Space

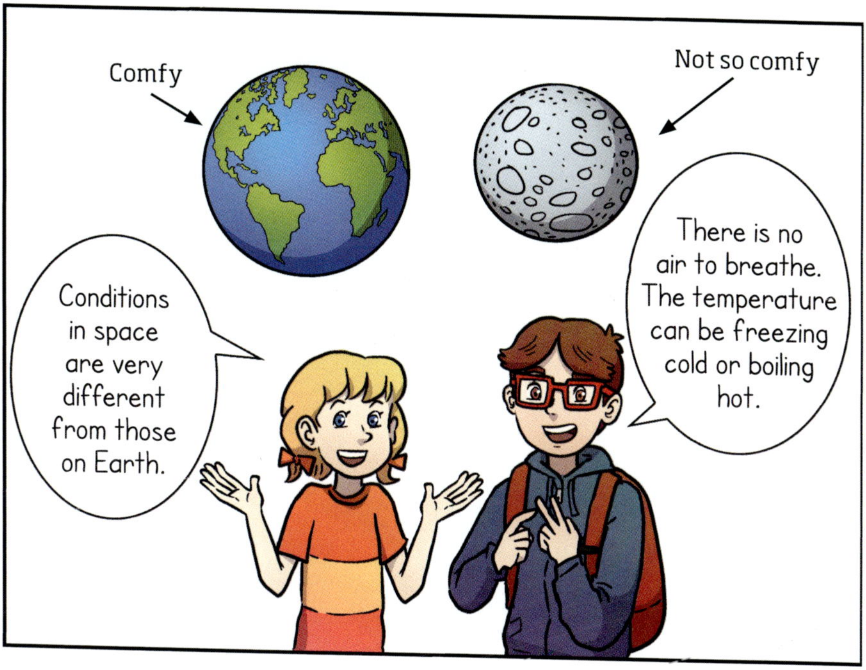
Comfy
Not so comfy
Conditions in space are very different from those on Earth.
There is no air to breathe. The temperature can be freezing cold or boiling hot.

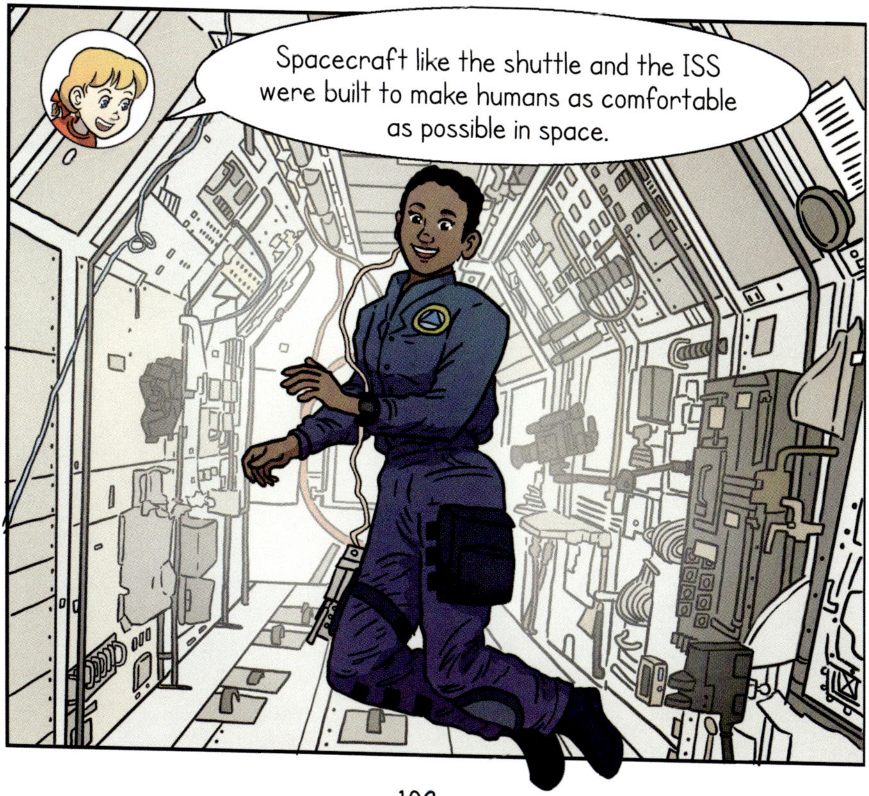
Spacecraft like the shuttle and the ISS were built to make humans as comfortable as possible in space.

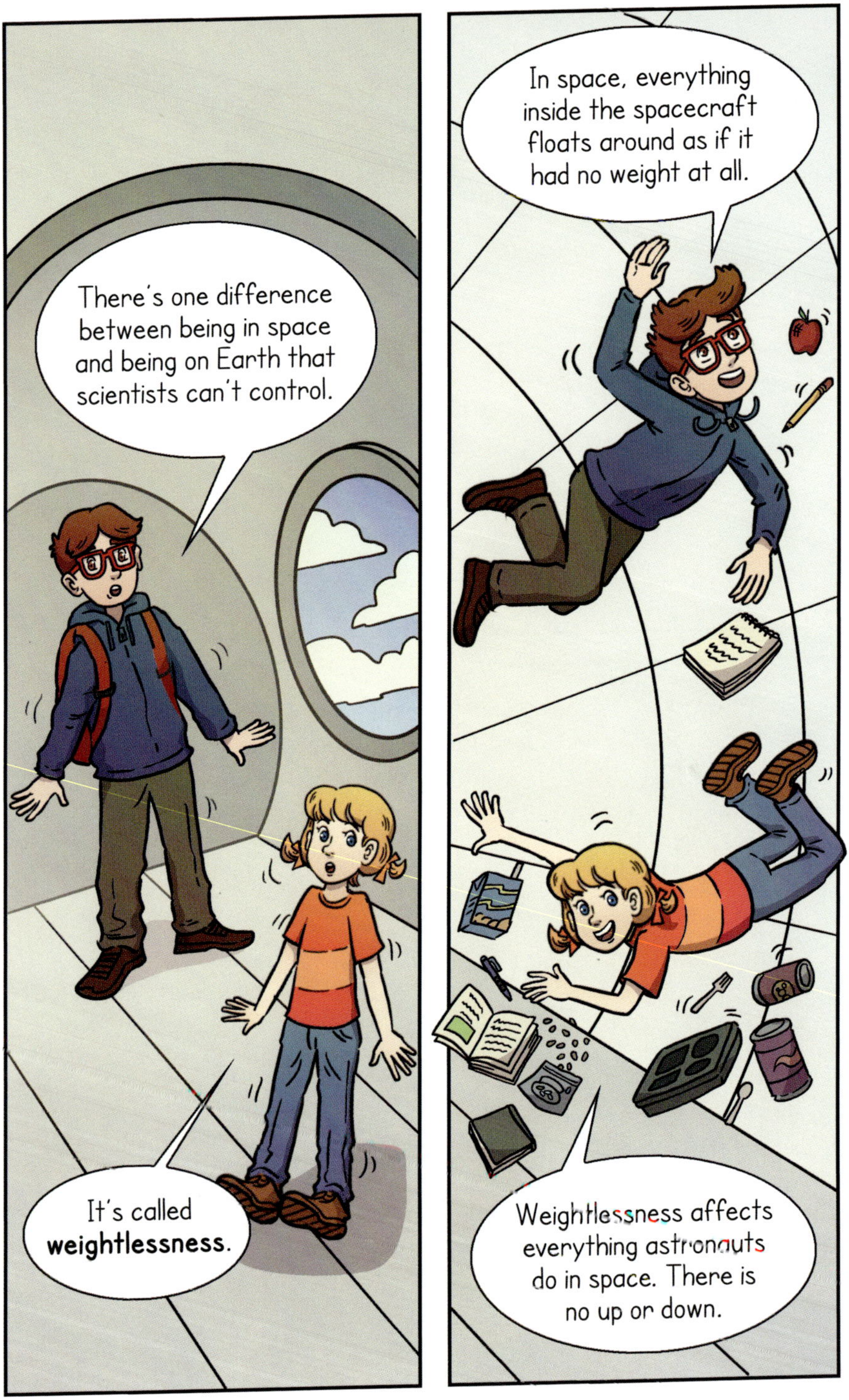
There's one difference between being in space and being on Earth that scientists can't control.
It's called **weightlessness**.
In space, everything inside the spacecraft floats around as if it had no weight at all.
Weightlessness affects everything astronauts do in space. There is no up or down.

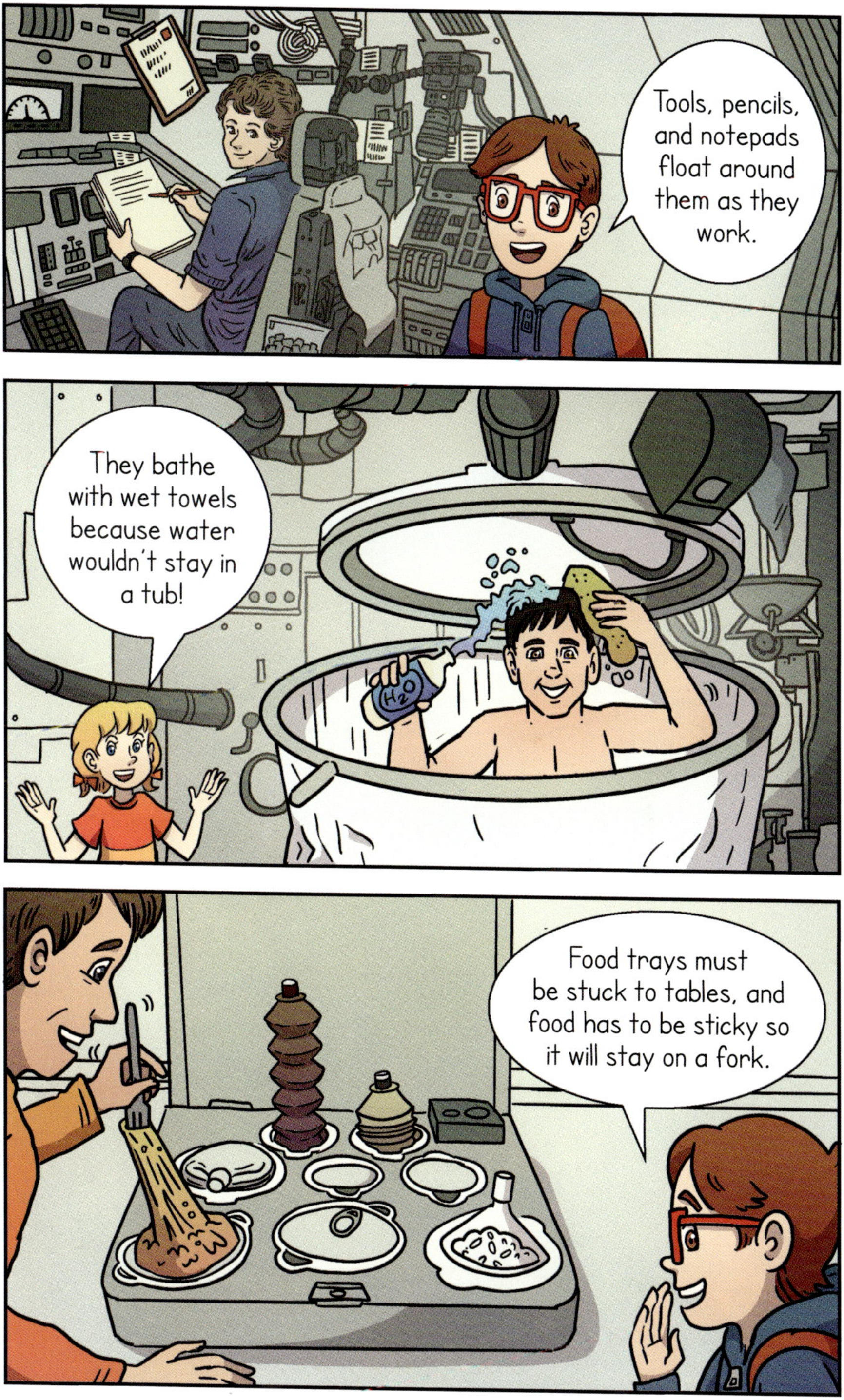

Tools, pencils, and notepads float around them as they work.
They bathe with wet towels because water wouldn't stay in a tub!
H_2O
Food trays must be stuck to tables, and food has to be sticky so it will stay on a fork.

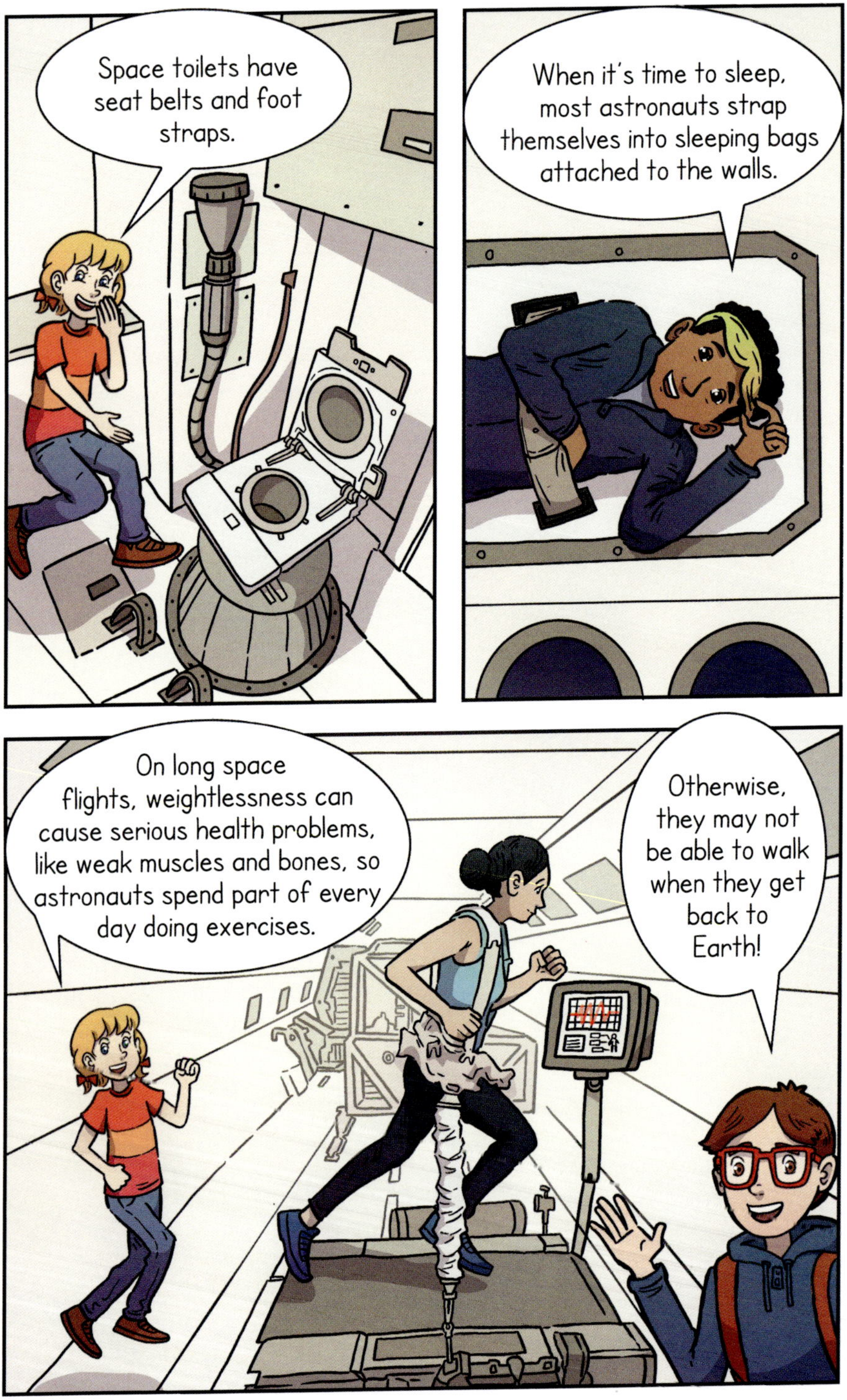
Space toilets have seat belts and foot straps.
When it's time to sleep, most astronauts strap themselves into sleeping bags attached to the walls.
On long space flights, weightlessness can cause serious health problems, like weak muscles and bones, so astronauts spend part of every day doing exercises.
Otherwise, they may not be able to walk when they get back to Earth!

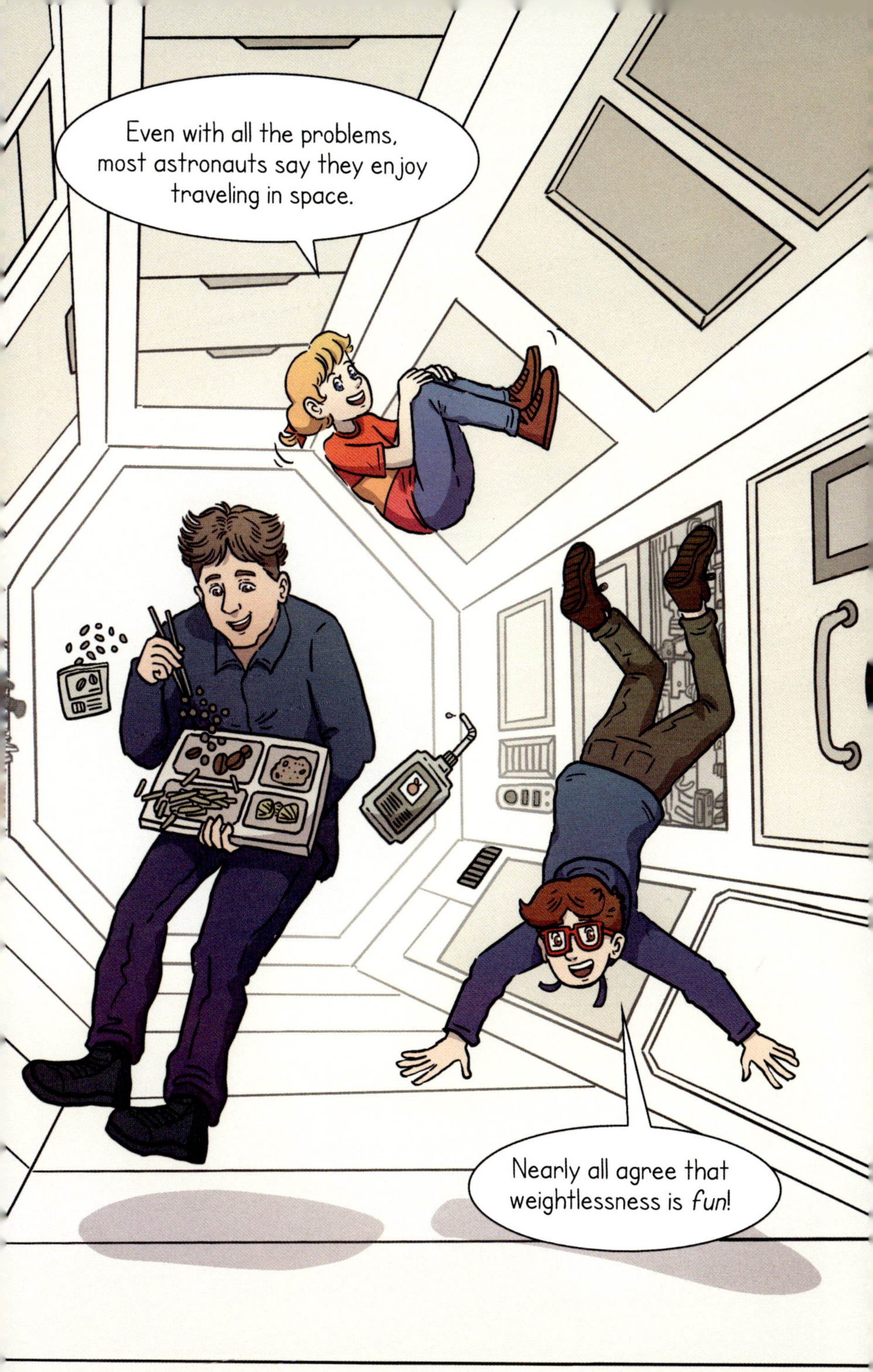
Even with all the problems, most astronauts say they enjoy traveling in space.
Nearly all agree that weightlessness is *fun*!

Life in Outer Space

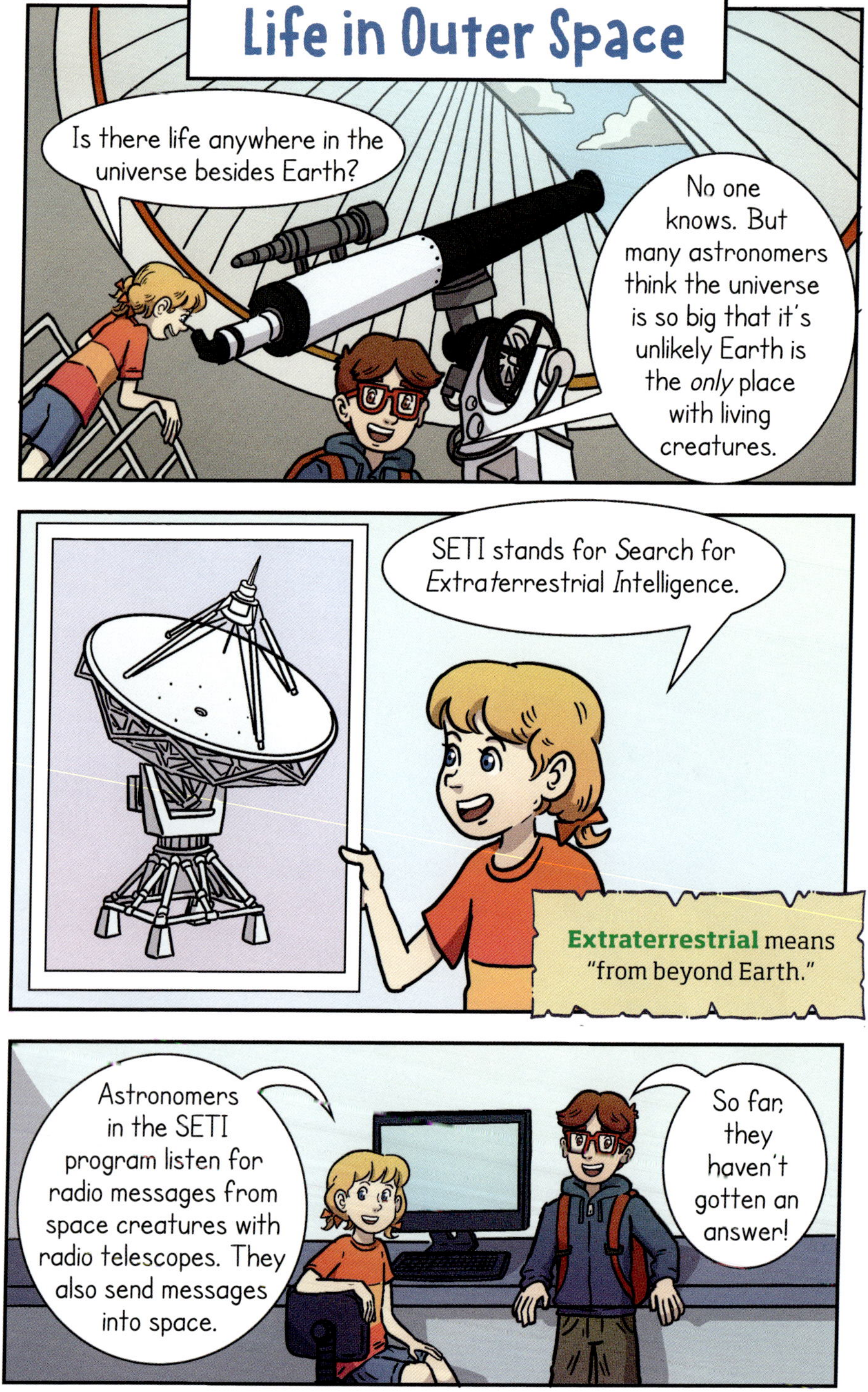
Is there life anywhere in the universe besides Earth?
No one knows. But many astronomers think the universe is so big that it's unlikely Earth is the *only* place with living creatures.
SETI stands for *S*earch for *E*xtra*t*errestrial *I*ntelligence.
Extraterrestrial means "from beyond Earth."
Astronomers in the SETI program listen for radio messages from space creatures with radio telescopes. They also send messages into space.
So far, they haven't gotten an answer!

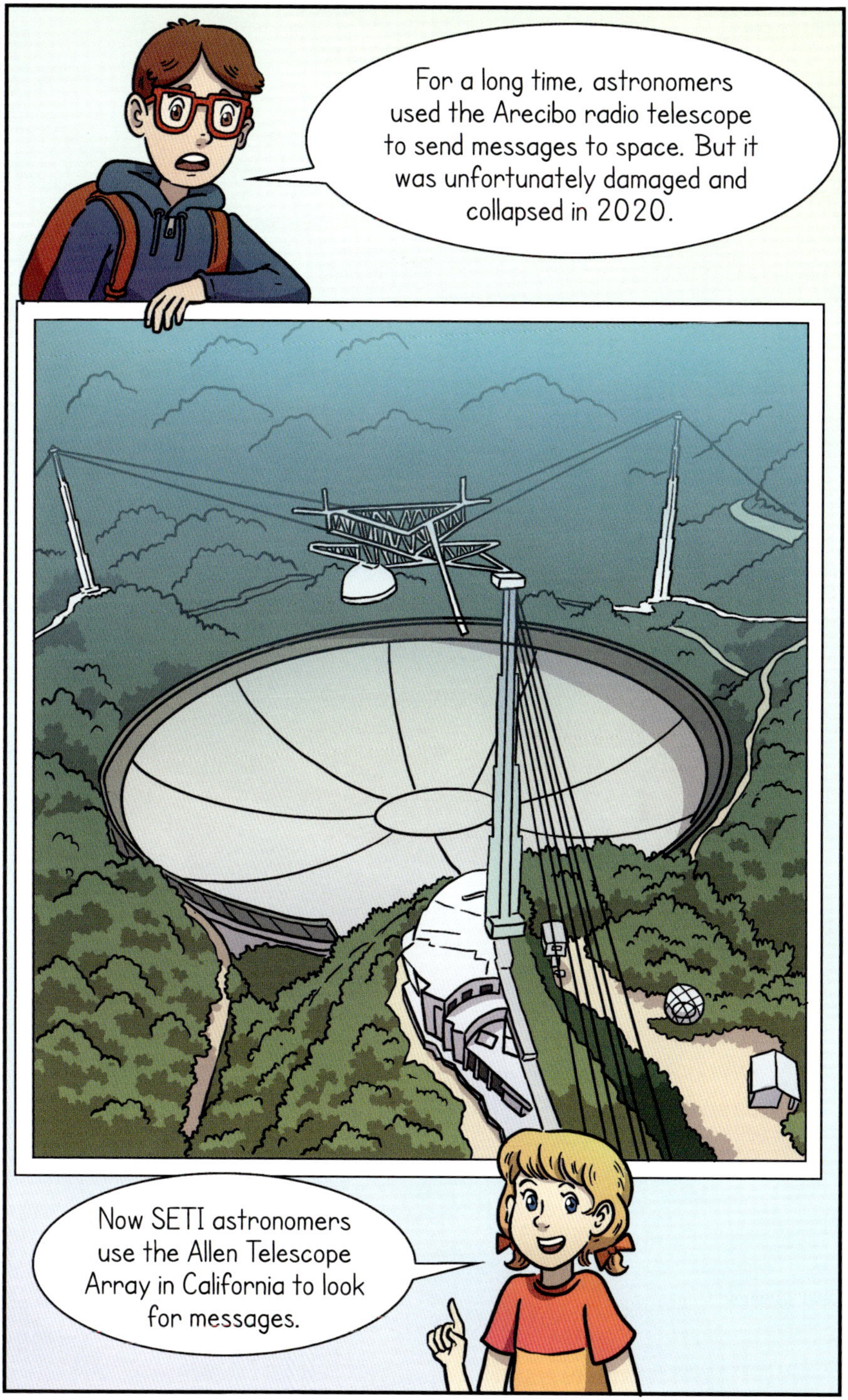
For a long time, astronomers used the Arecibo radio telescope to send messages to space. But it was unfortunately damaged and collapsed in 2020.
Now SETI astronomers use the Allen Telescope Array in California to look for messages.

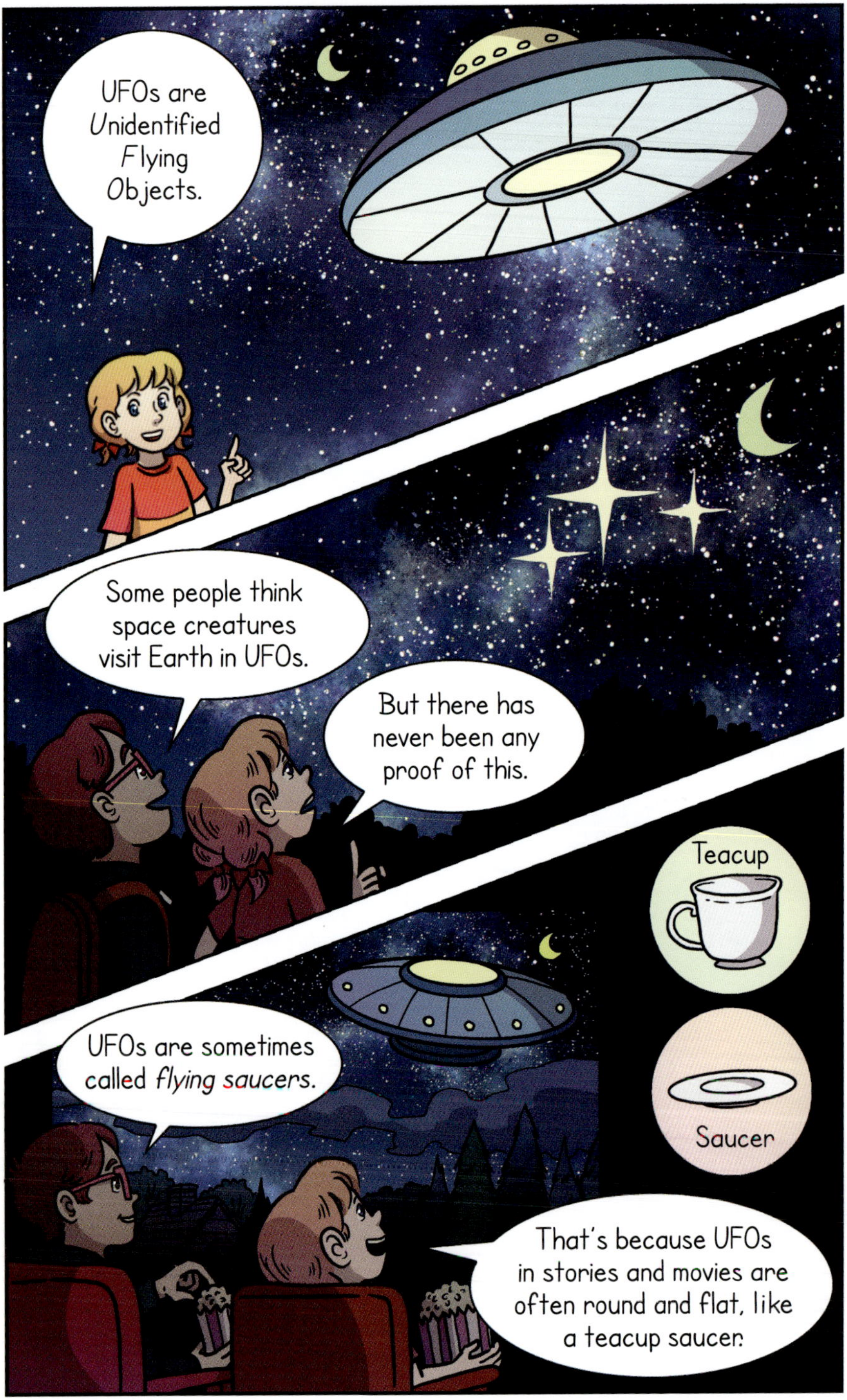
UFOs are Unidentified Flying Objects.
Some people think space creatures visit Earth in UFOs.
But there has never been any proof of this.
Teacup
UFOs are sometimes called *flying saucers*.
Saucer
That's because UFOs in stories and movies are often round and flat, like a teacup saucer.

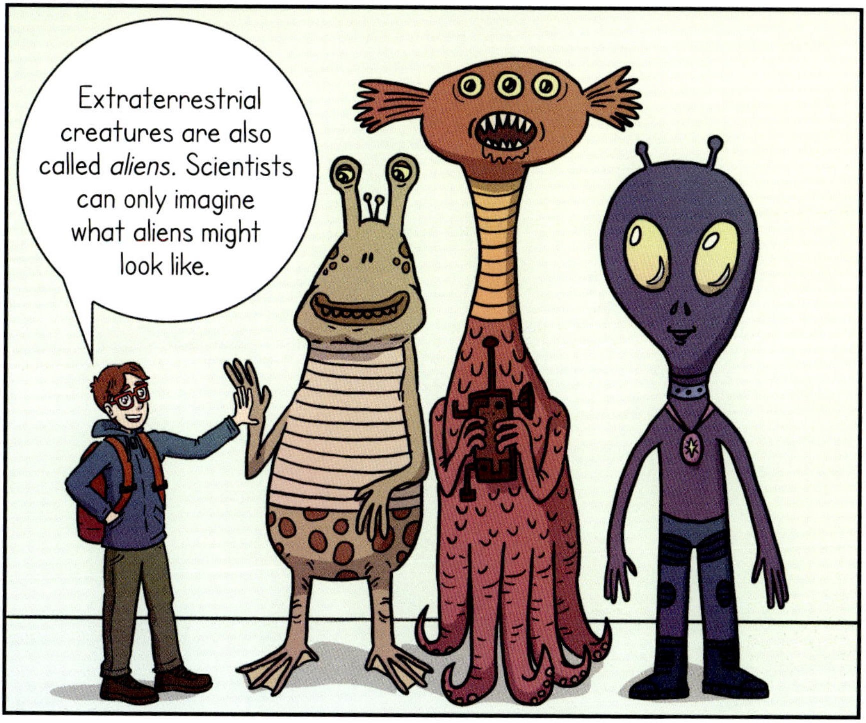
Extraterrestrial creatures are also called *aliens*. Scientists can only imagine what aliens might look like.

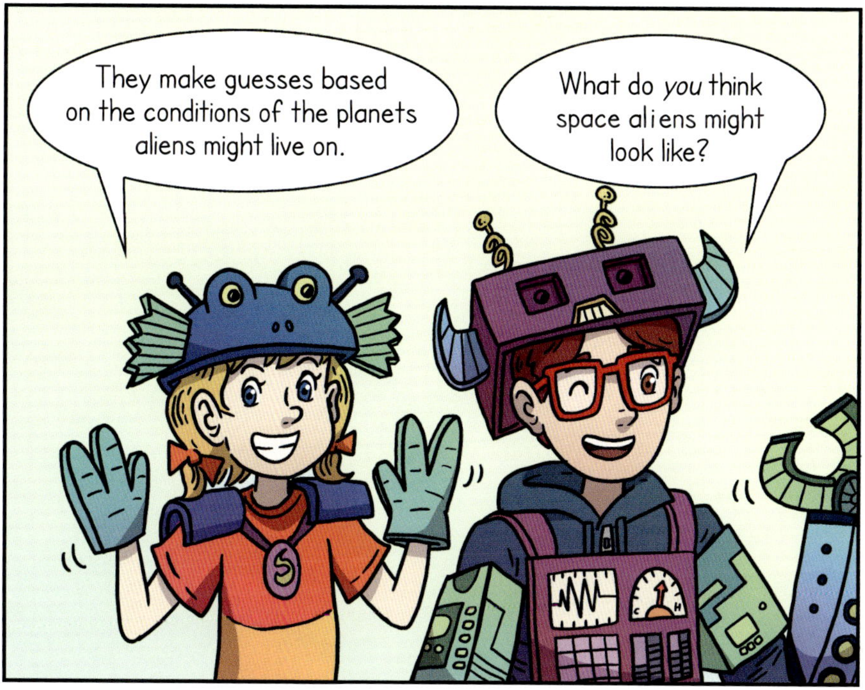
They make guesses based on the conditions of the planets aliens might live on.
What do *you* think space aliens might look like?

CHAPTER NINE

The Future

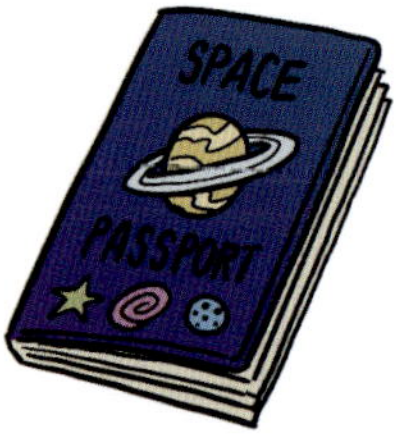
SPACE
PASSPORT

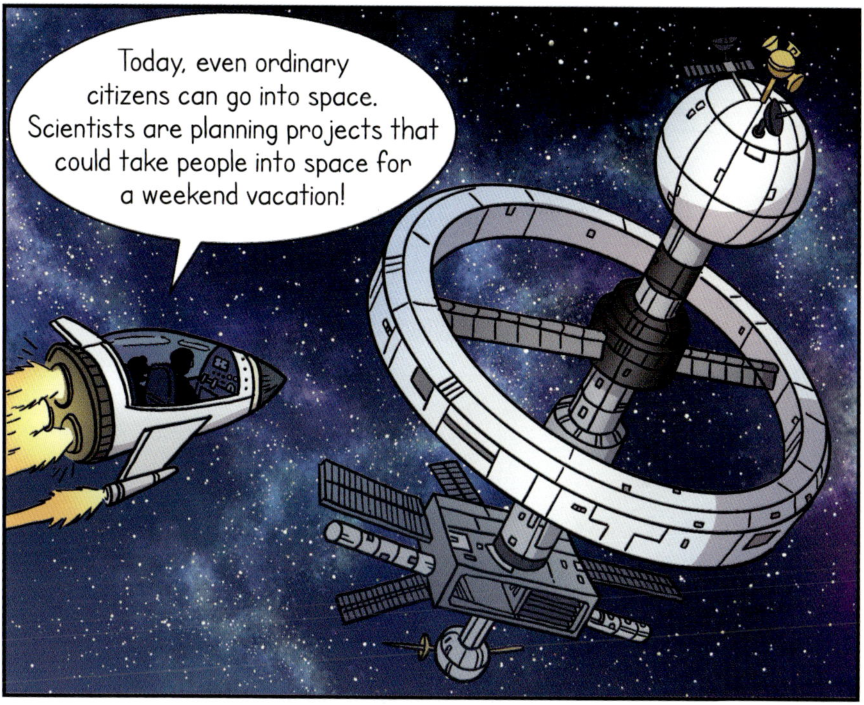
Today, even ordinary citizens can go into space. Scientists are planning projects that could take people into space for a weekend vacation!

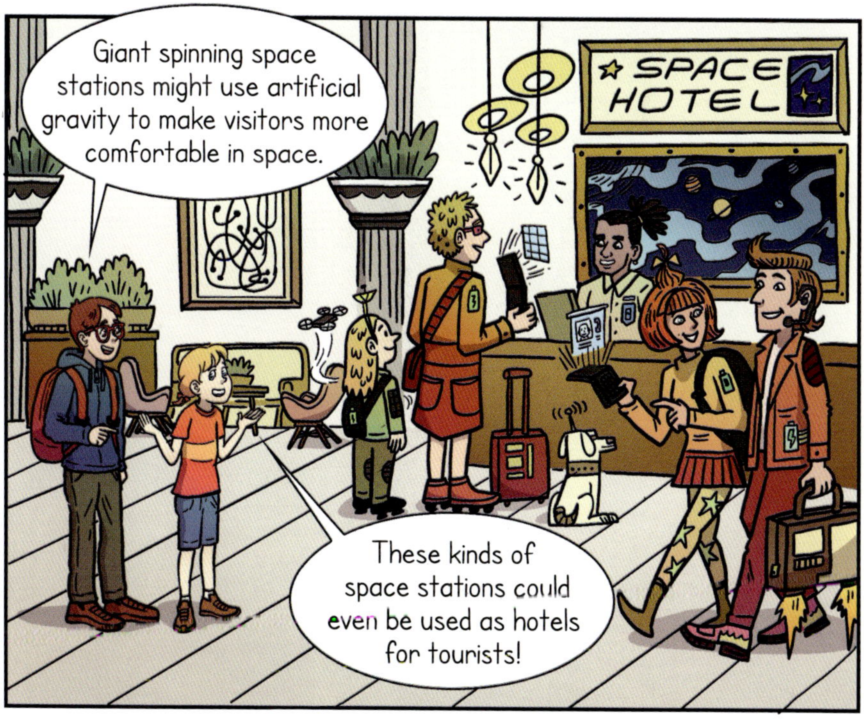
Giant spinning space stations might use artificial gravity to make visitors more comfortable in space.
SPACE HOTEL
These kinds of space stations could even be used as hotels for tourists!

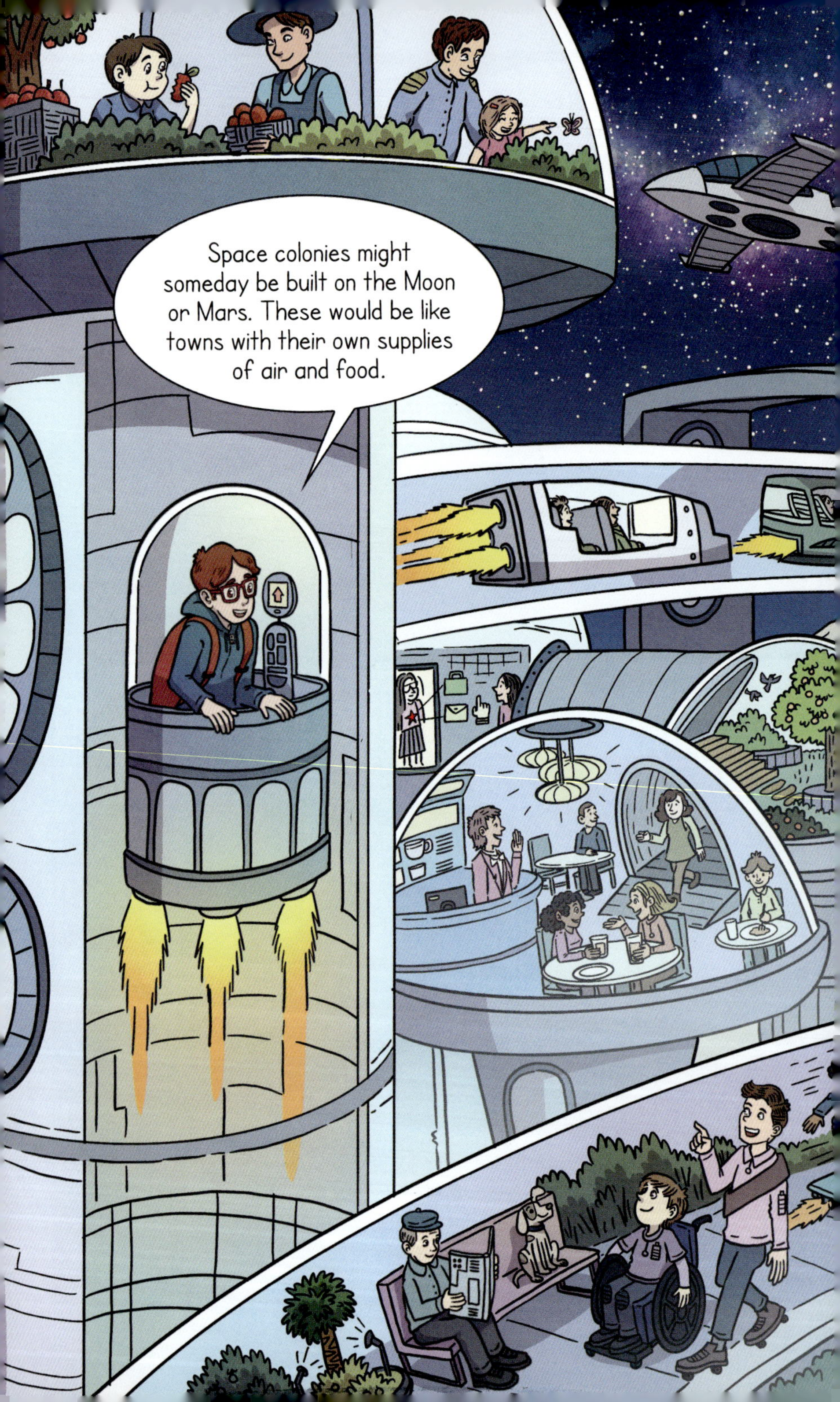
Space colonies might someday be built on the Moon or Mars. These would be like towns with their own supplies of air and food.

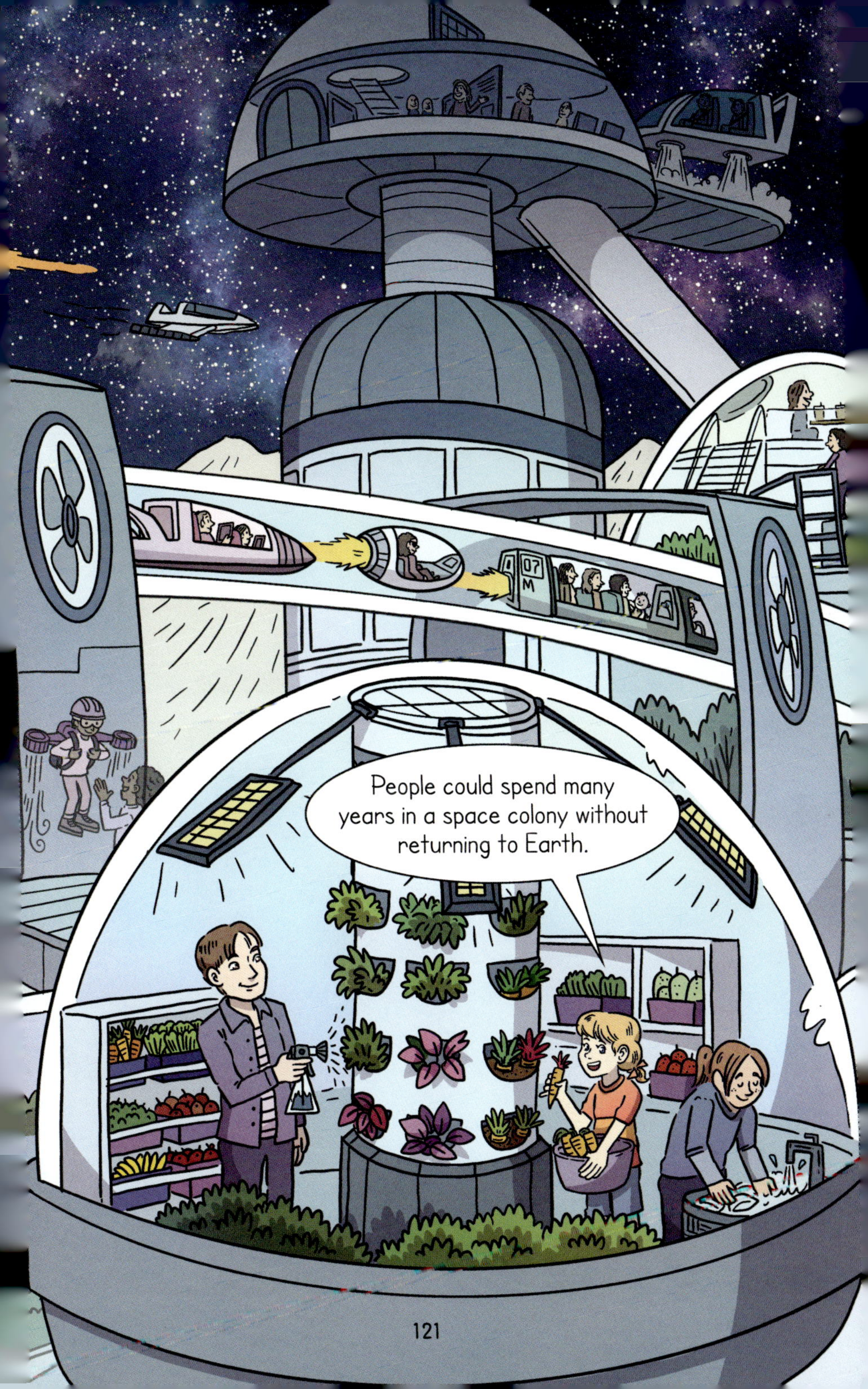
07
M
People could spend many years in a space colony without returning to Earth.

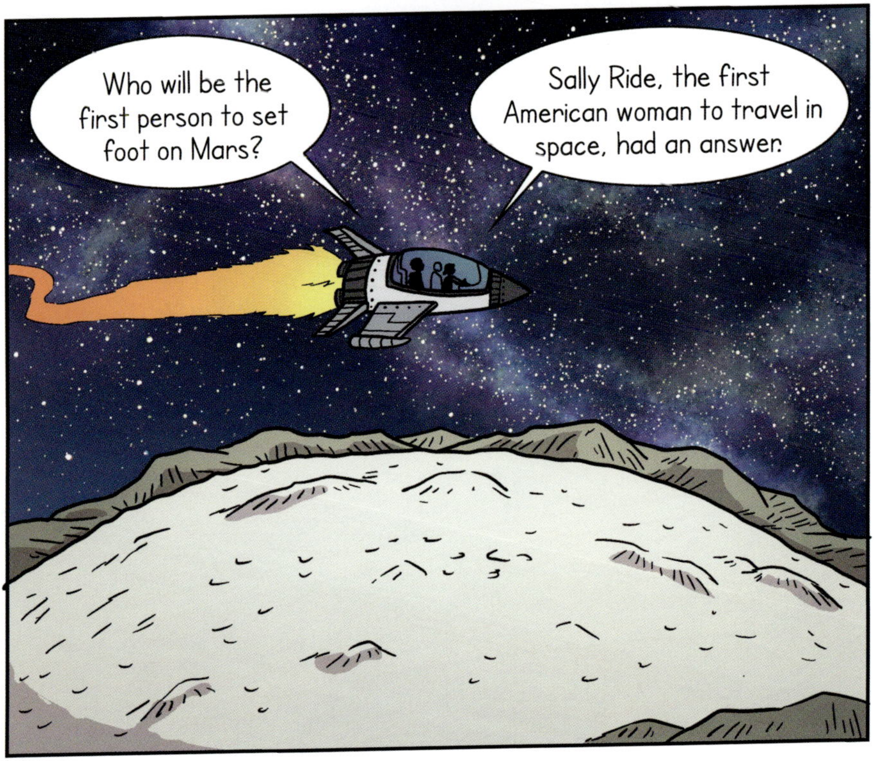
Who will be the first person to set foot on Mars?
Sally Ride, the first American woman to travel in space, had an answer.

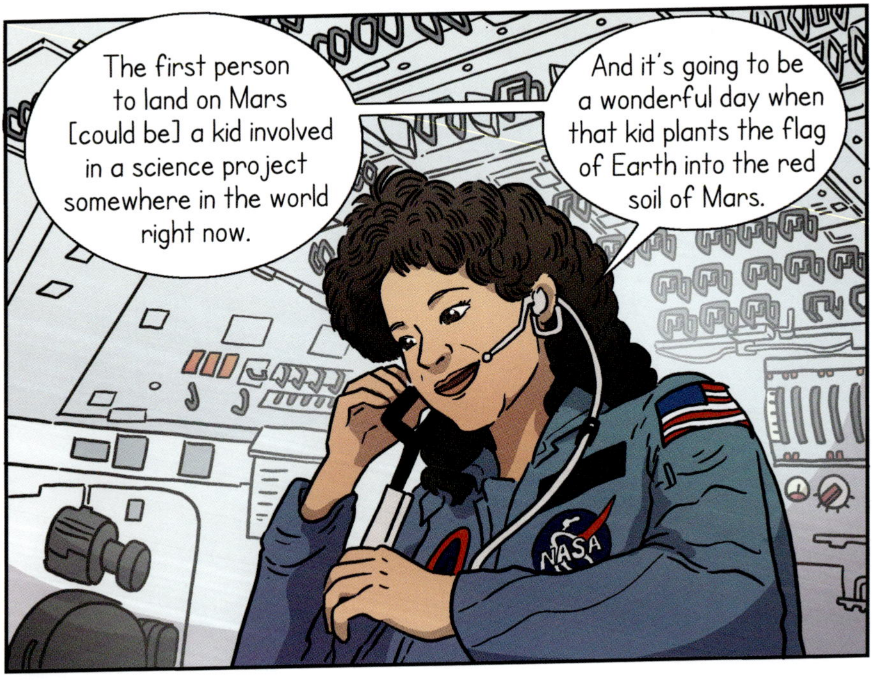
The first person to land on Mars [could be] a kid involved in a science project somewhere in the world right now.
And it's going to be a wonderful day when that kid plants the flag of Earth into the red soil of Mars.
NASA

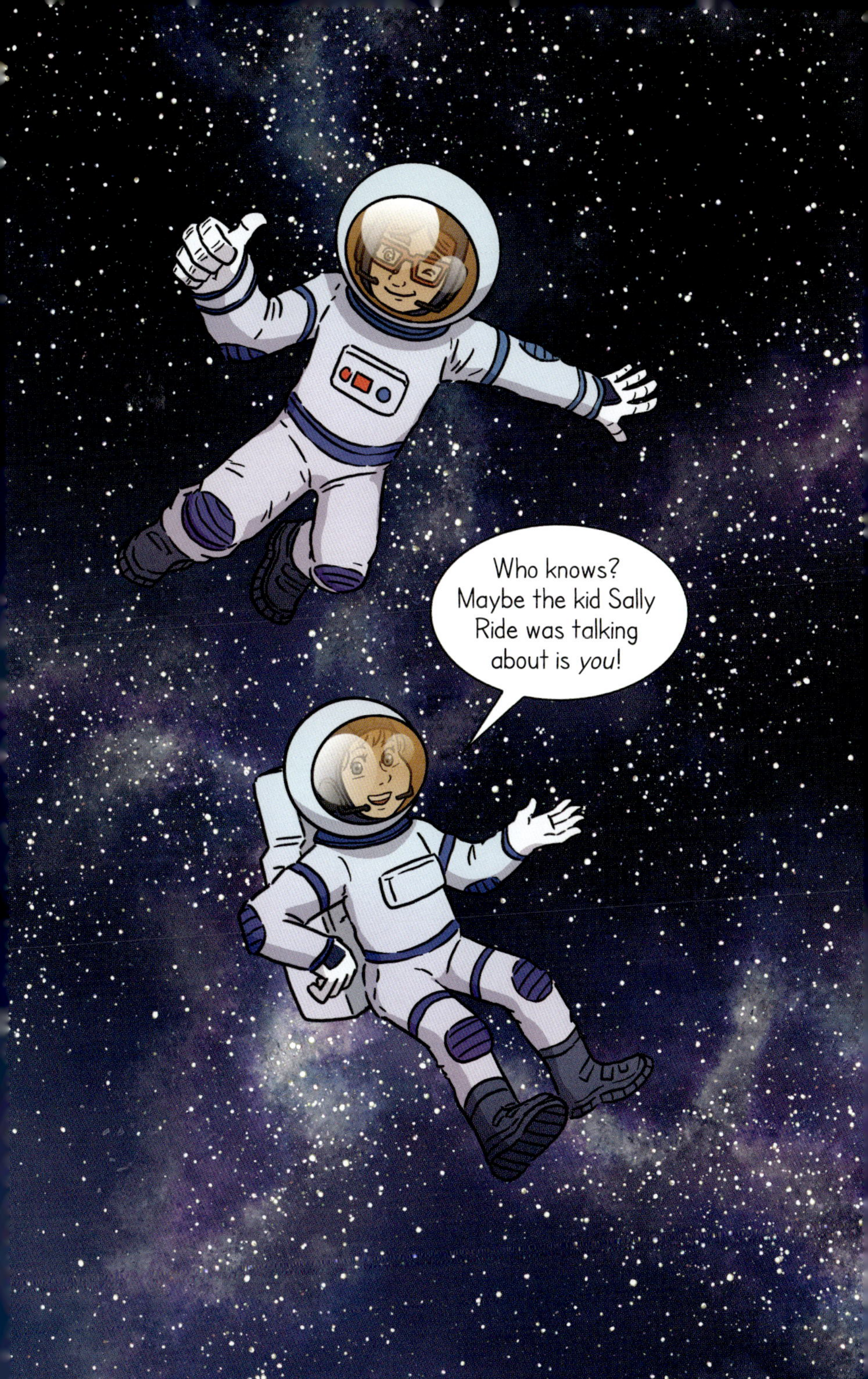
Who knows? Maybe the kid Sally Ride was talking about is *you*!

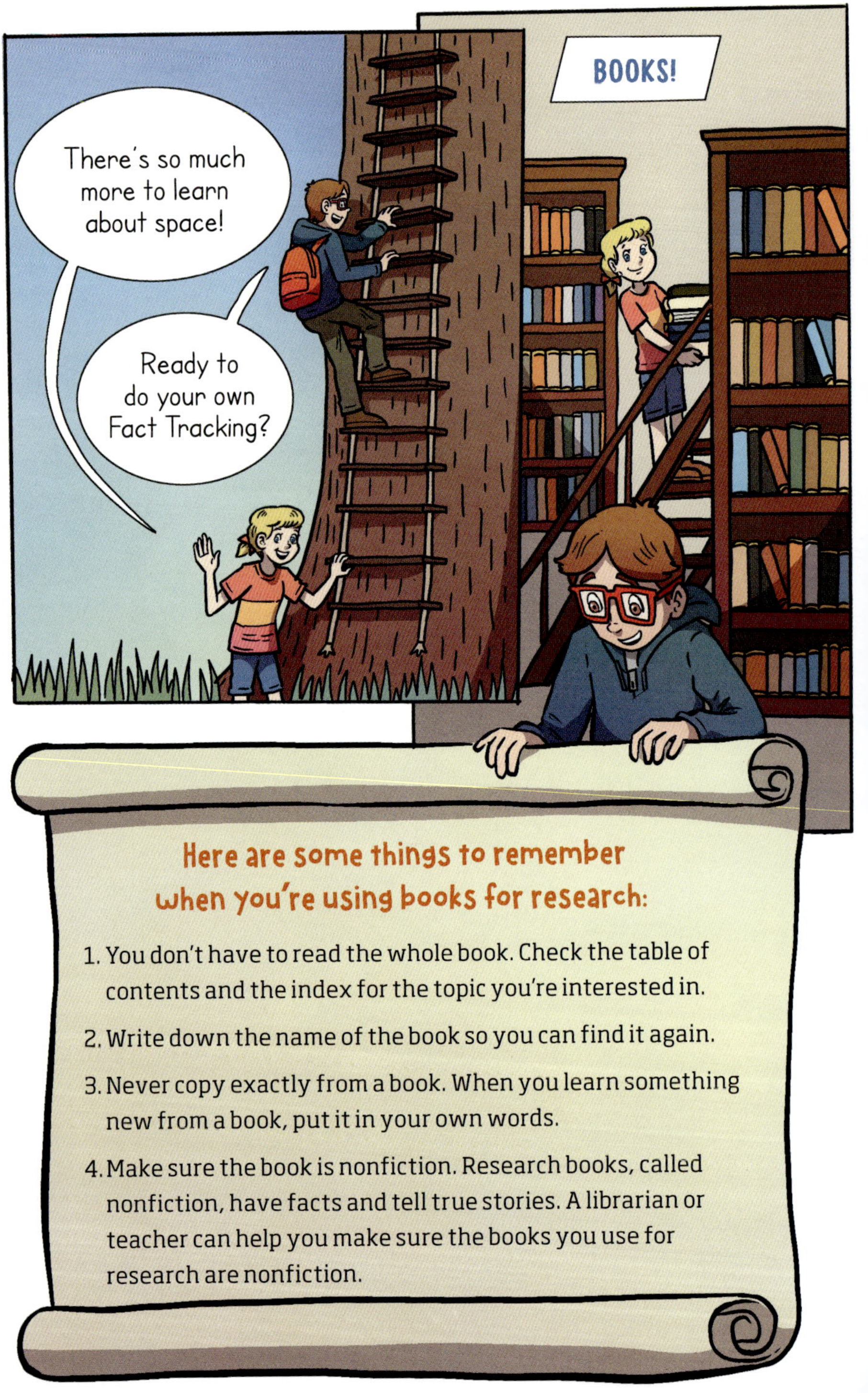
There's so much more to learn about space!
Ready to do your own Fact Tracking?
BOOKS!

Here are some things to remember when you're using books for research:

1. You don't have to read the whole book. Check the table of contents and the index for the topic you're interested in.
2. Write down the name of the book so you can find it again.
3. Never copy exactly from a book. When you learn something new from a book, put it in your own words.
4. Make sure the book is nonfiction. Research books, called nonfiction, have facts and tell true stories. A librarian or teacher can help you make sure the books you use for research are nonfiction.

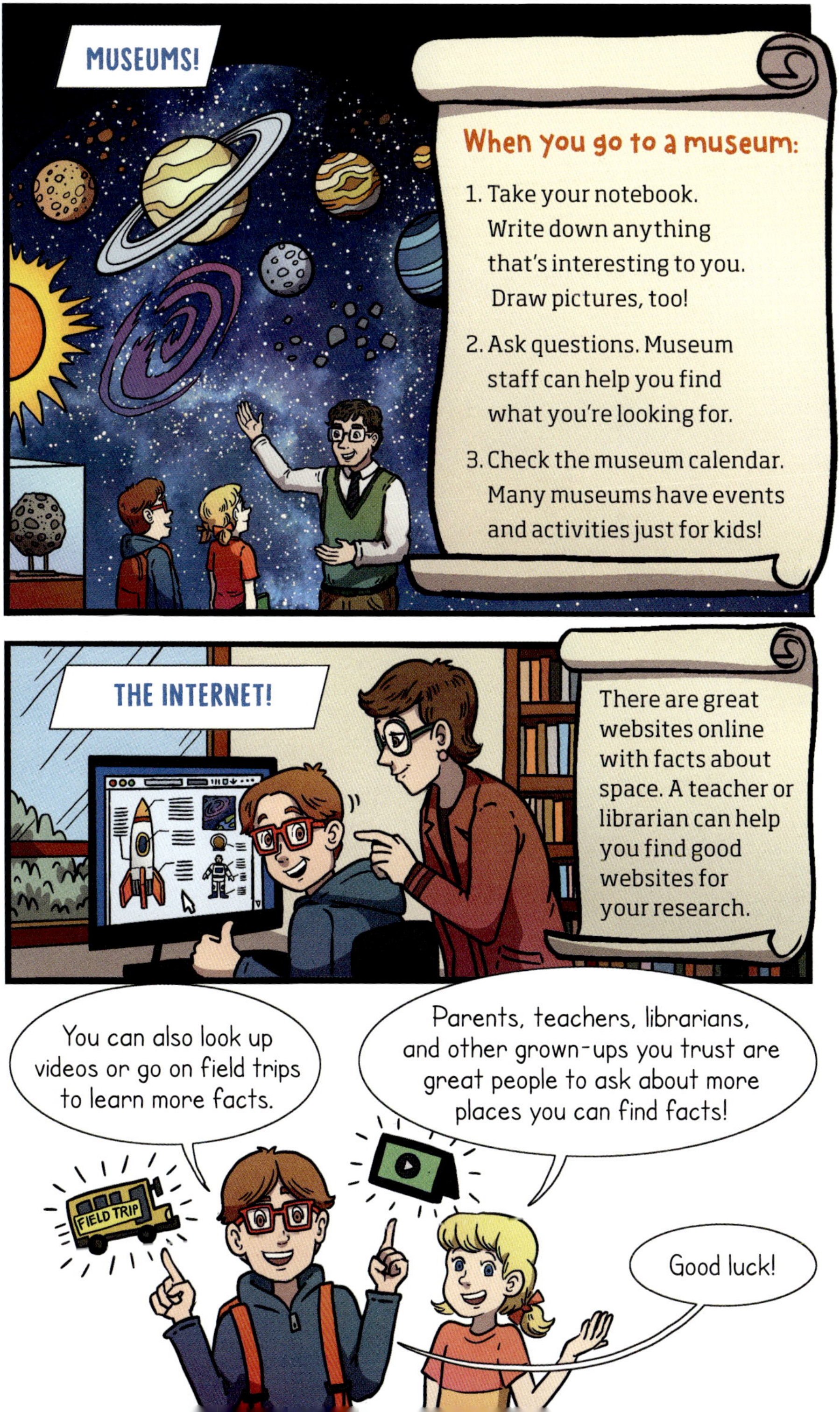
MUSEUMS!
When you go to a museum:
1. Take your notebook. Write down anything that's interesting to you. Draw pictures, too!
2. Ask questions. Museum staff can help you find what you're looking for.
3. Check the museum calendar. Many museums have events and activities just for kids!
THE INTERNET!
There are great websites online with facts about space. A teacher or librarian can help you find good websites for your research.
You can also look up videos or go on field trips to learn more facts.
Parents, teachers, librarians, and other grown-ups you trust are great people to ask about more places you can find facts!
FIELD TRIP
Good luck!

Don't miss the first Magic Tree House Fact Tracker Graphic Novel!

Available now!

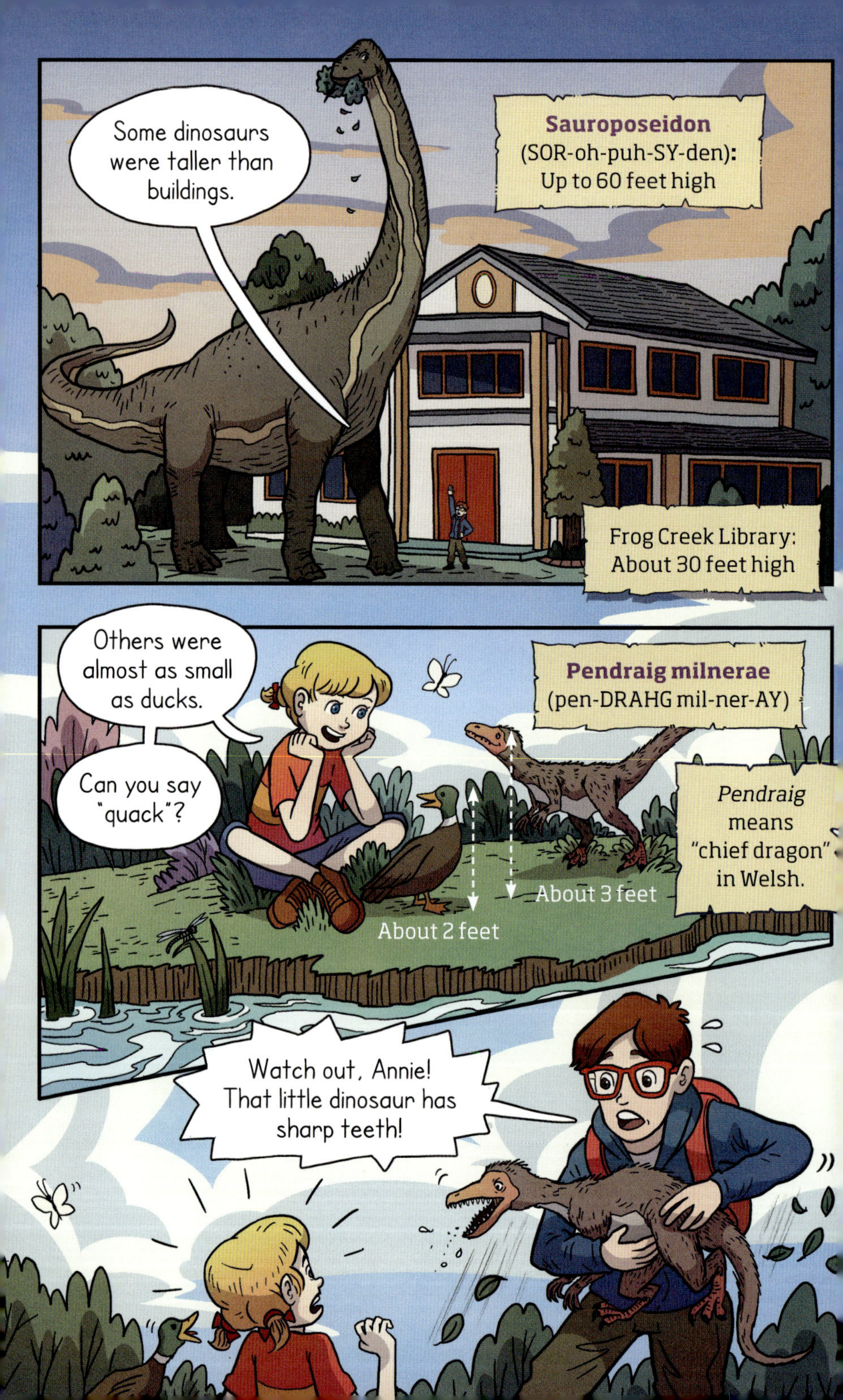
Some dinosaurs were taller than buildings.
Sauroposeidon (SOR-oh-puh-SY-den): Up to 60 feet high
Frog Creek Library: About 30 feet high
Others were almost as small as ducks.
Can you say "quack"?
Pendraig milnerae (pen-DRAHG mil-ner-AY)
Pendraig means "chief dragon" in Welsh.
About 2 feet
About 3 feet
Watch out, Annie! That little dinosaur has sharp teeth!

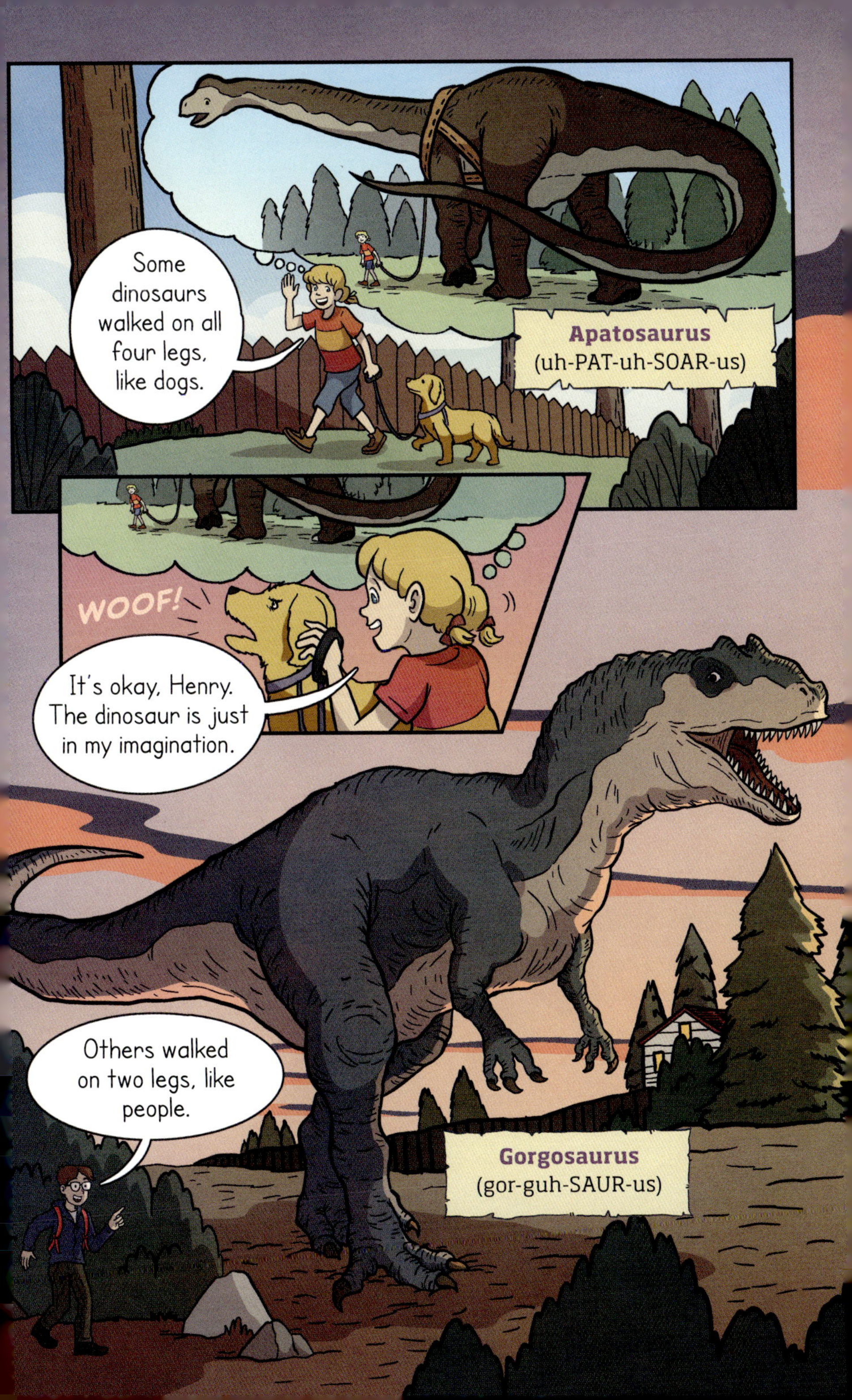
Some dinosaurs walked on all four legs, like dogs.
Apatosaurus (uh-PAT-uh-SOAR-us)
WOOF!
It's okay, Henry. The dinosaur is just in my imagination.
Others walked on two legs, like people.
Gorgosaurus (gor-guh-SAUR-us)

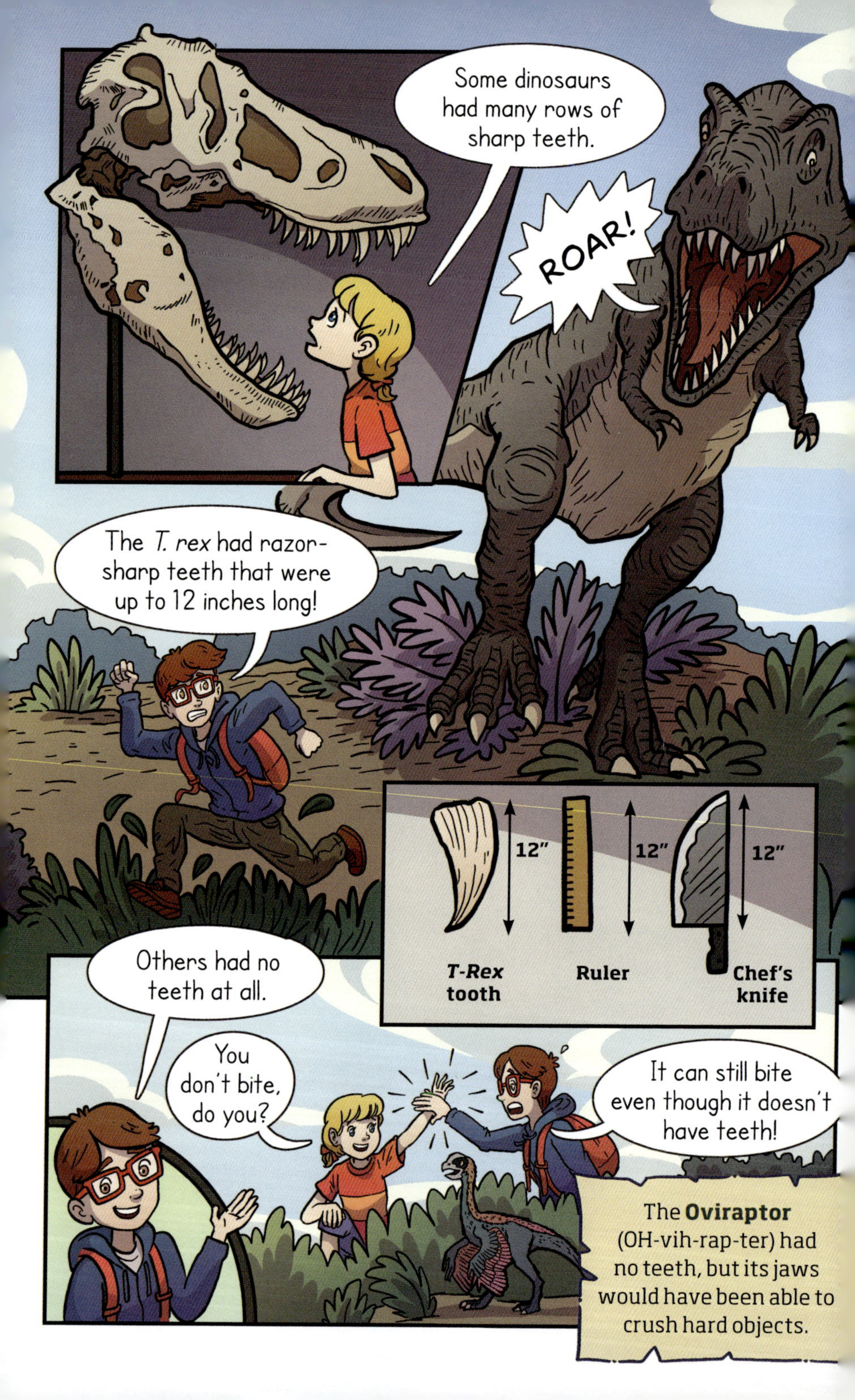
Some dinosaurs had many rows of sharp teeth.
ROAR!
The *T. rex* had razor-sharp teeth that were up to 12 inches long!
12"
12"
12"
T-Rex tooth
Ruler
Chef's knife
Others had no teeth at all.
You don't bite, do you?
It can still bite even though it doesn't have teeth!
The **Oviraptor** (OH-vih-rap-ter) had no teeth, but its jaws would have been able to crush hard objects.

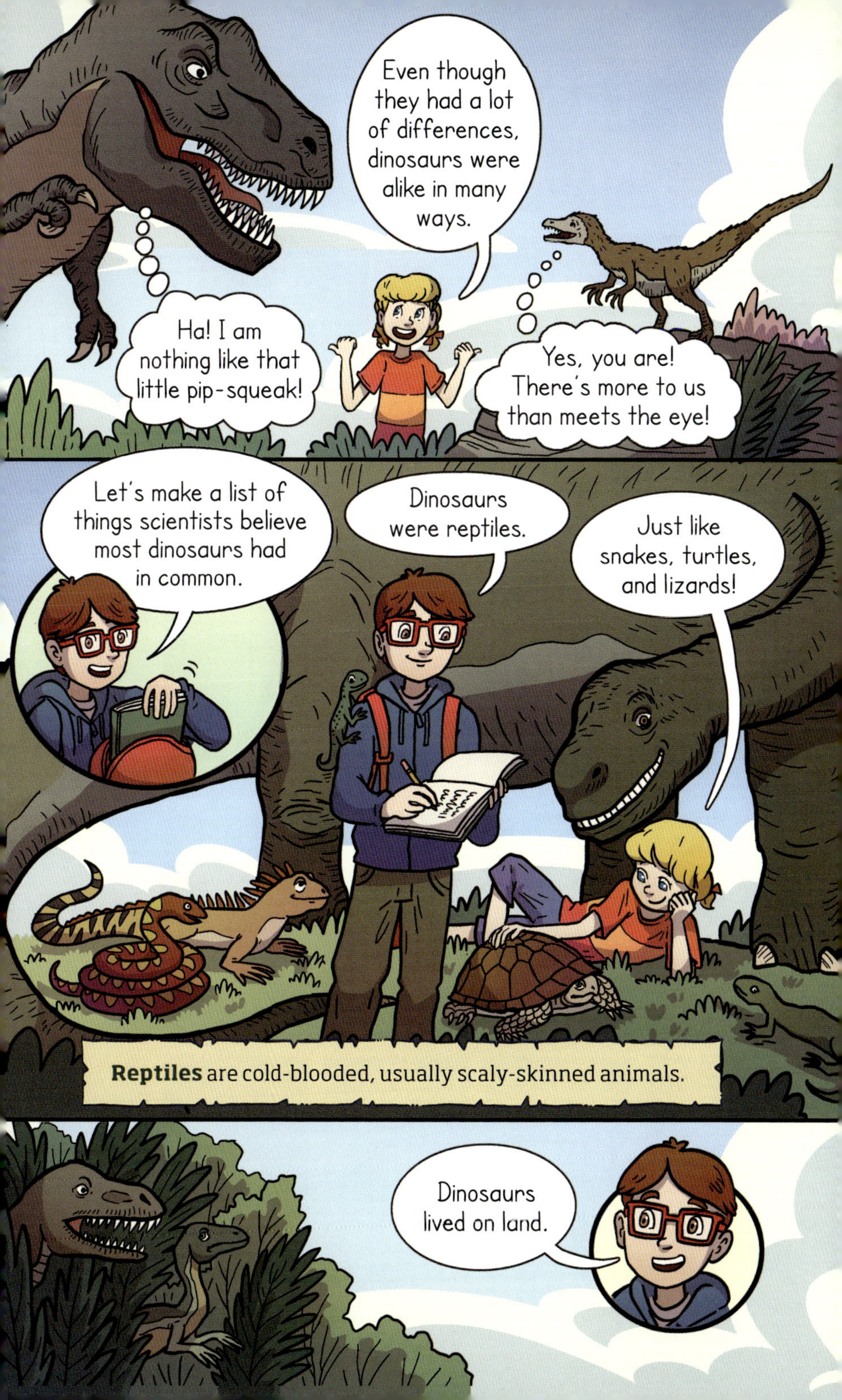
Even though they had a lot of differences, dinosaurs were alike in many ways.
Ha! I am nothing like that little pip-squeak!
Yes, you are! There's more to us than meets the eye!
Let's make a list of things scientists believe most dinosaurs had in common.
Dinosaurs were reptiles.
Just like snakes, turtles, and lizards!
Reptiles are cold-blooded, usually scaly-skinned animals.
Dinosaurs lived on land.

TRACK THE FACTS WITH JACK & ANNIE!

MAGIC TREE HOUSE FACT TRACKER
Dinosaurs
MAGIC TREE HOUSE FACT TRACKER
Knights and Castles
Will Osborne and Mary Pope Osborne
MAGIC TREE HOUSE FACT TRACKER
Mummies and Pyramids
Will Osborne and Mary Pope Osborne
MAGIC TREE HOUSE FACT TRACKER
Pirates
Will Osborne and Mary Pope Osborne
MAGIC TREE HOUSE FACT TRACKER
Rain Forests
Will Osborne and Mary Pope Osborne
MAGIC TREE HOUSE FACT TRACKER
Space
Will Osborne and Mary Pope Osborne
MAGIC TREE HOUSE FACT TRACKER
Titanic
Will Osborne and Mary Pope Osborne
MAGIC TREE HOUSE FACT TRACKER
Twisters and Other Terrible Storms
Will Osborne and Mary Pope Osborne
MAGIC TREE HOUSE FACT TRACKER
Dolphins and Sharks
Mary Pope Osborne and Natalie Pope Boyce
MAGIC TREE HOUSE FACT TRACKER
Ancient Greece and the Olympics
Mary Pope Osborne and Natalie Pope Boyce
MAGIC TREE HOUSE FACT TRACKER
American Revolution
Mary Pope Osborne and Natalie Pope Boyce
MAGIC TREE HOUSE FACT TRACKER
Sabertooths and the Ice Age
Mary Pope Osborne and Natalie Pope Boyce
MAGIC TREE HOUSE FACT TRACKER
Pilgrims
Mary Pope Osborne and Natalie Pope Boyce
MAGIC TREE HOUSE FACT TRACKER
Ancient Rome and Pompeii
Mary Pope Osborne and Natalie Pope Boyce
MAGIC TREE HOUSE FACT TRACKER
Tsunamis and Other Natural Disasters
Mary Pope Osborne and Natalie Pope Boyce
MAGIC TREE HOUSE FACT TRACKER
Polar Bears and the Arctic
Mary Pope Osborne and Natalie Pope Boyce
MAGIC TREE HOUSE FACT TRACKER
Sea Monsters
Mary Pope Osborne and Natalie Pope Boyce

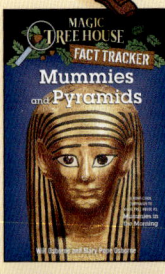

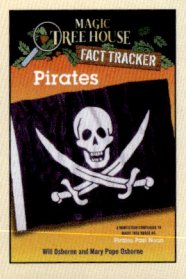

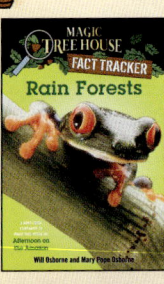

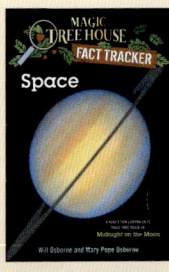

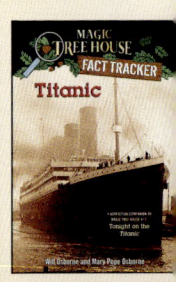

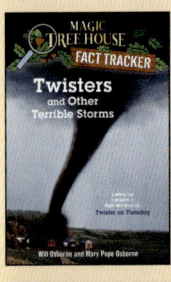

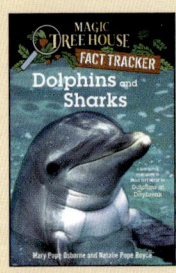

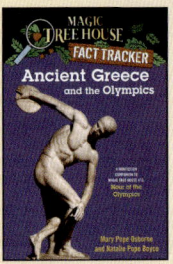

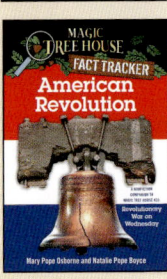

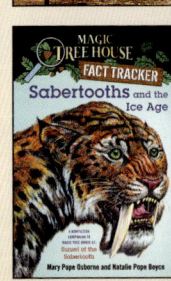

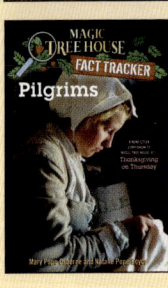

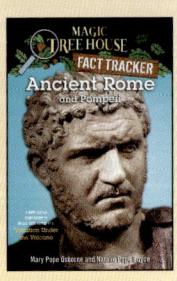

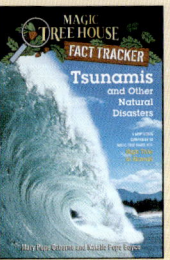

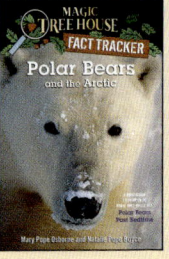

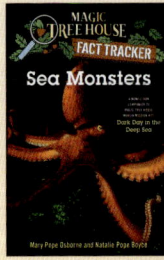

MAGIC TREE HOUSE FACT TRACKER
Penguins and Antarctica
Leonardo da Vinci
Ghosts
Leprechauns and Irish Folklore
Rags and Riches
Kids in the Time of Charles Dickens
Snakes and Other Reptiles
Dog Heroes
Abraham Lincoln
Pandas and Other Endangered Species
Horse Heroes
Heroes for All Times
Soccer
Ninjas and Samurai
China
Land of the Emperor's Great Wall
Sharks and Other Predators
Vikings
Dogsledding and Extreme Sports
Dragons and Mythical Creatures
World War II
Baseball
Wild West
Texas
Warriors
Benjamin Franklin
Narwhals and Other Whales
Mary Pope Osborne and Natalie Pope Boyce

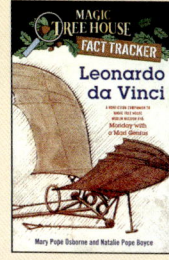

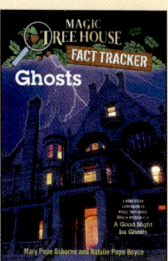

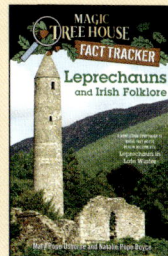

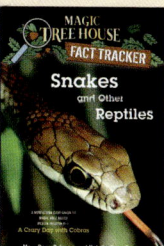

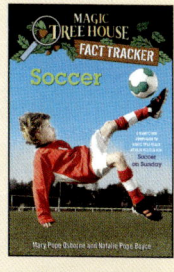

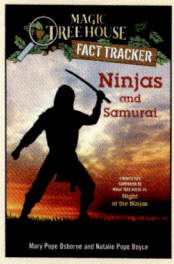

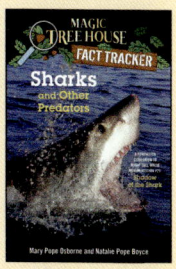

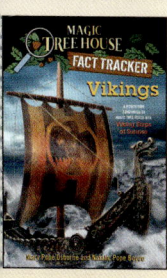

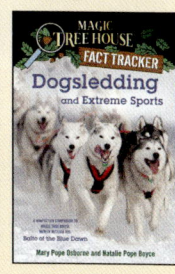

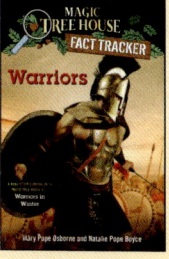

MARY POPE OSBORNE and **WILL OSBORNE** have coauthored eight nonfiction books for kids. Mary is the author of many novels, picture books, story collections, and nonfiction books. Her #1 *New York Times* bestselling Magic Tree House® series has been translated into numerous languages around the world. Will has worked as an actor, director, playwright, and author. He is the cocreator of numerous Magic Tree House® musicals, along with Randy Courts and Jenny Laird.

MEI NAKAMURA is an award-winning picture book, graphic novel, and middle-grade novel writer. She grew up on a shiitake mushroom farm in Maine before starting her career as an editor for Random House Children's Books. After over a decade, she moved back to her beloved home state, where she edits and writes books in her mountain home next to her husband, daughter, and two rescue dogs.

JOMIKE TEJIDO is an architect, artist, and award-winning illustrator and author who has made over a hundred children's books in his hometown of Manila, Philippines. When not making books, Jomike builds kinetic sculptures and paints on canvas. His art has been featured in twenty solo exhibitions and counting!